I0893318

LEATHERFACE VS. TRICKY DICK

THE TEXAS CHAIN SAW MASSACRE AS POLITICAL SATIRE

Martin Harris

HEADPRESS

A HEADPRESS BOOK
First published by Headpress in 2021, Oxford, United Kingdom
headoffice@headpress.com

LEATHERFACE VS. TRICKY DICK
The Texas Chain Saw Massacre As Political Satire

Text copyright © MARTIN HARRIS
This volume copyright © HEADPRESS 2021
Cover art, 'Face of America Leatherface' button, book design & layout © MARK MITCHELL : behance.net/markmjmitchell : instagram.com/markmillustrator
Proofing : Gareth Wilson

10 9 8 7 6 5 4 3 ~~2 1~~

The moral rights of the author have been asserted. The views expressed in this publication do not necessarily reflect the views of the Publisher.

All Rights Reserved. No part of this book may be reproduced, stored in a retrieval system, or transmitted, in any form or by any means, electronic, mechanical, photocopying, recording or otherwise, without prior permission in writing from the publisher.

Images are used for the purpose of historical review. Grateful acknowledgement is given to the respective owners, suppliers, artists, studios and publishers.

A CIP catalogue record for this book is available from the British Library

headpress

ISBN 978-1-909394-81-0 (paperback)
978-1-909394-82-7 (ebook)
NO-ISBN (hardback)

HEADPRESS. POP AND UNPOP CULTURE

Exclusive NO-ISBN special edition hardbacks and other items of interest are available at **HEADPRESS.COM**

★ Contents ★

FACE OF AMERICA
19
74
LEATHERFACE

"Yet there is still a vast difference betwixt the slovenly Butchering of a Man, and the fineness of a stroak that separates the Head from the Body, and leaves it standing in its place."

John Dryden

"A Discourse Concerning the Original and Progress of Satire"[1]

★ ★ ★ ★ ★

"This film kind of came out of the Watergate times. It was kind of inspired by it, in a lot of ways."

Tobe Hooper

on *The Texas Chain Saw Massacre*[2]

★ Introduction ★

IT WAS JUST PAST NOON on Friday, August 9, 1974 when an uncharacteristically tense Gerald R. Ford addressed the nation from the East Room of the White House. Typically a calm and measured public speaker, Ford's voice could be heard to quiver and even cracked a couple of times as he fidgeted behind the podium on which rested the speech he read. Emotion was evident on his face. At times it appeared as though he might be fighting back tears.

Moments before Ford had taken the oath of office and been sworn in as President of the United States. About a half-hour before that Secretary of State Henry Kissinger had received a one-sentence letter saying that Richard M. Nixon had followed through on his televised statement of the previous evening and resigned, the first president ever to do so in the nation's history.

Following expressions of humility and repeated allusions to the gravity of the moment, Ford at last referenced the remarkable and troubling sequence of events that for the previous two years had created unprecedented political turmoil and for many appeared to threaten the foundations of the country and its government.

"My fellow Americans, our long national nightmare is over," he said.

Ford was alluding, of course, to the protracted and painful Watergate scandal, the "internal wounds" of which he judged were "more painful and more poisonous than those of foreign wars."[3] At the time, Ford was perhaps the most congenial and conflict-averse politician on Capitol Hill, qualities that helped ensure his favorability with most lawmakers to succeed

Gerald Ford speaking in the East Room of the White House on August 9, 1974 shortly after taking office.

the disgraced Nixon. Those qualities also made Ford uneasy about that particular phrase, one that would soon appear in headlines and lead paragraphs of most reports on his speech before later becoming its most quoted line. "I wondered whether it was overly harsh on Nixon," Ford later wrote. Earlier he had asked his Chief of Staff Robert Hartmann whether they might wish to soften the statement.

"No, no," said Hartmann. "It's been a nightmare for everybody. For you, for me, for Nixon's friends and Nixon's enemies. For everybody in this country."[4]

Hartmann was right. Thinking back to how the scandal had been experienced by Americans, from the earliest reports of arrests at the Democratic National Committee headquarters at the Watergate Office Building to that final week of Nixon's presidency, that had been the word most commonly employed to describe the complicated, all-consuming crisis Ford was declaring at last to have concluded.

Watergate was a *nightmare*.

The scandal was a difficult, trying ordeal for all involved. There was the break-in, which turned out to be multiple break-ins, followed by the cover-up, then the cover-up of the cover-up. There was the tortuous, incremental unveiling of damning evidence despite the earnest efforts of Nixon and his men to combat that eventuality. There was the similarly drawn-out and sometimes contentious struggle between lawmakers over how to respond, as well as among those trying to interpret the complicated crime drama set in the White House and unfolding in their morning papers and on television day and night. There was the increasing fear of a constitutional crisis affecting the separation of powers and system of checks and balances. There was also the frequent petitioning of the courts to intervene, climaxing with a landmark case heard by the Supreme Court with the succinct yet symbolic name, *United States v. Richard Milhous Nixon*.

The scandal was a bad dream full of disorienting twists and turns and an ever-growing sense of dread, both for the American public and for those involved. In a memorandum later to become a testimony exhibit, White House Counsel John Dean recounted a meeting he had with John Mitchell, the former Attorney General who had headed Nixon's Committee for the Re-Election of the President at the time the Watergate break-in was discovered and during the initial effort to hide the White House's involvement. Dean was about to appear before a grand jury and wanted Mitchell to understand he felt he would have no choice but to reveal everything he knew, both to avoid perjuring himself and to prevent others from making him a scapegoat. "I told him that it was personally ruining my own life," Dean wrote. "I explained that I have always been the man in the middle of this nightmare, and that I meant no harm to anyone, but I had to start protecting myself."[5] Nixon himself experienced Watergate similarly, from the confusing beginning to the bitter end, as did others who, like Dean, would forfeit their own political futures in order to protect the president. Recalling one of his first conversations with his Chief of Staff H.R. "Bob" Haldeman to discuss the matter, Nixon wrote how "Haldeman said he felt like the whole thing was a nightmare," adding, "I agreed."[6] A recording of that very conversation would be later subpoenaed, although the president's legal team initially failed to realize they had been ordered to submit that particular tape. "It was a nightmare," Nixon wrote of the mistake, his frustration exacerbated by his knowledge of an eighteen-and-a-half-minute gap in the recording now destined to become known to the public.[7] And after it was all over—in that same East Room that very morning just a couple of hours before Ford spoke—Nixon delivered his own emotional speech when bidding farewell to the White House staff. "This was the nightmare end of a long dream," was how Nixon later described the moment, the ghastly conclusion to a remarkable political career.[8]

Richard Nixon saying farewell to staff in the East Room of the White House on August 9, 1974 just before leaving office.

The scandal was also a kind of persistent, evil presence that haunted the nation as its significance inexorably grew. Over the course of those two-plus years the term "Watergate" expanded into an all-purpose emblem connoting corruption in government, a catch-all confirming that public distrust in elected leaders was well founded.

Bad faith handling and insincere communication about the Vietnam War by previous administrations had continued under Nixon. The controversial publication of the *Pentagon Papers* in June 1971 clarified to all how those managing the war under Kennedy and Johnson had consistently misled both Congress and the public about the scope of the conflict and about internal pessimism regarding its potential for success. David Halberstam's *The Best and the Brightest* followed a year later, further fleshing out the story of the government's catastrophic failings with a damning epilogue addressing how Nixon had proven unable to avoid repeating those same mistakes throughout his first term. "There was, Americans were finding, no light at the end of the tunnel, only greater darkness," judged Halberstam.[9] The book was sitting atop the *New York Times* nonfiction bestseller list when the Paris Peace Accords were finally signed in late January 1973, although even as POWs began returning home it was evident the darkness had not been lifted. At a press conference a few weeks later, Nixon experienced a kind of epiphany as he recognized how the presumed end of one nightmare had seamlessly segued into another. "The questioning kept returning to Watergate with a relentlessness, almost a passion, that I had seen before only in the most emotional days of the Vietnam war," he would reflect. "For the first time I began to realize the dimensions of the problem we were facing with the media and with Congress regarding Watergate: *Vietnam had found its successor*."[10]

In "The Nightmare of Watergate," a *Wall Street Journal* op-ed published the day the public Senate Watergate Hearings chaired by Senator Sam Ervin began in May 1973, neoconservative commentator Irving Kristol summarized why the bewildering, logic-defying scandal had made even Nixon supporters like himself "more than a little frightened by Watergate."[11] Unlike previous examples of corruption in government with understandable motives and relatively accessible plotlines and characters, Watergate represented something both greater in scope and much more difficult to grasp. "This is not the first time that men around the President have abused their powers and violated our laws," noted Kristol. However, "what makes Watergate so extraordinary, is the sense that practically the entire White House staff, and perhaps even the President himself, have been living in a different world than the rest of us." It was as though America was just starting to realize its government wasn't just acting badly, it was acting as though it existed in an alternate reality not regulated by laws or even an adherence to reason. "People need to feel they understand their government, even if they find some of its behavior shocking," wrote Kristol. "An irrational government is the citizen's ultimate nightmare."

Such comments came before the full revelation of other "White House horrors" that predated the Watergate arrests on June 17, 1972. That was a phrase frequently used during the Senate Watergate Committee hearings by both witnesses and their inquisitors to describe a host of additional crimes, acts of political espionage, violations of citizens' constitutional rights, and abuses of power committed by White House staff. They also came before the uncovering of other "dirty tricks" by Nixon campaigners who themselves described their efforts as "ratfucking," the sensational testimony from "bag men" employed by White House staff to deliver hush money to Watergate defendants, and the later, brutish attempt by the president to halt the investigation, a failed gambit that instantly became known as the "Saturday Night Massacre." Eventually observers of all stripes would routinely refer to the scandal similarly, from labor columnist Victor Riesel decrying "the debilitating, disgusting and nationally destructive Watergate nightmare" (August 1973) to counterculturalist Hunter S. Thompson joking that thousands of Americans were writing television stations "to demand that this goddamn tedious nightmare be jerked off the air so they can get back to their favorite soap operas" (September 1973) to the venerable Pulitzer Prize-winning political writer William S. White hopefully speculating how Nixon might with "a little luck" still be able to pull off "an effective self-extrication from his Watergate nightmare" (January 1974).[12] Even before all that, Kristol perceived those involved in the scandal as part of "a wave of collective delusion, suspicion and paranoia engulfing the White House circles and overwhelming all the barriers that common sense erects against such a possibility: of an unreal reality imposing itself on the political process."

Above all, Kristol was unsettled by the inexplicability of Watergate, wanting more than anything to *make sense* of it, to cut through the complicated knots of break-ins and buggings, of payoffs and perjuries, of conspiracies and cover-ups and free himself of what had already begun to resemble the anxiety-causing uncertainty of a bad dream. After all, as Kristol concluded, "an incomprehensible government is the stuff out of which political nightmares are made."

★ ★ ★ ★ ★

In December 1972, Tobe Hooper was himself trapped in an uncomfortable situation from which he desired escape. Standing in the hardware section of the Montgomery Ward department store near Highland Mall in Austin, Texas, the filmmaker became aware of a throng of fellow patrons circling about him. "There were these big Christmas crowds," Hooper later recalled. "And god, I hate crowds. I hate them closing in on you. They were closing in and I was kind of like freaking. I just wanted to get out, get out of the crowd.... I was frustrated, and I found myself near a display rack of chain saws." In a flash he imagined himself peering through a camera lens. "I just kind of zoned in on it. I did a rack focus to the saws, and I thought, 'I know a way I could get through this crowd really quickly.'"[13]

Hooper avoided resorting to such antisocial mischief to rid himself of his crowd problem. However the moment did provide him inspiration to solve a different kind of puzzle.

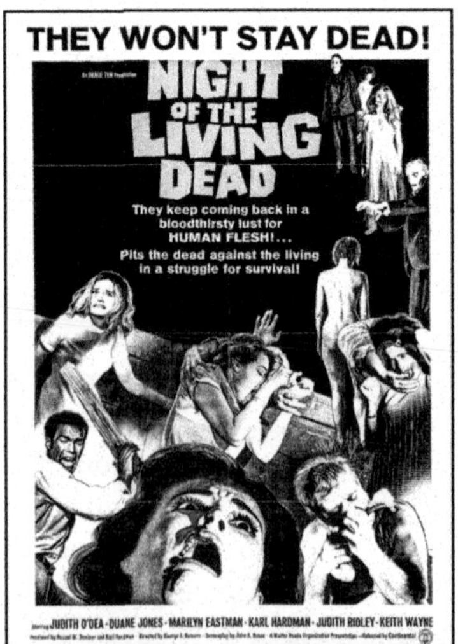

A poster advertising *Night of the Living Dead* (1968).

Having directed a couple of short avant-garde films, a number of commercials, a television documentary about the folk trio Peter, Paul and Mary, and one impressive though largely unseen experimental feature film, Hooper had been seeking an idea for a new project. He was already inclined toward the horror genre both out of personal preference and an understanding that horror allowed for the possibility of shooting a low budget feature with a chance at profitability. In interviews Hooper frequently

An early print ad for *The Texas Chain Saw Massacre* highlighting Rex Reed's favorable review.

listed as influences classic horror cinema like *Dracula* and *Frankenstein*, "Hitchcock's methods of manipulating an audience," particularly in *Psycho*, as well as the gruesome horror-themed EC Comics of the 1950s like *Tales from the Crypt*, *The Vault of Horror*, and *The Haunt of Fear*.[14] George A. Romero's 1968 film *Night of the Living Dead* provided a particular template as well after Hooper saw it at the student union at the University of Texas at Austin at a screening by Cinema 40, the campus film society.[15] "A crudely made film but very effective," judged Hooper, who ranked Romero's movie as one of the better horror entries of the previous decade.[16]

Perhaps a corresponding creepiness between the shoppers surrounding Hooper and the zombies besieging the cast in *Night of the Living Dead* had provided a kind of catalyst as well. In any case, that brief moment of holiday horror gifted the filmmaker an idea.

"I went home, sat down, all the channels just tuned in, the zeitgeist blew through, and the whole damn story came to me in what seemed like thirty seconds," said Hooper. "The hitchhiker, the older brother at the gas station, the girl escaping twice, the dinner sequence, people out in the country out of gas," all arrived in short order, providing Hooper with the essential elements of what would eventually become the plot of *The Texas Chain Saw Massacre*.[17] "I think the entire structure seemed to come in one package," he remembered, referring not only to the characters and several scenes but importantly to the notion of "everything tumbling back into itself" as frightened victims unwittingly staggered into terrifying traps from which every apparent exit carried them right back into danger—in other words, an exaggerated, elaborated version of Hooper's department store dilemma.[18]

By the time Hooper sat down with friend and collaborator Kim Henkel to construct a screenplay during January and February of 1973,[19] the pair were guided primarily by Hooper's initial vision of a story involving victims and villains clashing in an isolated, rural setting. The screenplay they produced contains practically all of what made it into the finished film. On a hot summer day in the heart of Texas, a wheelchair-bound brother and his sister are joined by three other young adults on a trip by van. They are visiting a cemetery where the siblings' grandfather was buried, having been prompted to do so after hearing some of the graves had been dug up and the corpses disturbed. After learning that their relative continues to rest peacefully, the travelers get back on the road. They pick up a hitchhiker who behaves strangely while relating how his brother and grandfather both used to work at the local slaughterhouse before the introduction of modernized killing methods made their jobs obsolete. His ride ends abruptly after he cuts his own hand with a knife and then slashes the brother's arm before being ejected from the van. Low on fuel they soon visit a gas station only to discover the tanks are empty and the owner is unsure about when the next delivery will arrive. They decide to pass the time by visiting the grandfather's abandoned house nearby, not heeding the owner's attempt to dissuade them by inviting them to stay and have some of the barbecue he cooks and sells at the station. Instead they take the food to go and proceed to the grandfather's house, and after a bit of exploring two of them wander to a neighboring house where they discover numerous parked cars hidden from view from the road. One enters the house and is shockingly killed by a hulking man who wears a mask made from human skin, the murder accomplished in seconds with just two blows from a sledgehammer. The other follows inside in search of her friend. After she sees the house strangely decorated with bones, skulls, and carcasses, she is suddenly accosted by the same man who brutally hangs her on a meat hook, then uses a chainsaw to carve the corpse of her friend in front of her. A third member of the group looking for the other two swiftly meets a similar fate, the killer needing just a single blow from the sledgehammer this time to accomplish the deed. Only the brother and sister remain, and as evening falls they become worried and begin to search for the others. Suddenly the mask-wearing man appears with the chainsaw and hacks the brother to pieces in his wheelchair before chasing after the sister. At one point she enters the killer's house that she then escapes by throwing herself through a second-story window. Eventually she finds her way back to the gas station and apparent safety, but the owner binds and gags her and transports her right back to the house where the others were killed. There she again meets the masked killer and the hitchhiker, both related it seems to the man who runs the gas station. Tied to a chair made of human bones, she is forced to endure a macabre parody of a dinner party as the guest of honor. There is a suggestion (never made explicit) that the meal consists of human flesh. They are joined by a fourth family member, Grandpa, who looks as though he could be over a century old. The torture appears about to conclude as members of the family converge upon the sister with the intention of killing her. They position Grandpa next to her with a hammer, ostensibly to demonstrate a skill once practiced at the slaughterhouse, but she escapes once more, again crashing through a window. Outdoors another chase ensues as the hitchhiker stabs her from behind with his knife while his masked brother races after with his whirring chainsaw. As dawn breaks they reach the highway where the hitchhiker is run over by an eighteen-wheeler. The sister flags down a pickup truck and jumps in the back, having at last escaped the masked killer who is left waving his chainsaw over his head in a kind of maniacal dance.

While Hooper drew upon other examples of commercial horror for inspiration, by most accounts Henkel was the one contributing the idea to fashion a plot from the early 19th-century German fairy tale "Hansel and Gretel" by the Brothers Grimm. In the story a brother and sister are lured to a strange house in the woods made of gingerbread, candy, and cake where a cannibalistic witch captures and imprisons them with the intention of eating them. Besides the core plot of siblings endangered by a monstrous villain in an isolated setting, a few other vestiges of the tale emerge in *Chain Saw* such as the discovery of bones of previous victims. Even though the children being abandoned in the woods by a father and evil stepmother is not part of the film's backstory, some might interpret the absence of parents as generally evoking a similar notion of the siblings being unable to rely on the older generation or any authority to help them. Meanwhile the most remembered detail from the fairy tale, the children using pebbles and then bread crumbs to help them try to keep from getting lost in the woods, is certainly at least connoted by the disorienting, claustrophobic circularity of *Chain Saw*'s plot, informed as it is by Hooper's idea of "the structural puzzle pieces" fitting together to emphasize "the way it folds continuously back on itself, and no matter where you're going it's the wrong place."[20] In interviews Henkel made a similar point about the film's narrative when succinctly describing the arrangement of *Chain Saw*'s parts.

"We referred to the way we put the story together as 'nightmare syntax,'" explained Henkel.[21]

It is clear that whatever other purposes the filmmakers had, principal among them was the desire to create a particular kind of commercial horror film, one designed to involve the viewer in a kind of "nightmare" of wrong turns punctuated by frightening revelations and mounting dread. Such an idea is communicated directly by the film's famous opening crawl introducing the "five youths, in particular Sally Hardesty and her invalid brother, Franklin" for whom "an idyllic summer afternoon drive became a nightmare." Importantly, the filmmakers also chose to eschew supernatural elements such as appear in the fairy tale, something Hooper initially entertained but Henkel successfully resisted, believing a more realistic story had a better chance of connecting with audiences. "The underlying social motivations get stripped out, if it moves in that direction, if you go with the supernatural," said Henkel.[22] Thus *Chain Saw* consciously presents a self-contained world that bears a strong and convincing relationship to the one inhabited by those who made the film and its first audiences. That notion is likewise underscored by the opening's presentation of the film as "an account of the tragedy" and assigning it a date ("August 18, 1973"), as well as a promotional campaign foregrounding the idea that *Chain Saw* is based on actual events ("What happened is true"). While the film's story is fictional, it nonetheless strives to present its characters and events in a believable way, inviting viewers to consider how it *could* have happened.

The emphasis on the story being based on actual events distinguishes *The Texas Chain Saw Massacre* from *Night of the Living Dead* and its fantastic story of reanimated corpses rising from the dead to feast on the living, although it should be said both films employ a "truth conceit" that coupled with other stylistic elements have inspired sometimes exaggerated descriptions of each as documentary-like. (In some cases those elements were by-products of low budgets, with Hooper and Romero's shared background directing documentaries certainly relevant as well.) Meanwhile the films do resemble each other in the way both present characters in isolated circumstances whose lives are threatened by a bewildering set of killers—that is to say, in both films the "nightmare" experienced by those under siege is constructed similarly, and unfolds similarly as characters are successively killed and the casts shrink. Indeed, in both films the essential plots of monstrous villains attacking and killing unlucky victims translate relatively easily into abstract terms. Faced with such superficially "simple" stories as well as the films' commercial aspirations (and successes), early critics were necessarily emboldened, encouraged even more by the exploitation leanings of both *Night of the Living Dead* and *The Texas Chain Saw Massacre*, signaled in over-the-top fashion by their titles. As a result, both films produced polarized responses often extreme in their scorn or praise, either dismissing the films as utterly meaningless and without value, or appreciating them as richly symbolic commentaries on contemporary society.

The dismissals are great fun, of course. Designed as they are to discourage viewing and thus inhibit further analysis, we chuckle at them in part because of our awareness of the films' subsequent rise in both critical estimation and historical importance. Released on October 1, 1968, *Night of the Living Dead* earned an angry response two weeks later from the *Variety* reviewer who characterized it as an "unrelieved orgy of sadism" that the Supreme Court might consider using as a guideline for defining "the pornography of violence."[23] Vincent Canby was similarly contemptuous in his *New York Times* review of what he called "a grainy little movie" featuring "nonprofessional actors" that "was made by some people in Pittsburgh."[24] Meanwhile Roger Ebert, then a relatively new critic writing for the *Chicago Sun-Times*, merely summarized the film's plot while focusing more intently on describing the trauma experienced by the young, impressionable children in the audience with whom he saw the film. Outraged over "kids who had no sources they could draw upon to protect themselves from the dread and fear they felt," Ebert used his review to lament over bad parenting, the "incompetence and stupidity of the censorship system," and the apparent money-grubbing of those who saw to it that the film "was scheduled for the lucrative holiday season, when the kids are on vacation."[25]

Six years later—to the day—*The Texas Chain Saw Massacre* premiered on October 1, 1974, and was promptly scorned in similar ways. "Craziness handled without sensitivity is a degrading, senseless misuse of film and time," declared Linda Gross in a contemptuous review for the *Los Angeles Times*.[26] In his *Monthly Film Bulletin* review, John Pym explicitly rejected attempts to assign meaning to the film (including those advanced by Hooper himself), finding *Chain Saw* "a tongue-in-cheek commercial shocker" best understood as "simply a contrived piece of nonsense studiously avoiding a point of view."[27] Stephen Koch's angry "Fashions in Pornography" piece for *Harper's Magazine* famously begins "*The Texas Chain Saw Massacre* is a vile little piece of sick crap" before designating the film "a particularly foul item in the currently developing hard-core pornography of murder." Koch echoes Pym's dim view of those attempting to find any significance or value in *Chain Saw*, finding it "a film with literally nothing to recommend it."[28] Ebert chimed in again as well, finding *Chain Saw* "a grisly little item... without any apparent purpose, unless the creation of disgust and fright is a purpose." Unlike Koch who calls the film "badly made," Ebert begrudgingly commends its technical proficiency, though still finds it "an effective production in the service of an unnecessary movie." In other words, there's nothing to see here, and certainly no reason to delve beneath *Chain Saw*'s gruesome surface. "It's simply an exercise in terror."[29]

Of course even as both films' commercial success provoked additional vitriol and hand wringing, they both also received positive critical response. Again, much as happened with alien invasion features of an earlier generation, the easily abstracted us-versus-them situations of both films readily invited the mapping of their stories onto contemporary conflicts. *Night of the Living Dead* was shot during the latter half of 1967 with post-production occurring during the first months of the new year, meaning the film was made with an awareness of it conceivably inspiring thoughts of the escalating war in Vietnam and protests against it at home, continuing battles over civil rights and the race riots of the "long, hot summer of 1967" and after, other internal clashes involving countercultural groups and factions opposing them, and even some of the same Cold War themes evoked by 1950s sci-fi. By the time the film premiered the assassinations of Martin Luther King Jr. and Robert F. Kennedy and the forceful response to protests at the Democratic National Convention in Chicago had with other events punctuated a year replete with violence and death, further thickening the context in which *Night of the Living Dead* was first viewed. J. Hoberman and Jonathan Rosenbaum cheekily summarized these many connections to contemporary horrors when suggesting "in 1968, the title of George Romero's film could have been a beatnik poet's metaphor for the 'CBS Evening News.'"[30]

Initial champions of *The Texas Chain Saw Massacre* primarily focused on its effective delivery of scares, paying little heed to deeper meanings. Rex Reed's early declaration of it as "the most horrifying motion picture I have ever seen" proved influential, thanks largely to quotes from his review being liberally incorporated into trailers and print ads. "This film is positively ruthless in its attempt to drive you right out of your mind and it accomplishes everything it sets out to do with brilliance and unparalleled terror," judged Reed. Writing for the *Cincinnati Inquirer*, Donald R. Berrigan praised the acting and direction of *Chain Saw*, calling it "a motion picture that makes *The Exorcist* look like a sissified Sunday School picnic," though warned parents of "the content of this soul-tearing production as it may affect the emotional development of the young, especially girls who are taught to be wary."[31] For the *Guardian*, critic Derek Malcolm likewise heralded *Chain Saw* as "a minor tour de force" and "first-class piece of sweat-inducing cinema," though insisted "it doesn't pretend to do anything more than scare the pants off you."[32]

Such visceral reactions were no doubt heightened by *Chain Saw*'s intense realism that commonly blunted any attempt at deeper analysis. However, for some viewers that same believability also helped spark curiosity regarding both the film's construction and significance, including the way it potentially provided some kind of judgment upon the culture that produced it. Sincere critical estimations first emanated from Europe where the film was chosen for inclusion in the Quinzaine des Réalisateurs (Directors' Fortnight) at the 1975 Cannes Film Festival. (While there, Reed remarked sardonically how critics were "showing 'The Texas Chain-Saw Massacre,' which played in drive-ins at home and is being hailed as masterpiece here."[33])

Later that year those putting together the program for the London Film Festival followed suit, with Malcolm joining Nigel Andrews and Alexander Walker to make *Chain Saw* a special Critics Choice selection. For Andrews, the "ferocious intensity" of Hooper's direction placed it in "a different class from its catchpenny rivals of the week," while Walker insisted the film "helps define a certain aspect of society today."[34]

Another British critic, Robin Wood, would later provide the most comprehensive detailing of *The Texas Chain Saw Massacre*'s achievement in his influential 1979 essay "An Introduction to the American Horror Film" where he argues "Hooper's cinematic intelligence... becomes more apparent on every viewing, as one gets over the initial traumatizing impact" of the film to recognize its artistry and thematic complexity.[35] Besides proving important to horror studies in general, Wood's essay became something of a starting point for a variety of readings exploring *Chain Saw*'s treatment of themes then emerging as central to the horror genre during the 1960s and 1970s. A few of these include ongoing generational conflicts ("parent-figures destroy 'children'") and "the specific notion of present and future (the younger generation) being devoured by the past"; how capitalist ideology necessarily exploits and degrades the proletariat, here represented by unemployed slaughterhouse workers ostensibly resorting to cannibalism for their survival ("the logical end of human relations under capitalism"); sexual repression and how "the release of sexuality in the horror film is always presented as perverted, monstrous, and excessive" (among other psychoanalytic readings); and questioning of the assumed "goodness" or normality of the "family unit" and how in *Chain Saw* "the monster is the family."[36]

Even while finding much beneath the surface to recommend the film, Wood still appreciates the trauma *Chain Saw* inflicts on a first viewing, with his explanation of *why* it is so unsettling sounding a great deal like Irving Kristol describing how an irrational, incomprehensible government frightened him so. "Uncontrol is emphasized throughout the film: not only have the five young victims no control over their destiny, their slaughterers (variously psychotic and degenerate) keep losing control of themselves and each other," explains Wood. "This is partly (in conjunction with the film's relentless and unremitting intensity) what gives *Massacre* to such a degree (beyond any other film in my experience) the authentic quality of a nightmare."[37]

★ ★ ★ ★ ★

Watergate was a nightmare. *The Texas Chain Saw Massacre*, a film conceived, written, shot, edited, and produced contemporaneously with the Watergate scandal, was explicitly constructed to be experienced as a kind of nightmare, and audiences then and now have repeatedly confirmed its success in that regard. As it happened, Hooper and Henkel commonly described their movie as having been inspired by the political scandal and even, in a way, "about" Watergate.

Hooper often spoke about how current events and contemporary issues necessarily found their way into his films. "I just think that film, for the serious filmmaker, is an osmosis of the times," he explained. "That's usually what I tap for my resources: I look around at what's happening politically and economically."[38] When making such a point about *Chain Saw*, Hooper invariably listed Watergate as foremost among the various external goings-on that had been incorporated into the film. That said, when referring to the relationship between the fictional film and factual material upon which he drew, Hooper typically avoided particulars, characterizing the process as a kind of non-specific assimilation ("osmosis") or a general capturing of the spirit of the period in which the film was made ("the zeitgeist blew through"). Thus while he claimed of *Chain Saw* "This film kind of came out of the Watergate times," and that "It was kind of inspired by it, in a lot of ways," he offered no guidance regarding exactly how the film was shaped by the scandal.[39] Henkel would be similarly suggestive about a connection existing between their film and the political story dominating headlines during the time it was made. In a 1982 feature about *Chain Saw* Henkel did share a clue about the relationship, although again mostly left it to viewers to fill in the blanks: "To the film makers, it was the blackest of black comedies, with some wry commentary on what Henkel called 'the moral schizophrenia' of the Watergate era."[40]

It is easy to imagine Hooper's tongue at least partly in cheek when responding to questions about *Chain Saw*'s meaning, especially when offering oblique explanations like "it's a film about meat."[41] Just as often Hooper would say the film came "straight out of the no gas thing,"[42] claiming the nation's gas shortage provided not only a key plot point but a kind of stimulus for the entire situation and story. Also frequently referenced by the filmmakers and others as source material is the story of actual killer and grave robber Ed Gein of Plainfield, Wisconsin, although from Hooper's own occasionally conflicting accounts he was likely only vaguely aware of Gein's story at the time *Chain Saw* was made. According to Hooper, when growing up in Austin relatives from Wisconsin would occasionally visit and frighten him with tales of a murderer who dismembered his victims, built furniture from the bones, and used the skin for lampshades and masks.[43] Such details correspond to the biography of Gein whose crimes were discovered in late 1957, his story more directly inspiring the character of Norman Bates in both the *Psycho* novel (1959) and film (1960), Ezra Cobb in *Deranged* (from early 1974), and much later Buffalo Bill in *The Silence of the Lambs* novel (1988) and film (1991). "We decided to have a *family* of Ed Geins," Hooper and Henkel would explain when asked about sources for *Chain Saw*, an idea that perhaps also indirectly linked the story to the Manson Family killings from a few summers before.[44] Following *Chain Saw*'s release, Henkel would additionally cite the horrific "Candy Man Murders" committed by serial killer Dean Corll during the early 1970s in Houston as yet another influence upon the film, although there, too, the link is uncertain given Corll's story only became widely known after he was killed by his accomplice, Elmer Wayne Henley, on August 8, 1973—that is, months after the screenplay was written and about three weeks into filming.[45] In any case, it is reasonable to assume details from real-life horrors such as these were in the filmmakers' minds, even if *Chain Saw*'s story was not directly based upon them.

Trying to pinpoint the degree to which these "resources" were genuinely being tapped when *Chain Saw* was made or the extent to which the film can be reasonably said to reflect them in a deliberate way can be an interesting exercise, although it is important not to let the pursuit of subtexts obscure the text itself. In *Chain Saw Confidential*, actor Gunnar Hansen who portrayed masked killer Leatherface alludes to various interpretations of the film, including those promulgated by the filmmakers. "When we were talking about the film, Tobe always considered it a political allegory and comedy," says

Chain Saw cinematographer Daniel Pearl. "He would say that over and over again. This is a comedy, this is political allegory," explains Pearl. "It was all about the gas shortage, the food shortage, and the shortages that were going to be coming about." With a measure of ironic distance, Hansen acknowledges conclusions of "academics who could see past the chain saw to recognize allegorical echoes of both the corrupting influence of the Vietnam war and the collapse of the American family. Oh, and also bourgeois sexual repression." Of course, however convincing such readings of *Chain Saw* might be, Hansen is himself most persuasive when ranking one above the rest. "What is *Chain Saw* about? At one level the answer is simple. When I am asked, I say it is about scaring the crap out of you," he says, adding how both Pearl and Henkel agree.[46]

It is important as well when exploring non-literal meanings of *The Texas Chain Saw Massacre* to keep in mind the filmmakers' comedic intentions. As noted, both Hooper and Henkel repeatedly insisted upon their purpose to mix humor with horror. Wood was again one of the few to draw attention to this characteristic early on, arguing that "Central to the film—and centered on its monstrous family—is the sense of grotesque comedy, which in no way diminishes (rather intensifies) its nightmare horror."[47] Most who watch *Chain Saw* with a critical eye share Wood's view that the consistently outrageous depiction of the family of villains and their interactions well conveys how "the film's sense of fundamental horror is closely allied to a sense of the fundamentally absurd."[48] The utterly mad dinner scene culminating in the futile attempt to have Grandpa strike the final killing blow (a "macabre farce," says Wood[49]) is one of several examples of the film's most intense and horrifying moments containing an undercurrent of dark humor—*if* the viewer is not too frightened to notice, that is. The presence of such comic elements within the film makes it all the more reasonable to approach "serious" themes or messages about contemporary contexts as having been similarly delivered with a grain of salt. Just as the killer Leatherface arriving at dinner wearing a suit and tie (to go along with a newly made-up skin mask) adds a kind of droll incongruity to the scene, so, too, is there something intrinsically amusing about earnestly declaring *The Texas Chain Saw Massacre* to be a political allegory, a manner of "dressing up" a low-rent exploitation horror flick as something more dignified.

A poster of Richard Nixon created by the Democratic Party during the 1960 presidential campaign.

Those accepting the invitation to interpret *Chain Saw* as an extended metaphor of Watergate necessarily face limitations when trying to equate characters and situations in the film too directly with those of the political scandal's dramatic narrative. In truth, the film's cast is too small and the plot too narrow in scope to provide enough onscreen evidence to allow one to pursue the allegorical reading with any great depth. For example, in pop culture writer Joseph Lanza's recent book-length discussion of *Chain Saw*'s connections to a variety of contemporary contexts, he considers how one character in particular—the gas station owner, listed as the "Old Man" in the credits—might function as a kind of stand-in for the embattled Richard Nixon.[50] Actor Jim Siedow's physical resemblance to Nixon as well as his character's status as a seeming authority figure desperately struggling to control his "men" encourage such a reading. So does the "moral schizophrenia" his character exhibits when vacillating between objecting to and endorsing the others' sadism, recalling as it does the self-conflicted sophistry Nixon and others constantly employed to justify their criminal misdeeds. Yet further connections do not readily follow, and Lanza correctly avoids trying to assign additional equivalencies to other characters in order to shoehorn *Chain Saw*'s narrative into a kind of awkward *roman à clef* of Watergate.

Despite Hooper's own claims about making a "political allegory," it is more accurate to describe *Chain Saw*'s relationship to Watergate as *satirical* insofar as the film employs humor and wit to present an exaggerated, grotesque version of the crimes and abuses perpetrated by Nixon and his co-conspirators and their unsettling effect on the American public. Read in this way, the film can be interpreted as picking up and running with the idea that Watergate was indeed the "ultimate nightmare," transforming the story of political corruption

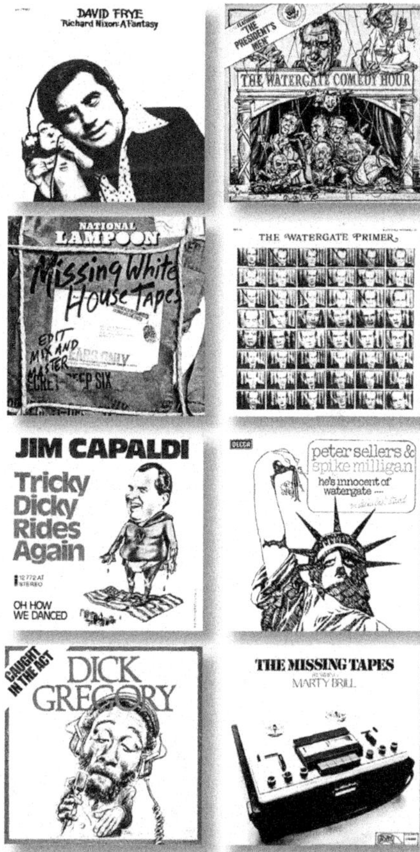

A sampling of Watergate-themed comedy and novelty records.

at the highest levels into a literal horror show. It goes without saying that *The Texas Chain Saw Massacre* is not *solely* about Watergate, and it would be unhelpfully reductive to claim as much. Yet a preponderance of both textual and contextual clues make clear that at least one of the filmmakers' intentions was for their nightmarish film to be understood as a kind of critical commentary on the nightmarish scandal. Some of the allusions to Watergate in *Chain Saw* are specific and deliberate, including (for example) the very first words spoken in the film when a radio news announcer reports a story involving indictments and a grand jury. Others are less on the surface, such as how the plot's circularity and "the way it folds continuously back on itself" recalls the infinite loop (or downward spiral) of the endless-seeming, every-turn-is-the-wrong-one Watergate story. In any case, the constant reminders, many of which attentive viewers in late 1974 were better positioned than we are to notice, well support the view that *Chain Saw* was made not just with an awareness of Watergate, but with a deliberate purpose to mock the scandal and those involved.

Reading *The Texas Chain Saw Massacre* as a Watergate satire might distinguish it from other low-budget horror films, but doing so aligns it right alongside many other contemporary cultural and media productions of the era. At the same time that Watergate produced genuine, existential distress among U.S. citizens over whether or not the republic would survive the trauma it was causing, it produced a multitude of parodies, spoofs, farces, caricatures, lampoons, and jokes ridiculing Nixon and others involved. Just as the scandal permanently damaged trust in government and presidential authority, it forever changed and emboldened political satire.

Nixon had been a prime target of satirists for his entire career as a politician. His vicious Congressional and Senate campaigns earned him the "Tricky Dick" nickname way back in 1950, with the fund crisis scandal and "Checkers" speech in 1952 affording him a momentary triumph though causing him subsequent vulnerability as a source of derision. Herbert Block's devastating "Here He Comes Now" cartoon from 1954 depicting then-Vice President Nixon crawling from an open sewer indelibly stamped him as a dirty politician. A poster created by the Democratic Party during the 1960 presidential campaign showing Nixon sporting a sinister grin next to the caption "Would YOU buy a used car from this man?" foregrounded his untrustworthiness. In the first presidential debate that year, the memorable contrast between a handsome and polished John F. Kennedy and Nixon appearing without makeup, perspiring, and in need of a shave added further to the ease with which Nixon could be reduced to caricature. His later rise to the presidency unsurprisingly increased the frequency of satirical treatments during Nixon's first term in office. There were a host of comedy LPs, including David Martin's sketches and songs *Richard the 37th: The Agnew and the Ecstasy* (1969), Orson Welles's scripture-themed oration *The Begatting of the President* (1970), and three very funny Nixon-themed titles by the comedian and impressionist David Frye, *I Am the President* (1969), *Radio Free Nixon* (1971), and *Richard Nixon: Superstar* (1971). Novelist Philip Roth wrote a book-length skewering of Nixon titled *Our Gang (Starring Tricky and His Friends)* that appeared late in 1971. There was even a play satirizing the president that ran on Broadway for two weeks in the spring of 1972, Gore Vidal's *An Evening with Richard Nixon* in which Vidal casts harsh judgment on the president via copious quotations from Nixon's own writings and speeches.

During that first term there also appeared a spate of comedic films that directly assailed the president. Renowned filmmaker Emile de

Antonio's 1971 documentary *Millhouse: A White Comedy* waggishly strings together archival footage from throughout Nixon's career, juxtaposing clips with other reporting and interviews to acerbic effect. According to de Antonio, after a hugely successful opening in multiple New York City theaters in late September 1971, the government successfully blocked further distribution of the film, thereby limiting its audience. ("That's the way hardball is played, and Nixon played hardball," said de Antonio, who would claim the film earned him a spot on the White House's infamous "enemies list."[51]) Fred Levinson's comedy *Hail* premiered at Cannes in May 1972, an inspired send-up in which a corrupt administration resembling Nixon's assassinates political opponents, introduces secret "detention camps" to imprison protestors, and conspires to eliminate Congress and the Supreme Court. Not released in the U.S. until 1973, a prologue suggests the "Federal Government banned" that film as well, causing it to be "forced out of distribution," although the claim has not been corroborated.[52] Similar stories surrounded the September 1972 farce *Another Nice Mess* directed by Bob Einstein (Albert Brooks's brother, later known as Super Dave Osborne) and co-produced by Tom Smothers who with his brother Dick drew Nixon's ire for anti-war segments and other political commentary on *The Smothers Brothers Comedy Hour*. Such material may have contributed to the decision by CBS to cancel the show in 1969, causing some to speculate the White House tried to suppress *Another Nice Mess* when it turned out to be a box office flop. The film stars Rich Little as Nixon and Herb Voland as Spiro Agnew who play the roles slapstick style as the comedy duo Stan Laurel and Oliver Hardy. In truth, the highly uneven film probably bombed all on its own, despite a cameo by a young Steve Martin as a trouble-causing hippie.

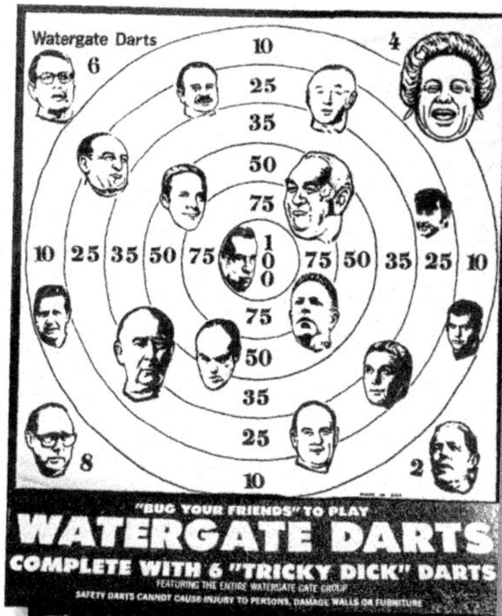

The Watergate darts game, one of several contemporary tie-ins satirizing the scandal.

Such examples of pre-Watergate Nixonian satire range from light-hearted jabs to more incisive attacks. However as Arthur Dudden argues in a historical overview of late 20th-century political humor, the glee with which Nixon was scorned during Watergate marked an important shift in tone and attitude for such criticism. "The laughter surrounding the Watergate affair was violent and destructive, a deeply skeptical ridicule without quarter," observes Dudden. "It was cynical, yet certain of its target, deadly in its accuracy. It declared unequivocally, as events proved, that a president of the United States for the first time in history was both a knave and a fool."[53] Such sentiments were voiced via a proliferation of buttons, t-shirts, novelty items, posters, and bumper stickers making Nixon the punchline ("Honk If You Think He's Guilty," "Four More Years, and Two Off for Good Behavior"). Humorists submitted satirical columns on a weekly basis, one of the most famous being Art Buchwald's "What to Say About Watergate" piece from July 1973 compiling a catalogue of excuses from which the president's supporters could draw: "Everyone does it," "The press is blowing the whole thing up," "The President was too busy running the country to know what was going on," "Franklin D. Roosevelt did a lot worse things," "What about Chappaquiddick?"[54] *The Watergate Cookbook* by N.Y. Alplaus (Jerome and Cynthia Rubin) included recipes for Nixon's Perfectly Clear Consomme, Ehrlichman's Cover-Up Casserole, and Mitchell's Sitting Duck. The Watergate Scandal card game, "a game of cover-up, deception and scandal for the whole family," sold out a first printing of 10,000 in four days.[55] The Watergate Game was a hit as well, a board and dice game in which "cheating is permitted" and the object was the same, namely, to be the last player not to go to jail.[56] There was also Watergate Darts inviting players to throw "'Tricky Dick' darts" at a board that featured "the whole Watergate gang" ("'Bug Your Friends' to Play"). On the literary front, Judith Wax used Chaucer as inspiration for her poetic "The Waterbury Tales" in which she replaced pilgrims with the Watergate cast of characters in a series of Middle English couplets.[57] George V. Higgins reworked his bestselling hard-boiled crime novel *The Friends of Eddie Coyle* into a book-length political commentary, *The Friends of Richard Nixon*. Even Marvel Comics' *Captain America* introduced a multi-issue storyline in early 1974 in which the titular hero uncovers a criminal conspiracy called the

"Secret Empire," tracing it all the way to the White House where resides the organization's leader, referred to only as "Number One" but obviously Nixon. Shockingly, the story arc ends in the Oval Office with Number One avoiding justice by shooting himself in the head.[58]

Meanwhile *Time* was telling its readers how in nightclubs "Comics across the country are milking Watergate for every plausible or implausible laugh that it is worth," adding "at least a dozen records and albums featuring Watergate humor have already been released."[59] Following an earlier report on "a gusher of albums and singles on the subject" in "Watergates Flood Market," an article in *Billboard* from the week *Chain Saw* began filming in July 1973 marveled at how no less than three Watergate-themed comedy records were appearing in the charts—Dickie Goodman's novelty single "Watergrate," Mort Sahl's comeback album *Sing a Song of Watergate*, and *The Watergate Comedy Hour* LP featuring sketches by Avery Schreiber, Jack Burns, Fannie Flagg and others.[60] Other novelty singles included Don Imus's "Son of Checkers" (a "break-in" record much like Goodman's featuring snippets of popular songs punctuating a faux news report), Tom T. Hall's lament "Watergate Blues" which made the country Top 20, Jim Capaldi of Traffic's angry rocker "Tricky Dickie Rides Again," and "Haldeman, Ehrlichman, Mitchell, and Dean" performed by a barbershop quartet dubbed The Creep (the commonly used acronym of the Committee for the Re-Election of the President) who in September 1973 performed the song on *The Mike Douglas Show*. Dick Gregory, Earle Doud, Marty Brill, and Peter Sellers and Spike Milligan all filled entire LPs with Watergate material, while Alen Robin, Richard Pryor, the Credibility Gap, and the Firesign Theatre were among other comedy acts devoting vinyl space to the subject. Within a week of the Saturday Night Massacre, Frank Zappa's band was premiering a new composition in their live show, the title of which communicated an unambiguous perspective on the president: "Dickie's Such an Asshole." Robert Klein addressed the scandal on his *Mind Over Matter* LP on a track called "Wallowing in Watergate," the title of which alludes to a phrase once used by an irritated Nixon to describe the country's obsession. Mark Russell makes a similar observation about the scandal's ubiquity on *Mark Russell's Wild, Weird Wired World of Watergate*, an LP chronicling a live performance of satirical songs and jokes from his residency at the Shoreham Hotel in Washington, D.C. Recognizing Watergate had begun to dominate his usual politics-focused act, Russell noted "I'm becoming a one-issue candidate here."

Among the better comedic treatments of Watergate was National Lampoon's album *The Missing White House Tapes* that collected material previously aired on its nationally-syndicated radio show while adding a side's worth of cut-and-paste tracks reordering Nixon's own words to hilarious effect (e.g., assembling phrases from Watergate speeches into an "Admission Speech" confessing to various crimes). Skits include an ongoing "Impeachment Parade" mocking an inauguration processional, a *Sesame Street* parody "Pennsylvania Avenue" starring Big Dick, the Shredder Monster, and Ervin the Frog, and "Mission Impeachable" spoofing the introduction to the popular spy drama with instructions being delivered to the Watergate burglars. However the best and most successful of the Watergate LPs was David Frye's *Richard Nixon: A Fantasy*, the fourth and final Nixon-focused album by Frye whose connection to Nixon was analogous to Vaughn Meader's to Kennedy. Despite radio and television networks' resistance to run ads for the album and Woolworth's refusal to stock it over worries it "might offend some people,"[61] *Richard Nixon: A Fantasy* spent 15 weeks on the *Billboard* Top 200 albums chart during the latter half of 1973, peaking at #45, and like *The Missing White House Tapes* it was nominated for a Grammy for Best Comedy Recording. The album weaves together a sequence of short sketches casting Nixon as "Five O'Clock Shadow," the central character in a gangster movie who escapes punishment following the Watergate break-in, but is subsequently caught and imprisoned, tried and found guilty, and ultimately sentenced to the electric chair. The witty story written by Frye, Gabe Kaplan, and others alludes to numerous films and television shows along the way (e.g., *The Godfather*, *Convicts 4*, *The Caine Mutiny*, *Perry Mason*), affording Frye the chance to showcase more than two dozen impressions. All is framed by Frye doing Walter Winchell as narrator of *The Untouchables* television series, and interestingly Winchell's sensational, alarmed introduction resembles *The Texas Chain Saw Massacre*'s opening crawl: "The story you are about to hear is unique in the annals of American crime." The album's conclusion also evokes *Chain Saw*, with Nixon narrowly escaping electrocution thanks to his finally waking up. That's right—it was all a nightmare.

Most contemporary Watergate satire (and much of it since) is characterized by similarly overt denunciation of Nixon, with even the most inspired examples typically marked by broad humor and indignant lashes leaving little doubt about the criticism being delivered. To evoke John Dryden's famous distinction between "railing" and "raillery" in his late 17th-century essay "A Discourse Concerning the Original and Progress of Satire," most Watergate satire falls into the former category of explicit and direct attack, unlike the more subtle, allusive type of satire Dryden believed to be both more difficult and more effective. "How easie it is to call Rogue and Villain, and that wittily?" he argued. "But how hard to make a Man appear a Fool, a Blockhead, or a Knave, without using any of those opprobrious terms? To spare the grossness of the Names, and to do the thing yet more severely, is to draw a full Face, and to make the Nose and Cheeks stand out, and yet not to employ any depth of Shadowing." Dryden further emphasized the difference with a vivid metaphor, characterizing name-calling and heavy-handed invective as the "slovenly Butchering of a Man" that carves up the target and generally demands little or no work from readers to grasp. Meanwhile the best raillery requires the "fineness of a stroak that separates the Head from the Body, and leaves it standing in its place"—in other words, is less blunt, more understated, and often needs the audience to exert some effort to discover the actual wound.[62] Dryden highlighted his poem *Absalom and Achitophel* (or one character from it, anyway) as his own best effort when it came to achieving such finesse, a political satire and allegory that ingeniously retells the Old Testament story of King David and his rebellious son as a way of commenting on a current succession crisis involving Charles II and the efforts of those seeking to make his illegitimate son heir to the throne. Interestingly, the essayist Joseph Addison would subsequently spark a debate among critics after pointing out that to him one of the chief pleasures of Dryden's poem and a primary reason for its popularity was the way it "gave the Reader an Opportunity of exerting his own Talents" by the intellectual exercise of deciphering how the surface-level story from the scriptures related to the contemporary political crisis.[63]

There is nothing subtle about the way Leatherface uses a chainsaw in *The Texas Chain Saw Massacre*. But there is a great deal in the film that is, including its commentary on Watergate and the Nixon administration, and as a result some effort is required to uncover *Chain Saw*'s many allusions to the scandal. What follows is an attempt to do just that and explore the filmmakers' assertions about *Chain Saw* being inspired in part by Watergate and even made with the intention of reflecting upon it in a critical way. Tracing connections between the details, characters, and plot of *Chain Saw* and the details, characters, and plot of Watergate is both entertaining and edifying, giving those who have seen the film many times something new to consider while also adding further to the overwhelming evidence that the film is much more than "simply an exercise in terror." Doing so also helps to recall just how unprecedentedly nightmarish and disturbing both the Watergate scandal and *The Texas Chain Saw Massacre* were for Americans—easy enough to forget after decades' worth of escalating horrors that have happened both in the movies *and* in presidential politics.

A word about the decision not to try to encapsulate *Chain Saw*'s satire in summary form and instead highlight discrete (and sometimes discreet) connections between the film and scandal that arise throughout the film. While *Chain Saw*'s engagement with Watergate is frequent and fairly consistent, it is nonetheless intermittent, presenting brief, suggestive comments that contribute toward a general criticism of the actions of Nixon and his cohorts without sustaining an overall, ongoing "argument" as, say, a genuine political allegory might have done. The young people being frightened and terrorized by the crazed family undoubtedly can be read as an exaggerated version of the trauma inflicted upon the American public by those responsible for Watergate, and many of the connections between the film and the scandal do relate to that overall thesis. But other references evoke different ideas about Nixon and Watergate that would have been necessary to exclude from that argument as tangential digressions. Such an approach would also have likely meant glossing over moments when the film references political and cultural issues not explicitly related to Watergate but nonetheless significant to its context.

I have also been steered in this direction by other examples of book-length "deep dives" into individual films that exemplify a kind of "granular" approach that lingers over minutiae with a magnifying glass in an effort to tease out underlying meanings. Other, non-traditional examples of meticulous, exhaustive, and even obsessive methods of interpreting individual films have provided inspiration as well. Internet publishing with no limits to word counts or the scope of one's inquiry has yielded countless examples of unbridled, fanatical dissection of films, a phenomenon also demonstrated by podcasts such as the many "movies by minute" shows that devote an entire episode to discussing each minute of a favorite film. The ease with which meaning-seeking viewers can themselves manipulate digital video has even led to interpreters making their own movies in response, replacing text-based criticism with visual analyses that in some cases are quite effective. Also worth mentioning are examples of what Chuck Klosterman has called "immersion criticism" in which passionate viewers find ways to argue "that symbolic, ancillary details inside a film are infinitely more important than the surface dialogue or the superficial narrative" in order to support elaborately idiosyncratic or, as Klosterman says, "usually insane" readings (e.g., *The Shining* as Stanley Kubrick's coded confession for having helped NASA fake the moon landings).[64]

Examples of the latter often insist upon unprovable and/or outlandish claims about intention, whereas the filmmakers' own affirmations of *Chain Saw*'s Watergate connection as well as evidence within the film directly invite my chosen path of inquiry. That said, on occasion I have permitted myself to wander slightly off the evidentiary trail of bread crumbs left by the filmmakers in order to fill in details of the stories of both *Chain Saw* and Watergate that are not otherwise covered. In this regard I am guided by the filmmakers' own consistently good-humored approach to the idea of infusing their film with suggestive subtexts and then finding out later what it signifies to others—or even to themselves. "I think we shoot a lot of stuff, and then 20 years later find out what it really meant," Hooper once said, acknowledging the process by which the passage of time can cause what originally seemed (or was intended to be) part of a film's background to subsequently emerge more front and center and cause primary messages and themes to recede in significance.[65] Some might find such a stance toward the film's interpretation ambivalent or even apathetic, while the more cynical might even align it with the apparent nihilism exhibited by *Chain Saw*'s story. I would instead regard such openness to a variety of readings as consistent with the filmmakers' generally mischievous attitude toward both the film and its potential meanings, an attitude that guided the entire production all the way back to Hooper's fantasy of chainsawing his way out of Montgomery Ward. It is in a similarly playful, non-dogmatic spirit that I approach the exploration of *Chain Saw*'s satirical response to Watergate and the many ways the "worlds" of both the film and the scandal overlap.

★ ★ ★ ★ ★

Exactly one month after Nixon announced he was resigning, President Ford once more addressed the nation. Again he spoke of nightmares, and a desire to end them. The tragedy of Nixon and his presidency "could go on and on and on," he said, "or someone must write the end to it." In order not to "prolong the bad dreams that continue to reopen a chapter that is closed," Ford announced he had decided to grant a "full, free, and absolute pardon unto Richard Nixon" for all offenses—known or yet to be discovered—committed by him during his tenure in office.[66]

On the one hand, the new president's action did effectively provide an "end" to the Watergate narrative, at least insofar as it resolved the central issue of Nixon's ultimate fate. But it hardly settled questions about the extent of Nixon's culpability, nor did it do anything to restore the nation's faith in their leaders or curb mounting distrust in government. Rather it had the opposite effect, ensuring more scrutiny and investigation as the American public endeavored to understand the significance of what it had endured. In a way, such a non-ending ending prefigured the abrupt, ambiguous conclusion of *The Texas Chain Saw Massacre* that premiered just three weeks later, a film in which the main character with whom the audience identifies survives, but so, too, does the mask-wearing villain from whom she very narrowly escapes.

The nightmare was over. But the effort to comprehend what had happened and what it all meant was just getting started.

Caught in the Vortex (0:00)

From the original trailer to *The Texas Chain Saw Massacre.*

AGAINST A BLACK SCREEN the first credit appears, like the rest (save the title) appearing in all lower case: "a vortex/henkel/hooper production."

Vortex, Inc. was a corporation—a production company—established by Kim Henkel and Tobe Hooper in order to manage the collection of profits and other business emanating from their film, *The Texas Chain Saw Massacre*. With Henkel the company's president and Hooper its vice president, the pair's administration would not be *quite* as embattled as the concurrent one headed by Richard Nixon and Spiro Agnew, although it was not without its own significant difficulties. When considering in retrospect the fate of the millions of dollars *Chain Saw* earned and the filmmakers' desperate, mostly futile efforts to obtain a rightful share, a company name evoking a downward spiral or black hole might seem grimly appropriate.

As detailed in a two-part 1982 *Los Angeles Times* feature by Ellen Farley and William K. Knoedelseder Jr., the story of the financing and distribution of *Chain Saw* is nearly as complicated and legally fraught as the tangled narrative threads produced by the Watergate scandal. Needing a budget with which to begin production, it was late spring 1973 when the filmmakers received $60,000 from entrepreneurial-minded businessman Bill J. Parsley in exchange for 50 percent ownership of the film and of any profits it might produce. At the time, the former Texas state legislator was Vice President for Public Affairs at Texas Tech University and had occasionally invested in independent films before. "I just like deals," Parsley explained when asked about his involvement in *Chain Saw*. "I like to put things together, whether it's oil or movies or whatever."[67] Warren Skaaren, the first-ever head of the Texas Film Commission established in May 1971, had put Hooper and Henkel in touch with Parsley who, after deciding he was interested in investing in the "little ol' horror movie" (as he described it), formed a financing corporation of his own called M.A.B. of which he owned two-thirds.[68] The filmmakers later sold another 19 percent of Vortex to a second company comprised of attorney Joe K. Longley and a few of his poker buddies who collectively contributed $23,532. That group's lack of expectation regarding the project was reflected in the name they chose for their company—P.I.T.S. (for "Pie in the Sky").[69]

Later when Henkel and Hooper convinced cast and crew members to accept payment in shares of Vortex, they apparently failed to clarify their company did not in fact own the entire film, but only 50 percent after the deal with Parsley, and even less following the subsequent one with Longley and his associates. "We didn't know about M.A.B. until two years later," explained Edwin Neal who portrayed the Hitchhiker in the film. "We knew there was a group of investors, but for all we knew they were part of Vortex."[70] As post-production editing stretched out over many months—much of it taking place in Tobe Hooper's living room—more money had to be raised, increasing the film's budget to about $125,000 according to most estimates, with Hooper later citing $155,000 as a final total.[71] With each additional contribution to the budget the actual percentage of the film owned by those holding "points" of Vortex further diminished. Thus any profits *Chain Saw* produced would have likely created problems down the road between Henkel, Hooper, the 20 or so cast and crew members, and other Vortex shareholders.

However the distribution deal subsequently arranged for the film was even more disastrous, all but ensuring those who made and originally invested in *Chain Saw* would receive little more than a pittance for a film Farley and Knoedelseder estimate earned $20–25 million at the box office during the first couple of years and "perhaps as much as $50 million at theaters around the world" by 1982.[72] It was Skaaren again who helped Henkel and Hooper land a distribution deal for the film after several major studios turned it down. Via a Hollywood contact, Skaaren had *Chain Saw* screened by a representative of the Bryanston Distributing Company of New York who quickly offered $225,000 to the filmmakers to distribute *Chain Saw* in exchange for 35 percent of the box office.[73] According to John "Joe Bob Briggs" Bloom, the deal was closed on the very day Nixon resigned from office (although in truth it was a few weeks later).[74]

Production still from *The Texas Chain Saw Massacre.*

Both Bloom and the *L.A. Times* writers supply further details about Bryanston and its novel marketing techniques to increase *Chain Saw*'s profile and help ensure its notoriety prior to its October 1974 premiere and afterwards. They also describe connections between Bryanston heads Louis and Joseph Peraino Jr.—called the "Piranha brothers" by some—and the Columbo crime family. When the great majority of the money collected by the distributors failed to find its way to the filmmakers or other investors, it eventually became clear Bryanston had no intention of honoring agreements made with the filmmakers, withholding most of the film's profits from the beginning. That meant when Vortex eventually did receive payments they were already small even before M.A.B. and P.I.T.S. received their portions. In his 2013 account *Chain Saw Confidential*, Gunnar Hansen who played Leatherface described the moment nine months after the film's release when he received his first payment due to him for his "small share in Vortex," and how dismayed he was to receive a check for just $47.07.[75] At the same time Neal was paid $28.45 for his 0.5 percent ownership of Vortex.[76] "See, that's where the massacre is... *after* the movie," commented Allen Danziger who portrayed Jerry.[77] Lawsuits would follow, with an initial settlement in 1977 also not honored by Bryanston.

"It could take a team of intelligence agents years to unravel the movie's trail and decode the legal paperwork left in its wake," conclude Farley and Knoedelseder.[78]

By the time Henkel and Hooper formed their company, the word "vortex" had already become a favorite choice of commentators to describe the swirling maelstrom of Watergate, challenging "nightmare"

A poster advertising *Deep Throat* (1972), Associate Director of the FBI Mark W. Felt.

as an all-purpose descriptor. An Associated Press item from early April 1973 highlights "Two big names caught in the hottening Watergate vortex," White House Counsel John Dean and Nixon's doomed-to-fail nominee to head the FBI L. Patrick Gray.[79] Others subsequently involved in the cover-up would be described similarly, such as Nixon lawyer Fred Buzhardt Jr. who found himself "Caught in Watergate Vortex" or SEC chairman G. Bradford Cook who "got caught up in the Watergate vortex and was compelled to quit, another young lawyer disgraced."[80] Meanwhile taking over as Director of the Office of Public Liaison after co-conspirator Charles Colson was dismissed in March 1973 was William J. Baroody Jr. who was later portrayed as gamely trying to rehabilitate the White House's reputation and relationships with labor "in all this Watergate vortex."[81]

One other Watergate-related coincidence concerning the film's distribution is worth mentioning. Prior to their involvement with *Chain Saw*, the Peraino family had earlier financed the hardcore pornographic film *Deep Throat* with Louis producing and father Anthony having supplied the film's paltry $22,500 budget. Employing mob connections for distribution and also extorting the film's profits from director Gerard Damiano, the family amassed a fortune from the X-rated film released just five days before the second Watergate break-in was discovered on June 17, 1972. *Deep Throat*'s status as a pop culture touchstone was further cemented when *Washington Post* managing editor Howard Simons began using the title as a nickname for reporter Bob Woodward's anonymous source within the executive branch who provided information to him about the developing scandal on "deep background."[82] Decades later in 2005, it was revealed that then Associate Director of the FBI Mark W. Felt had been "Deep Throat."

Writing Partners (0:00)

Kim Henkel and Tobe Hooper during production of *The Texas Chain Saw Massacre*.

Originally from Virginia, Henkel graduated from the University of Texas at Austin with a degree in English in 1969. It was around that time Henkel first met Hooper, an Austin native. Soon after Henkel collaborated with Hooper on the latter's first feature film *Eggshells*, appearing as a writer named Toz (credited as Boris Schnurr) and contributing extra dialogue, and the pair became best friends. "After that, Tobe and I talked about something off and on for several years and then we finally settled on the *Chain Saw* project," Henkel later recalled.[83]

Recounting the pair's writing process amid his commentary for a DVD release of *Chain Saw*, Hooper explained how Henkel "would come over to my house and I would sit in my little office and then Kim, he and I would talk and talk and he would go into the kitchen where the typewriter was and he would bang out pages and come out and we'd talk and talk more and he'd go back and bang pages out," a process Henkel remembers lasting "most of six to eight weeks" during the first part of 1973.[84] "What we did was sit down and talked through the script, worked through it scene by scene in terms of action, what was going to happen from one scene to the next, then I would go off and write the scene," explained Henkel. The pair managed to create a 160-page first draft by this method, eventually revising and paring it down to about 100 pages and titling the screenplay *Leatherface*.[85]

At the start of 1973, Hooper was 30 and Henkel 27. While they worked on their screenplay, articles reporting on the unfolding Watergate scandal by two other writing partners, Bob Woodward (who turned 30 in March 1973) and Carl Bernstein (then 29), continued to appear in the *Washington Post*. The first Watergate article to which the pair had contributed had been published about six months earlier.

At about 2 a.m. on Saturday, June 17, 1972, undercover policemen had discovered five men inside the offices of the Democratic National Committee headquarters located on the sixth floor of the Watergate Office Building in Washington, D.C. The men had broken into the DNC headquarters ostensibly to take photographs and plant listening devices, and all five were charged with felonious burglary and with possession of implements of crime. The *Washington Post* published a report on the incident in the Sunday morning edition, appearing on the front page under the headline "5 Held in Plot to Bug Democrats' Office Here." The byline went to Alfred E. Lewis, a long-time police reporter for the paper, although eight different reporters contributed to it including Woodward and Bernstein.[86] By Monday papers around the country had picked up the story and how the Federal Bureau of Investigation had already launched an investigation.

It was on Monday as well that White House Press Secretary Ron Ziegler deflected a question about the arrests with an offended-sounding dismissal. "I'm not going to comment from the White House about a third-rate burglary attempt," he asserted, characterizing the incident as "something that should not fall into the political process."[87] Three days later, President Richard Nixon himself held a press conference where he responded similarly when asked about the break-in. "As Mr. Ziegler has stated, the White House has had no involvement whatever in this particular incident," said the president.[88]

But even as initial denials were being delivered, links between those involved in the break-in and both Nixon's campaign and the White House had already been uncovered and were starting to be explored and reported. One of the five arrested at the DNC, James W. McCord Jr., was a former FBI and CIA officer then employed as security coordinator for the re-election committee. John Mitchell, Nixon's former Attorney General who in the spring left that position to become the committee's director, had immediately issued a statement insisting McCord and the other four men "were not operating either in our behalf or with our consent,"[89] though curiously Mitchell would give up managing Nixon's campaign two weeks later citing a need to spend more time with family.[90] Soon it was found two others who had organized the break-in had ties as well, ex-FBI agent G. Gordon Liddy who was also employed by the re-election committee, and ex-CIA agent E. Howard Hunt who had worked for the administration as

Bob Woodward and Carl Bernstein in the offices of the *Washington Post*.

a consultant and was listed in the White House directory. A few weeks later, Woodward and Bernstein reported a $25,000 cashier's check contributed to Nixon's campaign had been deposited directly into the bank account of one of the break-in suspects.[91] By the time of the Republican National Convention in late August, a grand jury charged with examining the case was poised to deliver criminal indictments and would do so in mid-September. That ensured the prospect of a subsequent trial would keep "the specter of the Watergate Caper" (as some had begun to style it) around until after the November election.[92]

For the remainder of the year and into the next, the administration's efforts to keep the focus away from Watergate were largely successful. As the incumbent, Nixon essentially avoided campaigning at all until the final weeks before the election. At an early October press conference he fielded a single question about Watergate and kept his answer brief, citing censure he had earned a couple of years before when commenting publicly on the trial of Charles Manson as reason to observe "the same single standard" and not talk about the indicted.[93] Even a detailed, two-night special report on Watergate delivered by Walter Cronkite on the *CBS Evening News* a week-and-a-half before the election did little to diminish the president's popularity, although the report would influence other news outlets eventually to begin paying attention to the story. For most of the 77.7 million Americans who voted for president in 1972, Watergate was a non-issue, and those who were aware of it mostly considered it a side story energizing a few "liberal" reporters working inside the D.C. beltway. As Timothy Crouse explains at the end of *The Boys on the Bus*, his book chronicling the 1972 presidential campaign and how it was covered, "the White House strategy was to make the issue out to be the *Washington Post* rather than the Watergate affair, and they succeeded."[94]

Nixon won re-election with ease, defeating the Democratic candi-

Original poster advertising *The Texas Chain Saw Massacre.*

date George McGovern by capturing 520 of 538 electoral votes and more than 60 percent of the popular vote. In January 1973 came the trial of the seven suspects, five of whom pleaded guilty, then at the end of the month McCord and Liddy were also found guilty of numerous charges. Even so, the American public remained unmoved by the developing story, with the White House's connection to Watergate still largely obscured to most. That same week headlines were taken up by news of the signing of the Vietnam Peace Agreement, a couple of days after which a Gallup poll reported Nixon's job approval rating had risen to 67 percent, matching the highest number he had achieved throughout his entire presidency.[95]

As the court turned to the sentencing phase, however, some believed key details surrounding the break-in's planning and purpose had remained hidden, with presiding Chief Federal District Judge John Sirica among the skeptics who still had questions about the defendants' motives and connections. "I was hoping that we would get answers to all of them," said Sirica after delivering the verdicts. "I don't know if we did or not."[96] Suspicions were strong enough to encourage the Senate on February 7 to vote 77-0 to create the Select Committee on Presidential Activities, a.k.a. the Senate Watergate Committee, "to conduct an investigation and study of the extent, if any, to which illegal, improper, or unethical activities were engaged in by any persons, acting individually or in combination with others, in the presidential campaign of 1972, or any campaign, canvass, or other activity related to it."

The committee began to contemplate potential witnesses. The White House considered its response and level of cooperation, starting to weigh the potential political fallout of the possibly public hearings to come. Then came Friday, March 23, the day of sentencing for the seven defendants. That was also the day a letter written by defendant James McCord to Judge Sirica was made public thanks to Sirica's dramatic reading of it aloud in court. Alluding to his own fraught legal situation ("I am whipsawed in a variety of legalities") and even doubts about his own personal safety ("Several members of my family have expressed fear for my life"), McCord presented a numbered list of shocking claims regarding the Watergate suspects' trial, including how they had been pressured to plead guilty and remain silent, that perjury had occurred, and that "Others involved in the Watergate operation were not identified during the trial."[97] The letter caused Sirica to postpone McCord's sentence, though he otherwise lived up to his "Maximum John" nickname by provisionally sentencing the other four burglars to 40 years in prison, Hunt to 35, and Liddy to a minimum of six years and eight months. In the wake of McCord's letter, others involved in what by then had been nine months' worth of effort to hide White House connections to the defendants were beginning to waver. The story that Woodward, Bernstein, and a handful of others had been pursuing was about to take over the nation's headlines, consuming Americans' attention without cessation for the next eighteen months.

Early in the pair's 1974 bestseller *All the President's Men*, Woodward and Bernstein describe how their famous collaboration began. "Woodward typed out the first three paragraphs of a story identifying one of the Watergate burglars as a salaried security coordinator of the President's re-election committee and handed it to an editor on the city desk," they recount (referring to themselves in third person). "A minute later, Bernstein was looking over the editor's shoulder, Woodward noticed. Then Bernstein was walking back to his desk with the first page of the story; soon he was typing. Woodward finished the second page and passed it to the editor. Bernstein had soon relieved him of it and was back at his typewriter. Woodward decided to walk over and find out what was happening. Bernstein was rewriting the story. Woodward reread the rewritten version. It was better."[98] The book was published June 15, 1974. A little less than two months later Nixon resigned, and a little less than two months after that *The Texas Chain Saw Massacre* premiered. (In April 2003, Woodward and Bernstein sold their "Watergate papers" consisting of notes, interviews, book galleys, letters, and other items produced by the pair from June 1972 through 1976 for the prodigious sum of $5 million. The purchaser? The University of Texas.)

Especially after the 1976 film adaptation directed by Alan J. Pakula, *All the President's Men*'s compelling presentation of journalists in action foregrounded the importance of both collaboration and corroboration when reporting, elevating to iconic status *Post* executive editor Ben Bradlee's famous maxim to "get it right." Meanwhile, the process by which Henkel and Hooper judged their work on the *Leatherface* screenplay was described by the latter in a way that emphasized the filmmakers' satirical intentions:

"When it was funny to us, we knew it was right."[99]

What Happened Is True. That Was a Lie (0:14)

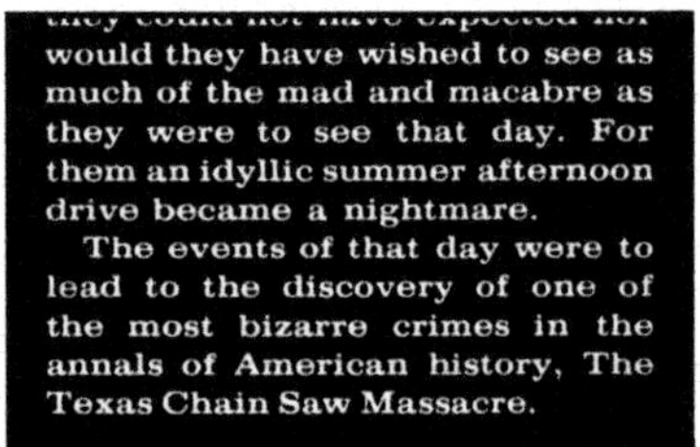

The opening crawl.

Following Hooper's directorial credit comes the famous opening crawl. The text is narrated by the actor John Larroquette in his first credited role.

"The film which you are about to see is an account of the tragedy which befell a group of five youths, in particular Sally Hardesty and her invalid brother, Franklin," Larroquette begins, implying *Chain Saw* to be based on an actual event. Much as viewers misremember the quotient of blood and gore subsequently shown, so, too, do commentators often mistakenly refer to the introduction as a literal claim of historical veracity, a confirmation of what was in fact only stated in the tagline of the film's original, effective poster: "What happened is true. Now the motion picture that's just as real."

Hooper later explained how he'd instructed Larroquette to "do his best at Orson Welles" when reading the lines.[100] While evoking Welles and his authoritative baritone as a model for a narrator was standard, it was doubly appropriate when one recalls games Welles himself played with audiences regarding verisimilitude. "We had no intention that anyone would believe this was a real event," explained Henkel. "This was supposed to be in the tradition of those overblown radio dramas of the '30s, like Orson Welles' *War of the Worlds*—we had no intention of actually deceiving anybody."[101] Audiences were nonetheless fooled, with many even today still believing *Chain Saw* is based on actual events. In *Chain Saw Confidential*, both Hansen and Henkel share multiple accounts of individuals insisting upon the story's veracity and knowledge of the "real" Leatherface's whereabouts (most often at the state prison in Huntsville, Texas).[102] In any event, the truth conceit could be strategically evoked to defend the film's brutality, and in fact the filmmakers did frequently point to real-life horrors as justification for those depicted onscreen. In other words, in a practical sense, saying "what happened is true" could function as a kind of "cover story."

The crawl does not appear in the screenplay and was only added near the very end of post-production, just about when the House Judiciary Committee opened formal impeachment hearings on May 9, 1974. Like Henkel, Hooper usually characterized the crawl as an irreverent bit of dissembling. Less playfully, he also connected it directly to more serious examples of dishonesty such as those being explored by lawmakers at the time.

"The opening of the film states: 'The story you are about to see is true.' That was a lie," said Hooper. "That was a response to being lied to by the government about things that were going on all over the world."[103]

One of the Most Bizarre Crimes in the Annals of American History (0:48)

The crawl concludes with Larroquette indicating that what we are about to witness represents "one of the most bizarre crimes in the annals of American history."

From the beginning, Richard Nixon's earliest statements about the break-in and arrests at the Democratic National Committee headquarters at the Watergate hotel in Washington, D.C. emphasized at once both the strangeness of the crime and his professed desire to uncover and present the true story of it.

Just four days after the Watergate arrests, Nixon was already privately recognizing in an Oval Office conversation with White House Chief of Staff H.R. "Bob" Haldeman how the oddity of the crime would likely intrigue those outside the D.C. bubble. "Anything that's as bizarre as this—and interesting—is going to be a national story," Nixon conceded.[104] He would use the same adjective to describe the break-in later in an August 1972 press conference. There the president proclaimed, "I can say categorically that his [White House Counsel John Dean's] investigation indicates that no one on the White House staff, no one in this administration, presently employed, was involved in this very bizarre incident." As Dean would later testify, the claim that he had conducted an investigation into the matter as well as other statements about the White House's cooperation with others' investigations were all false. In any case, amid the fabrications Nixon blithely professed a commitment to uncovering the truth: "We have indicated that we want all the facts brought out and that as far as any people are who guilty are concerned, they should be prosecuted."[105]

By the time Judge Sirica read James McCord's letter aloud in court, it was plain to all that while the original Watergate crime was certainly bizarre, the truth about the break-in and what had taken place both before and after it had yet to surface. From the last week of March through April 1973, the drama kicked into high gear as several involved in the break-in and/or cover-up started to break their silence with both prosecutors and lawmakers. McCord began cooperating with the court while also meeting with the Senate Watergate Committee. E. Howard Hunt was granted immunity by Judge Sirica and testified before the grand jury. Meanwhile Jeb Magruder, the deputy director of Nixon's re-election committee under Mitchell who had known about the break-in beforehand and was involved in efforts to hide White House connections after, had committed perjury during the Watergate defendants' trial. Knowing McCord's letter to Sirica alluded to him (among others), Magruder likewise decided to begin cooperating with prosecutors. During April, many others including Dwight Chapin (Nixon's Deputy Assistant), Gordon Strachan (aide and primary liaison between the White House and the re-election committee), David Young (Special Assistant to the National Security Council), Fred LaRue (campaign official and participant in both the planning for Watergate and the cover-up), Herbert Kalmbach (Nixon's personal attorney), and John Mitchell (former Attorney General and re-election committee director) would testify before the grand jury.

Meanwhile John Dean, after not having produced a Watergate

report previously, was again given the task to do so and at the end of March was sent to the presidential lodge at Camp David in Maryland for that purpose. Recognizing the White House's new strategy to portray him as chief orchestrator of the Watergate cover-up, Dean reported back that he could not produce the assigned report. Soon Dean on one side entered into negotiations with prosecutors to deliver testimony in exchange for immunity, and on the other did the same with the White House to settle upon terms for his resignation. After reassigning the task of leading the White House's nominal "investigation" of Watergate to Domestic Affairs Advisor John Ehrlichman, Nixon announced on April 17 that all members of the White House staff would be made available to testify before the Senate Watergate Committee. In the same statement, the president obliquely indicated "there have been major developments in the case concerning which it would be improper to be more specific now, except to say that real progress has been made in finding the truth."[106] More turmoil followed, with Dean quickly issuing a statement that he would not be made a "scapegoat" and the White House (via Ziegler) firing back that the process they were following was "not one to find scapegoats but one to get at the truth." Amid mounting stories of payments to Watergate defendants, a report that Nixon had been provided details of the cover-up many months before was greeted with a vehement White House denial on April 23. Three days after that came news that FBI Acting Director Patrick L. Gray had months before destroyed evidence supplied to him by Ehrlichman and Dean consisting of files secured from E. Howard Hunt's safe. One day later, Gray resigned. Later Gray would testify how nothing in his prior service had prepared him for the scandal that ultimately cost him his job, choosing a fitting metaphor to relate his victimhood: "I never expected to run into a Watergate in the service of a President of the United States and I ran into a buzz-saw, obviously."[107]

The head-spinning month concluded with Nixon delivering what would turn out to be the first of three formal "Watergate speeches," each of which punctuated periods when *The Texas Chain Saw Massacre* was written, filmed, and edited. In the speeches Nixon again characterized the Watergate crime as bizarre while also communicating his own disingenuous desire to uncover the truth behind it.

The first televised address came on April 30, 1973, not long after Hooper and Henkel had completed their screenplay, and the speech contained some bombshells. Nixon announced the resignations of his top two aides, Haldeman and Ehrlichman, his Attorney General Richard Kleindienst, and the dismissal of Dean. He also once more emphasized both the inexplicability of the original crime and his own efforts to discover and share the truth about what had happened. "I was appalled at this senseless, illegal action, and I was shocked to learn that employees of the re-election committee were apparently among those guilty," said Nixon before presenting himself as "determined that we should get to the bottom of the matter, and that the truth should be fully brought out—no matter who was involved."[108]

Richard Nixon delivers his first televised Watergate speech on April 30, 1973 in which he announced the resignations of Bob Haldeman, John Ehrlichman, and Richard Kleindienst and the firing of John Dean.

Within days the *New York Times* and other outlets were reporting how Haldeman, Ehrlichman, Dean, Mitchell, Magruder, and LaRue were *all* involved in the cover-up and would likely be indicted. The May 7th issue of *Newsweek* featured Haldeman and Ehrlichman on the cover looking every bit like mobsters with dark sunglasses under the headline "The White House in Turmoil." Inside the reporting included statements from John Dean, among them more indication that Nixon himself had known about the cover-up since at least the previous September. As the Senate Watergate Committee prepared to begin its work, Elliot Richardson, Nixon's nominee to replace Kleindienst as Attorney General and the current Secretary of Defense, appointed former Solicitor General Archibald Cox to serve as the Special Prosecutor for the U.S. Department of Justice. Cox was charged with investigating "all offenses arising out of the 1972 Presidential election," including "allegations involving the President, members of the White House staff, or presidential appointees and any other matters assigned to him by the Attorney General."[109]

The president was saying he wanted to get to the bottom of it. Plenty of others were about to try to do the same.

From May 17 through August 7 came nearly all of the "first phase" of the Senate Watergate Hearings intended to concentrate primarily on the break-ins at the Watergate and subsequent cover-up. With a couple of exceptions, practically all of the major and minor figures appeared—35 witnesses in all, testifying over 37 days with each session lasting from a few hours up to six or seven. One more witness, E. Howard Hunt, testified in late September to round out the first phase. After that more hearings continued all of the way into November as nearly 30 more mostly ancillary witnesses testified about campaign practices and "dirty tricks" (the second phase) and campaign finance (the third phase). The hearings were televised live during the days with coverage rotated among the three major networks (ABC, CBS, and NBC), then replayed every night in full on PBS, providing Americans more complicated storylines and characters than the soap operas the hearings preempted.

As witnesses continued to provide testimony behind the scenes to Sirica and the grand jury, the public hearings made headlines throughout the summer, foregrounding the scandal and inspiring an ongoing national conversation about government corruption and Nixon's own possible culpability. Most who testified were cooperative and forthcoming, the major exceptions being Mitchell, Ehrlichman, and Haldeman. The most damning testimony for those three and for Nixon, too, came from John Dean, who for an entire week at the end of June captivated the country with his detailed recollection of all he knew about the planning for the DNC break-in and the considerable efforts by many to hide the White House's involvement. Then in mid-July came the stunning revelation of a secret White House taping system, confirmed by the testimony of former Deputy Assistant Alexander Butterfield. Dating back to early 1971, recording devices had been installed in the Oval Office and Cabinet Room in the White House, in Nixon's office in the Executive Office Building, and eventually at Camp David, with phone lines in most of those locations and elsewhere tapped as well. Thousands of hours of recordings had been made, including those capturing conversations involving Nixon and staff members that were the subject of testimony from Dean and others. The discovery of these tapes would fundamentally alter the trajectory of the Watergate narrative going forward, with legal battles over access to them lasting a full year.

Taking advantage of the committee's summer recess, Nixon delivered his second Watergate speech on August 15, 1973, about four weeks into the filming of *Chain Saw*. There the president objected to allowing the White House recordings to be made public, arguing that conversations involving the president must be kept confidential so "that he would be able to talk openly and candidly with his advisors about issues and individuals." Also, as he did in the earlier speech, Nixon stressed he "had no prior knowledge of the Watergate break-in" (a claim ultimately never disproved) and that he "neither took part in nor knew about any of the subsequent cover-up activities" (a claim later shown to be false). "That was and that is the simple truth," he insisted. Nixon also once more characterized what had occurred at the Democratic National Headquarters to have been a peculiar aberration, an unfortunate and isolated action by "a few overzealous people" that unfortunately had managed "to tar the reputation of the millions of dedicated Americans of both parties who fought hard but clean for the candidates of their choice in 1972."[110]

Nixon's gave his third and final Watergate speech on April 29, 1974 while *Chain Saw* was still being edited some eight months after filming wrapped. As it happened, in that address Nixon revealed he had been doing some editing himself in response to another effort to subpoena tapes, this time by the House Judiciary Committee. With approximately 50 black three-ring binders stacked behind him, Nixon announced an intention to make public carefully edited transcripts of White House tapes he maintained would "show that what I have stated from the beginning to be the truth has been the truth," namely that he himself was not involved in the cover-up and that he was unaware of it until having been told about it by Dean in a March 21, 1973 meeting.[111] This speech concentrates primarily on Nixon's effort to counter Dean's testimony that Nixon had known of the cover-up as far back as September, leaving unsaid the absurdity of the crime in lieu of addressing the genuine crisis it created. Despite Nixon's impassioned plea to the "American people" to accept his professions of innocence and interpret the soon-to-be-published transcripts as evidence of such, their publication would hardly absolve him of wrongdoing, and in fact only served to inspire new doubts regarding his culpability and fitness to remain in office.

Richard Nixon delivers his third and last televised Watergate speech on April 29, 1974 in which he presented soon-to-be-published edited transcripts of White House recordings.

In late July 1974 came the unanimous Supreme Court ruling forcing the White House to submit subpoenaed tapes and other materials to a federal district court, and on August 5, 1974 came the public release of the contents of the so-called "smoking gun" tape of his June 23, 1972 conversation with Haldeman about instructing the CIA to block the FBI's investigation of the Watergate break-in. That conversation proved all of Nixon's other statements about being unaware of any cover-up activities to have been false. It also again demonstrated Nixon's early desire to emphasize the episode's oddity as part of the cover story meant to dissuade the FBI from exploring the break-in further by indicating vaguely its connection to other CIA-led operations. As Nixon instructed Haldeman, "just say this is sort of a comedy of errors, bizarre, without getting into it."[112]

Later after resigning and when writing in his memoirs about the Watergate break-in, Nixon again foregrounded the strangeness of the crime which for him seemed both impractical and illogical. "The whole thing made so little sense. *Why?* I wondered. Why then? Why in such a blundering way? And why, of all places, the Democratic National Committee?"[113] Nixon was still echoing his very first response to the crime, partly recorded in scribbled comments on a memo written by Ron Ziegler the day after the initial arrests in which the White House Press Secretary first characterized the break-in as a "third-rate burglary."

"He understated," wrote Nixon by way of correction. "*Attempt* at burglary. Bizarre business."[114]

Another Saturday Night Massacre (1:03)

Furthering the "What happened is true" conceit, a date next appears to

The New York Times
NIXON DISCHARGES COX FOR DEFIANCE; ABOLISHES WATERGATE TASK FORCE; RICHARDSON AND RUCKELSHAUS OUT
Kissinger Meets Brezhnev on Mideast Cease-Fire Plan

Headlines the day after the "Saturday Night Massacre" of October 20, 1973.

suggest what is about to be shown occurred on August 18, 1973—a Saturday.

Gunnar Hansen notes in *Chain Saw Confidential* how literal-minded viewers mistaking the crawl's implied claim as genuine would be disappointed to learn the film was still being shot on that date (and thus could not possibly be based on real events). He also notes how the date happened to have been the 22nd birthday of actress Teri McMinn who portrays Pam. According to Hansen, McMinn recalls that as the final day of shooting, a detail others have also reported, "although there's some debate about precisely when we started and wrapped filming," says Hansen.[115] In *The Texas Chain Saw Massacre Companion*, Stefan Jaworzyn reports "the film began shooting on 15 July 1973 and took anywhere from 32 days to eight weeks" to complete, though adds that "it's a measure of how traumatic the shoot was that most err towards a longer period."[116] (In the 1988 documentary *The Texas Chain Saw Massacre: A Family Portrait*, Hansen recalls filming lasting from July through early September.[117])

In addition to having helped with the film's financing and distribution, Warren Skaaren—later a major Hollywood screenwriter whose credits would include *Beverly Hills Cop II*, *Beetlejuice*, and *Batman*—is most often acknowledged as the source of the film's sensational title. According to John Bloom's account, Skaaren's suggestion came "just one week before principal photography commenced" in July 1973.[118] However, Austin film historian Alison Macor reports the idea for the title came much later, "a few months into the editing process," which would mean either late 1973 or during the first half of 1974.[119] Sound man Wayne Bell similarly recalls "it was only late in the post-production process that this name came out."[120] According to Larry Carroll (originally the film's co-editor with Hooper before being replaced by Sallye Richardson), production manager Ron Bozman phoned late one night to interrupt Hooper and Carroll's work. He had "called in the midst of a poker game in Houston and had a good bit to drink, it sounded like," reports Carroll who says he then handed the phone to Hooper. "I was looking at Tobe and his eyes suddenly start to glow. He looks at me and says, '*The Texas Chainsaw Massacre.*' My understanding was that Ron was telling people the stories [from the film] and someone in the poker game came up with the title."[121] Hansen relates the story a little differently, suggesting Skaaren had thought of the title during a poker game and the next day phoned Bozman with it.[122] In any case, Macor confirms how "most people connected with the film credit Skaaren for the title change," and that nearly everyone also agreed *The Texas Chain Saw Massacre* was an improvement over other working titles such as *Saturn in Retrograde*, *Head Cheese*, *Stalking Leatherface*, and *Leatherface*.[123]

Exactly nine weeks after the date the events of the film take place came the infamous "Saturday Night Massacre," a phrase swiftly employed by media to refer to the series of remarkable events that occurred on the evening of Saturday, October 20, 1973. Earlier that day, Richard Nixon ordered his Attorney General Elliot Richardson to fire Special Prosecutor Archibald Cox following an afternoon press conference in which Cox described a compromise offer by the White House to supply summaries of transcripts of the White House tapes rather than the tapes themselves as not complying with a court order. But Richardson refused to carry out Nixon's directive, citing how during his confirmation hearings six months before he had assured lawmakers the Special Prosecutor would be allowed to act independently and could only be removed for "extraordinary improprieties" of which Richardson judged there had been none. Instead Richardson resigned his position, then Deputy Attorney General William Ruckelshaus resigned as well after also refusing to fire Cox. Finally the next Department of Justice official in line of succession, Solicitor General Robert Bork, carried out Nixon's wishes and fired Cox. A constitutional crisis followed, prompting serious discussion of the possibility of impeachment for Nixon's obstruction of justice and abuse of presidential power.

Whether the film's title was suggested before or after Nixon's Saturday Night Massacre is likely without consequence for anyone hoping to establish a causal link. That is to say, the fact the film happens to depict a literal massacre taking place on a Saturday and partly at night is in all likelihood a coincidence. While the group doesn't necessarily appear part of the day-to-day working class, it makes narrative sense to set on a weekend their road trip to inspect Sally and Franklin Hardesty's grandfather's burial site following a report of vandalism and grave robbing. (Incidentally, the original screenplay includes dialogue indicating the group had been traveling for some time throughout the Western U.S. "Kind of a vacation, looking for land too," says Franklin, seeming to suggest a commune-like arrangement among the five. In the film, however, these references were cut and only a day trip is implied.[124]) Even so, the word "massacre" in the film's title certainly had more significance to contemporary moviegoers than simply to invite a kind of lurid sensationalism that proved beneficial at the box office. That is because the word also carried meaningful political connotations that support a reading of the film as a negative commentary upon a corrupt and destructive administration.

In the "Saturday Night Massacre" entry of his political dictionary, Nixon speechwriter William Safire recounts the episode before quoting Leonard Garment, then White House Counsel and successor to John Dean, figuratively describing the resulting scene in graphic terms: "There was blood all over the floor." Explains Safire, "the blood image—as a 'massacre'—quickly took hold," and by Monday the phrase had already become "locked into Watergate terminology" as an unmistakable criticism of Nixon and his actions.[125] In a 2017 article for the *Washington Post*, Amy B. Wang attempted to determine the phrase's origin, noting how it first appeared in a *Post* article by David S. Broder published two days after the event. In fact, Broder's usage indicates the phrase had already been in circulation when he employed it: "The prevailing White House view was that time is on the side of the President, that as the shock of what is being called the 'Saturday night massacre' wears off, the legality and propriety of Mr. Nixon's actions will be broadly endorsed by Republicans."[126] Wang shares others' speculation that humorist and *Post* columnist Art Buchwald might have coined the phrase.[127]

Safire adds how other usages of the word "massacre" throughout American history similarly had a "sloganizing" effect (e.g., the Boston Massacre, the St. Valentine's Day Massacre). In the entry Safire does *not* mention more recent massacres such as the Hue Massacre at the start of the Tet Offensive that saw thousands of South Vietnamese summarily executed by the Viet Cong and North Vietnamese Army from January 30 to February 28, 1968. Neither does Safire mention the My Lai Massacre of March 16, 1968 in which American soldiers injured, raped, and killed hundreds of South Vietnamese civilians in one of the most notorious episodes of the Vietnam War, nor the Kent State Massacre (also called the "May 4 Massacre") in which the Ohio National Guard shot and killed four students on the Kent State campus on May 4, 1970 amid a protest against the Cambodian Incursion launched four days before. The massacre in Hue dramatically widened the credibility gap between Lyndon B. Johnson's earlier optimistic statements regarding the war's progress and the devastating reality. Meanwhile in the case of the latter two events the term was employed to describe representatives of the U.S. government delivering horrific and disproportionately grievous harm upon undeserving victims, with analyses of both events also frequently containing specific criticism of the Nixon's ongoing management of the protracted conflict in Southeast Asia. Another event undermining Nixon's claims of progress toward peace in the Middle East was the Munich Massacre of early September 1972 in which a Palestinian terrorist group called Black September took 11 members of the Israeli Olympic team hostage at the Summer Olympics in Munich, Germany before ultimately killing them all. As Rick Worland points out in an analysis of *Chain Saw*, by including the word "massacre" in the title "a low-budget horror movie managed to grab patrons and call up some of the bitterest social and political schisms of the day."[128] Indeed, at the time *Chain Saw* was made nearly all of those references connoted criticisms of American government in general and the Nixon administration in particular.

EXTRA
HOUSTON CHRONICLE
MARKETS
Sniper Kills 14; Wounds 29 From UT Tower; Slain by Policeman
Student's Wife, Mother Dead
DJ Stock List Plunges 12.20

Reporting on the Texas Tower Massacre of August 1, 1966.

One other precursor massacre no doubt prominent in the filmmakers' minds was the August 1, 1966 tower shooting at the University of Texas at Austin. After knifing to death both his mother and wife, ex-Marine Charles Whitman climbed to the 28th floor of the

Main Building on campus, a.k.a. "The Tower," and from its observation deck used an assortment of weapons to fire down upon individuals for more than an hour-and-a-half before he was shot dead. All told Whitman killed 15, a total including one unborn child and a victim whose death 35 years later was also ruled a homicide at Whitman's hands, and injured 31 more. Soon the event was described as either the University of Texas Massacre or the Texas Tower Massacre.

Hooper was himself on campus that day, and in the commentary for a DVD release of *Eggshells* (in which the tower appears early in the film) he tells how when individuals on the ground fired upwards at Whitman "the clock was being shot and the bells were chiming."[129] In a piece written for the *Austin American-Statesman* after Hooper's passing in August 2017, friend Marcia Zwilling recalled "Tobe's story about being on campus the day Charles Whitman started shooting from the tower," and how "As Tobe left a building, an officer shoved him back inside and told him to stay put. The officer turned and walked away—and moments later was instantly shot dead."[130] Hooper's friend Ron Perryman, who assisted filming *Chain Saw*, was also present during the shooting, and in fact several of his photographs taken that day appear in the August 12, 1966 issue of *Life* magazine.[131] Coincidentally, *Chain Saw* cast member Allen Danziger was on campus at the time as well. "I was driving down Guadalupe Street on my way to cash a cheque when he was killing everybody," Danziger later recalled. "I was on a motor scooter, and a cop yelled at me to get off the street!"[132]

In fact, the only objections to the newly proposed title raised by those involved with making the film had more to do with the word "Texas" than "Massacre," with Carroll and the film's art director Robert Burns wondering about the "the state's already fragile reputation" following the assassination of President John F. Kennedy in Dallas in 1963 and the tower shooting.[133]

Flash Photography in the Dark (1:26)

A few moments in *The Texas Chain Saw Massacre* recall the experimental approach of Hooper's first film, *Eggshells*. Subtitled "An American Freak Illumination," *Eggshells* was barely screened at the time it was made aside from showings in Austin and at a few nearby locations, although it was recognized with an award at the 1971 Atlanta International Film Festival.

Eggshells is an obscure relic of the psychedelic avant-garde with affinities to *Easy Rider*, *Alice's Restaurant*, *Medium Cool*, and other countercultural cinema of the era influenced by *cinema vérité*. However unlike those films *Eggshells* frequently abandons plot altogether in favor of presenting abstract, impressionistic episodes involving a group of Austin hippies inhabiting a commune house apparently haunted by what Hooper would later mischievously describe as a "crypto-embryonic hyper-electric presence."[134] Inspired scenes include an impossibly aerodynamic paper airplane, a character appearing to swordfight himself thanks to some clever and complicated editing, a self-painting room achieved by stop motion animation, a romantic pursuit through the woods involving an incredible number of multi-colored helium-filled balloons, and a climactic scene in which a man (played by Henkel) drives his vehicle into an empty field and sets it on fire, then strips nude and gallops away as it explodes behind him. While nowhere near as gripping or affecting as *Chain Saw*, *Eggshells* nonetheless demonstrates Hooper's command of a remarkable variety of unorthodox cinematic techniques, some of which resurface to prove especially effective when deployed in the service of advancing an intensely realistic story like *Chain Saw*.

A poster advertising *Eggshells* (1969).

The film in fact begins with an example of such stylized cinema. After keeping theatergoers in total darkness for more than 20 seconds, an unsettling sequence follows that appears to dramatize the efforts of Edwin Neal's character, the Hitchhiker, to dig up graves and take photographs of the corpses, although the character is never shown. One initially hears shoveling, heavy breathing, wood cracking, and the sound of someone straining. Then comes a flash and camera clicking accompanied by an eerie whining sound that has been described as a pitchfork scraping along the edge of a table. More flashes and whines follow, revealing gruesome images of decomposed human remains.

Wayne Bell had helped with the sound on *Eggshells*, and was the boom operator and handled post-production sound on *Chain Saw* in addition to working with Hooper on the score. In interviews Bell has explained how different sounds for the film were created, captured, and mixed, including how they employed a lap steel guitar, a five-string double bass with a broken neck, children's toy instruments, cymbals, and other "lo-fi" sources later manipulated with tape speed changes and echo effects.[135] One exception was the scraping sound, which Bell describes as not being lo-fi while also refusing to disclose its source. "I call it the 'stinger,'" says Bell, "which you hear in the opening scene and again at the climax of the film. A lot of people have asked me about this sound, but it is so signature to that film, I kind of like to keep it that way."[136] Soon we will learn about the graves being disturbed, and a little after that we see the Hitchhiker using his camera, thereby enabling us to recognize the significance of the opening. Later Hooper would tell how the sequence was "meant to give you a piece of the puzzle that you are about to assimilate, and to kind of freak you out a little bit, and to give you some disturbing, foreboding clues as to what you're about to see."[137]

In testimony before the Senate Watergate Committee given on May 17, 1973, the first day of the televised hearings, Sergeant Paul W. Leeper described the scene when he and other officers encountered five well-dressed men in the offices of the Democratic National Committee on the sixth floor of the Watergate Office Building at around 2 a.m. on Saturday, June 17, 1972. According to Leeper, the men carried bags containing "various items, cameras, bulbs, clamps for clamping the cameras to the desk, walkie-talkies, things of this sort."[138] Former FBI agent G. Gordon Liddy had devised and helped direct the DNC break-in in order to gather "political intelligence" for the re-election committee. In his 1980 autobiography *Will*, Liddy tells how an earlier break-in on May 28 had involved both the installation of listening devices and the taking of photographs, including shooting two rolls' worth of 36-exposure 35-mm film of material found in DNC Chairman Lawrence O'Brien's desk.[139] The return trip on June 17 also involved what Liddy describes as a "massive photographic assignment" requiring the men to carry cameras and "special lights," although in that instance the picture-taking had yet to commence when the trespassers were caught.[140]

Both *The Texas Chain Saw Massacre* and the story of Watergate therefore begin with the discovery of a relatively minor offense that ultimately leads those investigating it to find evidence of much more grievous crimes. Also, in both cases the latter crimes are committed in order to prevent the disclosure of earlier ones, a connection highlighted further by the way both stories begin with flash photography in the dark.

One of a Series of Indictments (2:16)

"All the News That's Fit to Print"
The New York Times
LATE CITY EDITION
FEDERAL GRAND JURY INDICTS 7 NIXON AIDES ON CHARGES OF CONSPIRACY ON WATERGATE; HALDEMAN, EHRLICHMAN, MITCHELL ON LIST
COLSON IS NAMED
A Question of Veracity of the President Is Indirectly Raised
Heath, Trailing Labor Party In Britain, Declines to Resign
MITCHELL JUDGE HALTS TRIAL HERE
Nixon Urges Quick Trials, Cautions on Prejudgment

Reporting on the indictments of the second "Watergate Seven."

After the opening crawl, the very first words spoken in *The Texas Chain Saw Massacre* uncannily evoke Watergate. As the camera zooms out from a close-up to a wider shot of a rotting, unearthed corpse wired atop a gravestone with another corpse's head in its lap, a radio announcer can be heard off screen reading the tail end of a news report.

"It is believed that the indictment is only one of a series to be handed down as the result of a special grand jury investigation," he says.

Actual news reports delivered on that day included references to Watergate, among them continued responses to Nixon's second Watergate speech given the previous Wednesday. CBS Radio's *The World This Week* program of August 18, 1973 described how Nixon's claim of ignorance regarding the Watergate break-in and subsequent cover-up efforts "was not convincing to a lot of Americans," with one poll showing only "22 percent of those questioned feeling the President had told everything he knows."[141] From there the report tells of continuing efforts of Special Prosecutor Archibald Cox to obtain the White House tapes and the administration's unwillingness to comply. Meanwhile a front page story in the *New York Times* that day explained how Nixon's lawyers had filed a brief on Friday declaring the tape recordings need not be handed over should the president deem it harmful to "governmental interests" to do so.[142]

For anyone watching the film in late 1974 or soon thereafter, the radio announcer's report would immediately bring to mind Watergate given the preponderance of indictments that resulted from the scandal. On September 15, 1972 came the grand jury's original indictments of the five men who had been arrested after breaking into the DNC and of their two accomplices, E. Howard Hunt and G. Gordon Liddy. Later on March 1, 1974 another grand jury (the third impaneled during the scandal) indicted the other "Watergate Seven" as well, a group including John Mitchell, Bob Haldeman, John Ehrlichman, Charles Colson, Gordon Strachan, Robert Mardian (an aide to Mitchell), and Kenneth Parkinson (counsel for the re-election committee), with Nixon additionally named an unindicted co-conspirator. In all 69 different people would be indicted for crimes associated with Watergate, more than two-thirds of whom would serve jail time.

A Crime Is Discovered (2:23)

A "grisly work of art" found in the Newt cemetery.

The radio announcer next delivers "this hour's top news story," a report on the grave robbing, evidence of which is being shown on the screen as he speaks. He describes what we are seeing as "a grisly work of art," adding that "subsequent investigation has revealed at least a dozen empty crypts, and it is feared more will turn up as the probe continues." The cemetery is located in "the small rural Texas community of Newt," a fictional place located in the also fictional and suggestively named Muerto county (i.e., "Dead County" or "Dead Man County").

"Evidence indicates robberies have occurred over a period of time," the announcer continues. A sheriff named Jesus Maldonado is said to have offered no further details of "the ghoulish case" other than to confirm "evidence linking the crime to elements outside the state." A common surname in Texas and the southwest as well as Mexico, "Maldonado" literally means "badly given" or "ill-favored" and has been used as a nickname for an ugly or ignorant person, an early indicator that in the world of the film, the police likely should not be counted upon to maintain order. The report ends with the announcer noting how "residents have reportedly converged on the cemetery, fearing the remains of relatives have been removed," thereby making clear to the audience why Sally and Franklin and their friends later go there. Meanwhile "the investigation at the scene continues."

As happened following the June 17, 1972 arrests at the Watergate, the initial discovery of a crime in *Chain Saw* becomes linked to a larger pattern of illegal activity. Like the previous mention of grand jury indictments, here again the viewer is immediately invited to think about ongoing criminal inquiries, the uncovering of broad conspiracies, and the unreliability of elected officials, all topics that would call forth the political scandal that had dominated American media for more than two years.

A Word Cut in Two (3:31)

The Watergate Office Building.

Both at the end of the opening crawl and when the film's title is finally shown onscreen, "chain" and "saw" appear as two words. The same is true in the trailer and TV spot. Yet on the original poster and in other advertising created by Bryanston, "chainsaw" appears a single word, as is the case with all of the subsequent sequels and remakes. No particular significance was intended by the discrepancy, apparently.

The Watergate Office Building inside of which the Democratic National Committee headquarters was located is part of the Watergate complex of six buildings that occupy about 10 acres in the D.C. neighborhood of Foggy Bottom overlooking the Potomac River. Situated near an actual water gate built in the 1830s to enable canal boats' passage from the Potomac up the canal into Rock Creek Basin, the complex took nearly a decade to construct with the last of the buildings opening in 1971. There are competing stories regarding the origin of the name, although more than one point to a "Water Gate Inn" that had operated nearby from 1942 to 1966.

A Sinister Force (4:01)

The hot August sun, where it all begins.

The radio newscast continues throughout the opening credits, backed by an ominous, rumbling soundtrack of Bell and Hooper's audio experiments. Behind the words the red splashes on black might initially suggest blood cells under a microscope, although eventually it becomes clear we are looking at solar flares—in fact, stock footage purchased by the filmmakers from NASA in Houston during the final days of post-production. To confirm, the sequence ends with a crosscut to a shot of the sun shining brightly against a black sky as though viewed through a full aperture solar filter.

"That was influenced by my thinking about solar flares' and sunspots' reflecting behaviors," Hooper would later explain. "That's the reason the movie starts on the sun."[143]

It's a variation on the classic horror movie trope of a full moon affecting human behavior and inciting catastrophes to come, only in this case it is the sun that drives people mad. The idea prefigures a later discussion of astrology and its influence, the most commonly known element of which is a person's sign or "sun sign" as determined by which of the 12 zodiac constellations appears behind the sun at the time of a person's birth. As Hooper's statement suggests, the solar flares in particular are being referenced as specifically affecting people's behavior, an idea that unlike horoscopes has actual scientific support. A massive solar storm in early August 1972 had captured the public's attention by disturbing electrical grids in North America, disrupting satellite transmissions, and even causing the accidental detonation of naval mines off the coast of North Vietnam (although the latter was only made known after the declassification of documents many decades later).[144] In early May 1973 the government issued a report that "immense solar flares bombarded the earth with such unprecedented levels of energy last August that they disrupted some defense communications and may have caused homing pigeons to become lost." The severity of those storms was said to be "surprising" because they had occurred during a relatively quiet period in the current solar cycle.[145] When sufficiently large, these bursts of radiation create fluctuations in magnetic fields strong enough to affect the Earth's magnetosphere and cause power outages and blown transformers. Thankfully the atmosphere absorbs the radiation and protects us on the planet's surface from harmful effects, but some studies have nonetheless argued magnetic fluctuations caused by solar storms can still potentially affect heart rate and blood pressure and thus impact human health. The original screenplay places even greater emphasis on the sun, making it the film's first shot "larger than the frame and white hot." The first line of dialogue in the film that comes a couple of minutes later underscores the idea of the sun's menacing effect when the wheelchair-bound Franklin Hardesty complains "This heat is just driving me crazy."

Following the grave robbing story, the radio news report runs through a rapid series of items described in the screenplay as "an unusual number of natural disasters." We hear how storage units at an oil refinery near the Texas-Louisiana border have exploded, killing three. A cholera epidemic in San Francisco is up to 40 confirmed cases. A suicide in Houston has prompted an outbreak of violence. A 16-story building in downtown Atlanta has collapsed, killing 29. A man and woman are dead in Gary, Indiana, the man's genitals having been removed. The reports are read by Levie Isaacks, a local television news reporter and friend of Henkel's.[146] His straightforward yet slightly-alarmed sounding delivery resembles the televised reports of the dead rising to feast on the living in *Night of the Living Dead*, both of which could be said to satirize actual news reports of sensational crimes and violence. The compilation of horrors is over-the-top in an obvious way, meant to grab the attention of viewers otherwise preoccupied by the visuals in order to encourage thoughts of a seemingly imminent apocalypse perhaps somehow related to those ominous solar flares.

Most overlook this cosmic explanation for the nightmare about to be experienced by the group, and indeed the film only suggests it in a hinting way. Early reviewers certainly passed over it when insisting upon the absence of any apparent cause for the killer family's actions, often adding how such lack of explanation serves to ratchet up the horror of the story. That said, to say "the sun made them do it" hardly provides much comfort.

It is human nature to try and locate causes for strange or incomprehensible events, as well as to fill in gaps in fanciful ways whenever rational explanations elude us. Among the many inexplicable moments of Watergate, one of the most tantalizing concerned the surprise disclosure of an eighteen-and-a-half minute gap occurring amid a tape recording of the very first conversation between President Nixon and his Chief of Staff H.R. "Bob" Haldeman following the arrests at the Watergate. The pair had met in Nixon's private office in the Executive Office Building on Tuesday, June 20, 1972 for nearly an hour-and-a-half to discuss a wide range of topics. In mid-July 1973 came the revelation of the secret taping system, and a week later both the Special Counsel Archibald Cox and the Senate Watergate Committee separately subpoenaed nine of the tapes thought to include key conversations related to the break-in and cover-up. After many refusals and delays, the White House finally offered its "Stennis Compromise" which would involve Senator John C. Stennis, a Democrat from Mississippi, being allowed to listen to the tapes in order to confirm the accuracy of transcripts prepared by the White House. (That the 72-year-old Stennis was hard of hearing provoked added cynicism about the compromise.) The refusal by Cox to abide by the offer led to the Saturday Night Massacre discussed above, after which a chastened Nixon finally agreed to provide the tapes to Judge John Sirica and a new Special Prosecutor was appointed, Leon Jaworski. However in November it was discovered two of the nine subpoenaed tapes were either lost or never existed, and a third—the one of Haldeman and Nixon's June 20, 1972 conversation—contained that mysterious gap.

On the morning of November 21, 1973, the president's lawyers met with Jaworski to tell him about the gap. By that afternoon they were meeting with Judge Sirica to inform him as well. "It doesn't appear from what we know at this point that it could have been accidental," Fred Buzhardt Jr. said to Sirica with regard to the erasure, adding, with embarrassment, that according to Haldeman's meeting notes the topic of discussion during the missing segment of the recording was Watergate.[147] Sirica soon launched a public inquiry in open court to discover the erasure's cause. During grand jury testimony, Nixon's secretary Rose Mary Woods shouldered blame for having possibly erased up to five minutes of the tape by accident. However audio experts ultimately determined that the erasures had been made in several segments—at least five, and as many as nine—strongly suggesting the destruction of evidence to have been deliberate. Only a small number of individuals other than Woods had access to the tape. The fact that Nixon was one who did *and* that he possessed an obvious motive for hiding the conversation led many to believe the President himself had made the erasures.

Alexander Haig, White House Chief of Staff from May 1973 until shortly after Nixon's resignation in August 1974.

Various theories were explored both then and since, but the precise cause of the erasure has remained a mystery. On December 6, 1973, Alexander Haig who had replaced Haldeman as Nixon's Chief of Staff testified as part of Sirica's inquiry to share what he had learned during various discussions of the erasure with Nixon, his lawyers, and others in the White House over the previous weeks. Haig described how in one meeting with the President's counsel they expressed puzzlement over the different tones that could be heard during the gap. "That suggested that some outside source of energy had been applied to the tape," something Haig described as "the devil theory." As "they could not account for the energy source," it was speculated that Woods may have recorded over one part of the tape, then "a sinister force came in and applied the other energy source and took care of the information on the tape."

Nervous laughter followed Haig's statement. "Has anyone ever suggested who that sinister force might be?" asked Sirica. Haig replied no one had.[148]

Some understood Haig as here making a veiled reference to his boss. Whatever was intended, it was an explanation straight out of a horror movie. According to Haig, after reports of his testimony were published he began receiving letters from "demonologists all over the country."[149] Meanwhile in the White House a secretary who worked for Nixon's speechwriters, Jan Barbieri, humorously acknowledged the episode by pasting a photo of Bela Lugosi on a lampshade with the caption "Sinister Force."[150]

No Explanation for the Attack (4:47)

Tobe Hooper during production of *The Texas Chain Saw Massacre.*

The news stories are not only thematically linked by violence and horror, but also by a consistent lack of causes for the death, disease, and destruction being reported. Much as the initial grave robbing story is presented as an unresolved mystery, each of the other items also omit accompanying explanations. No reason is given for the oil storage units exploding. The story of the cholera outbreak ends with the phrase "is responsible for the disease," but the soundtrack's loud volume obscures whatever cause might have been revealed. The "outbreak of violence" in Houston is said to puzzle police who can offer "no explanation for the attack." The firm responsible for the fallen building insists "there's no explanation" and "no logical reason for the collapse." Nor is any reason given for the killings and mutilation in Indiana.

For Hooper, both the horror and the inexplicability of these stories directly commented on life in America, circa 1973, satirizing in particular the unsettling and often bewildering Watergate scandal as well as the foreboding it caused. "I was reacting to life around me, as I knew it," explained Hooper decades later in a 2014 interview. "The film was, to me, a part of what I felt like we were moving into in the future," he said. "An example of that is that in the van the news is on the radio a couple of times and the news has these horrible stories on it about things like an office building in Atlanta collapsing." Uncertainty about the capability or trustworthiness of those in power understandably provoked apocalyptic thoughts, here articulated as a seemingly commonplace litany of catastrophes. "These things really weren't happening in the '70s, but now they are—and three or four times a day. So it was a reflection of my feelings about the political environment."[151]

The world, it seemed, was falling apart, and those in charge couldn't be counted on to stop it. Even worse, they might be causing it.

How to Read Roadkill (4:51)

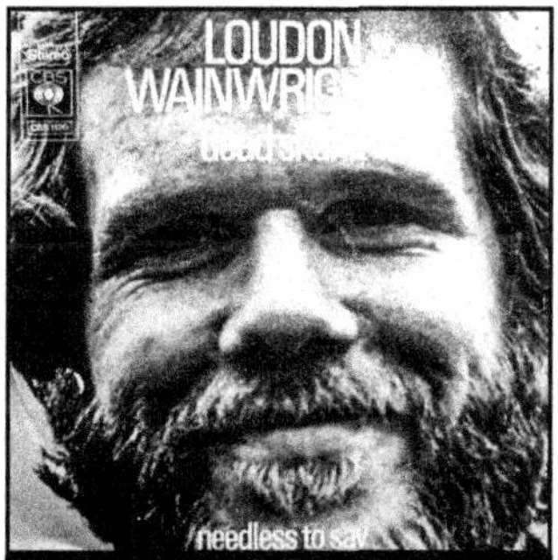

Loudon Wainwright III's hit novelty single from late 1972, "Dead Skunk."

The shot of the sun cross-fades to a close-up of a dead armadillo on its back on the highway. The screenplay originally called for "the long dead and putrid carcass of a dog." In fact such a scene was filmed, although it was decided that was "too horrible" of an image with which to begin.[152] In any event, the shot adds to the already growing collection of *memento mori* populating the prologue.

On a DVD commentary recorded in 1996, Hooper at one point identifies two primary influences for *Chain Saw*. One is Watergate, while the other is directly evidenced by the shot of a dead animal on the road. "There was this song called 'Dead Dog in the Middle of the Road,'" says Hooper. "Stinkin' to high heaven," interjects Gunnar Hansen. "Yeah... and it said nothing, but then again I guess it said everything," Hooper adds.[153]

Here Hooper misremembers the title of Loudon Wainwright III's "Dead Skunk," a novelty hit released in late 1972 that gained considerable airplay during the first months of 1973 while Hooper and Henkel were writing *Chain Saw*, peaking at #16 on the Billboard Hot 100 the last week of March. (In later interviews, Hooper would correct the reference.[154]) The song features an upbeat tempo humorously mismatched with lyrics describing a disgusting assortment of roadkill (including a dead dog), all punctuated by a sing-a-long chorus telling of "a dead skunk in the middle of the road stinkin' to high heaven." Wainwright often claimed he wrote the song in 15 minutes, making it somewhat ironic that in a career lasting five decades, "Dead Skunk" was his only single ever to chart.

One possible cause for the surprise popularity of "Dead Skunk" was the fact that some listeners associated the song with other protest-minded folk music of the era, interpreting it as a Watergate-inspired reference to the stench of corruption exhibited by the President and his cohorts. "It's about Nixon, isn't it?" listeners would ask the singer-songwriter, to which he "would humor them, saying: 'That's right! How did you ever manage to figure it out?'"[155] In truth, however, Wainwright's intentions with "Dead Skunk" were playful, not political. Confronted in an interview with readings of the song as a comment on man's destruction of nature, an attack on the church, and "an allegory about Nixon," Wainwright offered a shrugging response. "'Well, OK,' says Wainwright with open palms. 'But for me, it was just about a dead skunk lying there in the highway.'"[156]

The song's curious reception reflects Watergate's overwhelming influence upon popular culture during the time it played out. Not only did the scandal elicit conscious responses from various artists and performers, but it also encouraged Watergate-inflected readings of cultural products even when such commentary had not been intended. The popular misinterpretation of "Dead Skunk" as political diatribe also makes Hooper's coupling of the song with Watergate as primary influences upon *Chain Saw* seem less idiosyncratic.

It's All Downhill From Here (6:16)

In the distance behind the armadillo occupying the bottom half of the frame, an out-of-focus green van can be seen pulling over to park on the side of the highway. Having begun with an animal apparently struck dead by a vehicle, our introduction to the story's characters involves one of them very nearly being killed by a passing truck.

There is a cut to low-angle shot of the entire Ford van, and we see Kirk (William Vail) open the side door and put down wooden planks to allow the wheelchair-bound Franklin (Paul Partain) to exit the vehicle. Kirk hands Franklin an empty tobacco can, then steps aside to allow him to relieve himself. A quick, short sequence of shots shows Franklin from various angles, then Kirk observing a fast-approach-

A still from *Eggshells* reveals a Nixon poster hanging by the front door. The photo is the same used in a poster advertising the Moratorium Marches of mid-November 1969.

ing red eighteen-wheeler that skirts close enough to kick dirt up over the van. A startled Franklin shouts as he suddenly begins rolling uncontrollably down an embankment, ultimately being spilled from his chair at the bottom of the hill. As Franklin's sister Sally (Marilyn Burns) calls out in fright, Kirk rushes to Franklin's side to see if he is okay.

It is an unsettling scene, in part because of the way it immediately signals a willingness on the part of the filmmakers to place a handicapped character in such peril. For some interpreters the menacing eighteen-wheeler serves as a multi-purpose symbol of American capitalism, corporate culture, and/or the destructive effects of modern machines' burgeoning supremacy over man. However for most the incident primarily functions as more foreshadowing for the later shocks, as well as perhaps the downward slide into misfortune and then terror the characters will soon be forced to endure. With their first appearance the group is shown to be endangered, a disquieting prelude to the horrors to come.

The "five youths" are in truth young adults. Among the actors, Teri McMinn who portrays Pam was the youngest, as already noted turning 22 during filming, while the oldest, Allen Danziger who portrays Jerry, also had a birthday during the shoot, turning 31. Together they represent the same younger generation to which the filmmakers themselves belonged and which Hooper had examined previously in *Eggshells*. In that film the young characters who live together in a commune-like (and possibly haunted) "hippie house" are presented as naïve and vulnerable, full of imagination and idealism though poorly positioned to help either themselves or society as a whole. The film begins with a Vietnam protest, after which an engaged couple sharing a bathtub has a rambling conversation about America for which the woman's pleading question "What's wrong with this country?" serves as the theme. "It's flipping out," her fiancé responds. From there they discuss her father "preaching about how America is really good" and her futile efforts to counter that opinion. The conversation ends with her recognizing their dependence on their father's money and how if they challenge her "old man" too severely (or simply run away), "we'll starve to death." Worth noting as well is a photo of Nixon hanging next to the front door of the house. Though only fleetingly shown, it is nonetheless recognizable as a familiar image of the president smiling and holding a silver plate containing the Great Seal of the United States. The photo is best known from its use in a much-reproduced poster advertising the massive Moratorium Marches that took place in San Francisco and Washington, D.C. on November 15, 1969 where it appears next to a contrasting photo of Nixon with lips tightly clenched beneath the headline "Would you buy a used WAR from this man?" In *Eggshells*, only the smiling Nixon photo is displayed, perhaps having been cropped from the poster—an ambiguous detail possibly reaffirming the persistence of Nixon's authority. There may be a "crypto-embryonic hyper-electric presence" lurking in the basement, but Nixon and his influence seem to be haunting the house as well.

The Texas Chain Saw Massacre similarly presents the younger generation as at risk and lacking the means or awareness to protect themselves. When the family of villains later emerges, the threat they pose in part appears generational with the putative head of the household identified as "Old Man" in the credits and their revered patriarch (Grandpa) an apparent centenarian. The film is, as Robin Wood puts it, a story in which "parent-figures destroy 'children.'"[157] The group also represents the American public, generally speaking, with various indicators later aligning Leatherface and other family members with Nixon and his men. By late summer 1973, Watergate had served to transform the administration into something increasingly monstrous, and with no ready resolution to the crisis in sight, doom-laden pronouncements were commonplace. Case in point, in a New Year's Day article for the *New York Times* to kick off 1974, Hunter S. Thompson lamented what he described as "these five downhill years of the Nixon Presidency," adding how the seeming lack of any "real opposition or realistic alternative to Richard Nixon's cheap and mean-hearted view of the American Dream" represented "the horror of American politics today."[158]

Saturn in Retrograde (6:43)

Pam explains why Saturn, a malefic planet, is a particularly bad influence right now because it is in retrograde.

Franklin appears to have escaped injury from his fall, as soon the five are back in the van and on the road with Franklin complaining loudly about the heat.

Sitting on the floor of the van, Pam picks up her copy of the 1969 edition of Llewellyn George's book *A to Z Horoscope Maker and Delineator* and earnestly reads aloud a passage to Jerry while he drives. "The condition of retrogradation is contrary or inharmonious to the regular direction of actual movement in the zodiac and is in that respect evil," she reads. "Hence, when malefic planets are retrograde—and Saturn's malefic, okay?—their malefice is increased." When Jerry starts to object, Pam persists, clarifying how Saturn is not just a "bad influence," but particularly so because it is currently in retrograde. The passage Pam reads is not invented. It is exactly as it appears in George's thick reference work, a bestseller first written and published by George's own company in 1910 and largely credited with having helped introduce astrology to a mass audience in America, with new editions continuing to sell in great numbers well after George's death in 1954.

The 1969 edition of Llewellyn George's *A to Z Horoscope Maker and Delineator.*

Art director Robert Burns remembered *Saturn in Retrograde* as having once been considered as a potential title for the film ("hippiedom at work," cracked Burns), a choice that would have foregrounded the idea of a cosmic cause or "sinister force" precipitating the mayhem in a much more explicit way than is the case in the finished film.[159] Such a film title would not have been that out of step with the times, given the prevalence then of references to astrology and horoscopes in popular culture. Astrology has been popular in the

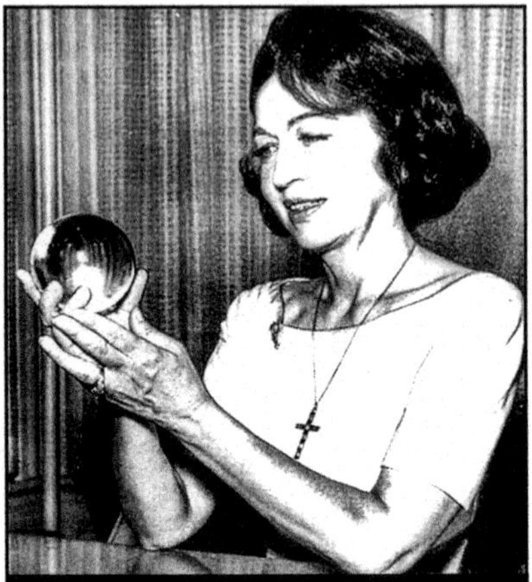

Celebrity astrologer and White House guest Jeane Dixon.

United States since the 19th century, although the association of the pseudoscience with psychology starting around the mid-20th century helped its cultural acceptance reach a peak of sorts during the 1970s. Other factors frequently cited as causing individuals to seek unorthodox belief systems are also often cited as having affected the spike in interest in astrology during this period, including the general decline in the influence of organized religion, increasing economic uncertainty, and a current political crisis. (These same influences, along with others like social media and dating apps, have been mentioned as helping fuel the recent resurgence in the popularity of astrology among millennials.[160])

At the time *Chain Saw* was made, the most popular name in astrology was Jeane Dixon, her fame having been well established thanks to her many predictions regarding political figures.

Dixon's most famous prediction came in a feature on her that appeared in a May 1956 issue of the Sunday supplement *Parade* where it was reported "for the 1960 election, Mrs. Dixon thinks it will be dominated by labor and won by a Democrat. But he will be assassinated or die in office 'though not necessarily in his first term.'" In that same article, Dixon reportedly looked favorably on Richard Nixon's future political prospects: "Vice President she considers underestimated. The crystal ball 'shows his shadow encircling the world.'"[161] Of course, for every correct prediction Dixon made there were dozens that missed the mark, including later in 1960 when she covered her bases by declaring Kennedy would *lose* the election to Nixon.[162] Nonetheless, in 1965 Dixon's celebrity was further enhanced by a book about her written by Washington-based political reporter Ruth Montgomery titled *A Gift of Prophecy* that reportedly sold over three million copies. As Montgomery would later tell it, an executive director at the publishing house "insisted on deleting most of my references to Jeane Dixon's wrong predictions," thus making the book a less than accurate portrayal of Dixon's prophetic prowess.[163] Prior to her involvement with Dixon, Montgomery had been a respected journalist and somewhat of a pioneer as a woman in a male-dominated field. She even traveled as part of the press corps covering Vice President Nixon's trip to the Soviet Union in 1959 where occurred his famous "kitchen debate" with Nikita Khrushchev. However in 1969, Montgomery left her career in political reporting to become a psychic herself.

Dixon continued to write (or have ghost written) several bestselling titles while penning a widely syndicated astrology column. She also became a close friend of Rose Mary Woods, Nixon's longtime secretary, and through that connection managed to deliver a variety of predictions regarding politics and national security directly to the president. In fact, Dixon herself even earned at least one half-hour meeting with Nixon and Woods in the Oval Office on May 4, 1971. A recording of the meeting reveals an uncomfortable and unconvinced-sounding president fumbling to respond to a series of quickly-spoken and strange statements from his guest, including Dixon reporting to him how she had known back in 1949 of "God's plan for you, for you to be president of the United States."[164] The next year following the Munich Massacre at the Olympics in September 1972, a recording of a short meeting between Woods and Nixon reveals his secretary sharing a warning told to her by Dixon that "there's gonna be some killing here in America." "Killing?" asks Nixon, sounding alarmed. "Bombing of Jews," Woods continues, adding how Dixon further predicted he would earn criticism from the Jewish community for not having defended them adequately. Nixon responds with insensitivity, arguing "there's one hell of a lot of people that just frankly are not all that interested in how much Jewish support people got" and that many "think the Jews are causing it themselves and they think they overreacted to the Olympic thing."[165] Even so, two days later in the Oval Office Nixon met with his National Security Advisor Henry Kissinger who during a discussion of the incident in Munich brings up the idea of a forming a government-wide, anti-terrorist committee. In his response, Nixon mentions how "Rose talks to this soothsayer, Jeane Dixon, all the time, she was in," then proceeds to embellish upon his visitor's prophecy with more specific worries. "They are so desperate," says Nixon of the terrorists, "they could kidnap somebody, they could shoot somebody... we have got to have a plan." The president wonders what would happen should Israeli Prime Minister Yitzhak Rabin be kidnapped and his captors "then ask us to release all blacks from prisons throughout the United States and we didn't and they shoot him?" Again stressing the need for "contingency plans for hijacking, for kidnapping, for all sorts of things that could happen around here," Nixon advises Kissinger "to look into it."[166] Kissinger did follow up and create such a committee, though it would meet only once before evolving into a less formal "working group" consisting of members of the State Department, the FBI, and the CIA. Modest as it was, it was the very first example of an interagency group focused upon counterterrorism in American government.[167]

The extent of Saturn's influence upon what awaits the young adults traveling down a Texas highway en route to a rural cemetery might be up for debate. But during the early 1970s, there was no arguing that astrology's influence extended to nearly every corner of the country, including inside the White House.

Expletive Deleted (7:28)

A long shot reveals the van approaching the cemetery where Sally and Franklin's grandfather is buried and the grave robbings have occurred. The original screenplay here contains a couple of pages' worth of dialogue among beer-drinking locals referred to generically as "Red," "Cowboy," "Beer Belly" and so forth, one of only a few examples of sequences appearing in the screenplay that did not make it into the finished film. Their speech contains profanities, starting with Red saying "I wouldn't give you jackshit for ever one o' them turds" and complaining about "civil rights my ass" and "Them sombitches in Wash-

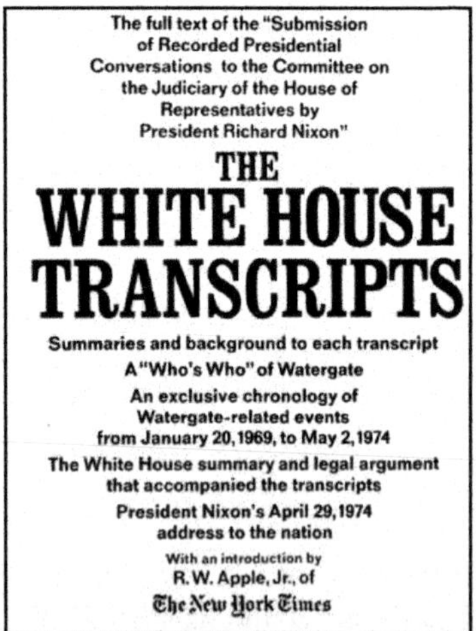
The full text of the "Submission of Recorded Presidential Conversations to the Committee on the Judiciary of the House of Representatives by President Richard Nixon"

THE WHITE HOUSE TRANSCRIPTS

Summaries and background to each transcript
A "Who's Who" of Watergate
An exclusive chronology of Watergate-related events from January 20, 1969, to May 2, 1974
The White House summary and legal argument that accompanied the transcripts
President Nixon's April 29, 1974 address to the nation
With an introduction by R. W. Apple, Jr., of The New York Times

The White House Transcripts, first published late April 1974.

ington." Others chime in to criticize "them fat ass lawyers" and to champion corporal punishment ("I can remember my daddy taking a stick to my young ass a time or two"). Only a revised version of the sequence's concluding line made it into the film, yet another ominous portent spoken by a drunk on the ground whom Franklin hears mumbling: "Things happen hereabout they don't tell about. I see things. You see, they say it's just an old man talking. You laugh at an old man. There's them that laughs and knows better."

The finished film in fact contains very little profanity—"damn" and "hell" are said a handful of times, and "shit" twice (and only once clearly when grumbled later by the Old Man). There is also no nudity and relatively little bloodletting, even when compared to contemporary exploitation titles. Such self-censoring was part of Hooper's earnest attempt not only to avoid an X rating for *Chain Saw* from the Motion Picture Association of America's ratings board, but to be given a PG rating rather than the R it eventually received. In 1972, the MPAA revised its still relatively new ratings system to G (General Audiences. All ages admitted.), PG (Parental Guidance Suggested. Some material may not be suitable for pre-teenagers.), R (Restricted. Under 17 requires accompanying parent or adult guardian.), and X (No one under 17 admitted.). Hooper's effort to avoid any age restriction for the film's audience seems amusing in retrospect, as do his stories of having described to the MPAA scenes in advance in order to solicit guidance to help the film earn the PG. "During shooting I was calling the MPAA every week," says Hooper. "I'd say, 'Look, I want to get a PG, and I need to hang a girl on a meat hook. How can I do this?"[168]

"It's not the crime, it's the cover-up" is perhaps the best known truism (or cliché) produced by Watergate. The scandal featured dozens of instances of individuals who made their circumstances worse by attempting to hide or obscure actions they or others had committed. One of the last, most extensive examples of such self-sabotage came at the end of April 1974 with the publication of *The White House Transcripts*, a carefully curated selection of 46 transcripts selected from thousands of hours of recorded conversations involving Nixon and his staff that occurred from mid-September 1972 to the end of April 1973 (an eight-month swath from the two-and-a-half years the secret taping system was in operation), along with a couple of presidential statements and a press briefing. Three million copies of paperback editions were sold within one week, with sections and even the entire text in some instances appearing thereafter in the nation's newspapers. The publishing of the transcripts was the White House's response to multiple subpoenas to hand over tapes, the most recent having come two weeks before when Watergate Special Prosecutor Leon Jaworski asked Judge Sirica to subpoena 64 recordings and the U.S. District Court complied with the request. Intended as a grand gesture of transparency made after many months of battling to keep the tapes hidden from the public, *The White House Transcripts* not only failed to provide Nixon a boost of support, but instead provoked more reason to doubt his fitness to remain in office.

Even after being sanitized, the frank and unsparing discussions revealed a disturbing siege mentality having taken over the White House, with Nixon in particular emerging as a vindictive, scheming, and above all immoral leader. They also made even more concrete episodes already familiar to the American public through the Senate Watergate Hearings of the previous year, including those involving the collection and distribution of funds to pay off the Watergate burglars, constant explorations of the reach of executive privilege and possible use of clemency and pardons, and strategies to limit the access of both legislators and the courts to information and evidence. Such a negative impression was deepened by Nixon's accompanying refusal to hand over the subpoenaed tapes (invoking executive privilege to do so), prompting a vote by the Senate Judiciary Committee declaring the transcripts' publication an insufficient response to the subpoenas. That would produce another order followed by a White House appeal, which in turn forced the Supreme Court to decide the matter. Newspapers across the country responded to the book with op-eds calling for Nixon's resignation or arguing for impeachment, while those not going that far nonetheless strongly denounced the president's failings as revealed in the transcripts. Republican lawmakers, including those still clinging to their support of Nixon, also expressed dismay. Chief among them was Senate Minority Leader Hugh Scott, who after reading the transcripts characterized them as a "deplorable, shabby, disgusting and immoral performance" by everyone involved, including the president.[169] Even the evangelist Billy Graham, a longtime Nixon supporter, was disgusted by *The White House Transcripts*, and after reading them "just wanted to throw up."[170]

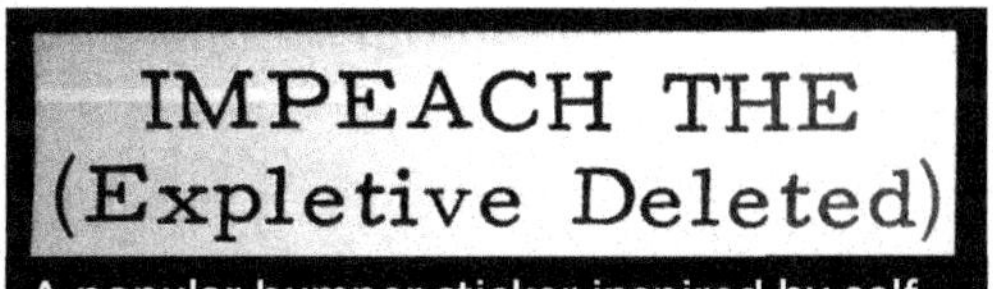

A popular bumper sticker inspired by self-censorship in *The White House Transcripts*.

Missing sections from conversations predictably earned special attention. Former White House Counsel John Dean shared how there were "major deletions" throughout the transcripts, including one from the September 15, 1973 conversation in which he participated that "omitted a long conversation about using the Internal Revenue Service to attack enemies."[171] Later in July, a couple of weeks before the Supreme Court ruling at last forced Nixon to comply and provide the original recordings, the House Judiciary Committee published its own transcripts of the eight recordings that had been made available to them, thereby revealing dozens of other omissions clearly intended to hide Nixon's own culpability. For instance, in a March 21, 1973 meeting between Nixon, Dean, and H.R. Haldeman, the White House's version includes an exchange in which Dean observes "there have been some bad judgments made" and recognizes how the scandal will continue "to burden this second Administration" or term. At that point *The White House Transcripts* neglects to include a line from Nixon that those who created the House Judiciary Committee's transcript had heard: "We're all in on it."[172]

Another editorial decision earning both censure and ridicule was the frequent choice to remove certain uses of profanity or offensive language in favor of the designations "(expletive deleted)" or "(expletive omitted)." Stories differ as to who decided upon the censorship, with some saying Nixon himself made the deletions and others suggesting either White House Counsel Fred Buzhardt Jr. or Press Secretary Ron Ziegler was responsible. In any event, the more than 120 instances of such omissions in *The White House Transcripts* proved more damaging than would have been the case had the offending words been left unexcised. As Nixon biographer Stephen Ambrose notes, the deletions "gave an entirely erroneous impression of Nixon's ordinary language" by promoting "the idea that Nixon swore like a muleskinner."[173] For example, in the White House's version of that same March 21, 1973 conversation between Nixon and Dean discussed above, the latter explains to the president how "the Cubans" used in the Watergate break-in were the same men "used for this California Ellsberg thing"—that is, the September 1971 burglary of *Pentagon Papers* leaker Daniel Ellsberg's psychiatrist's office in what proved an unsuccessful attempt to collect information damaging to Ellsberg. "I don't know what the hell we did that for!" says Nixon, and Dean replies "I don't know either." Nixon then asks "What in the (expletive deleted) caused this?" For most readers, the missing word or phrase suggested a profanity more severe than the "hell" appearing just above. In truth, as the House Judiciary Committee's transcript and the now-available tape itself reveals, the uncensored question from Nixon was "What in the name of God caused this?"[174] While Nixon was often quite coarse and offensive on the tapes, most of the deletions involved mild profanity or taking the Lord's name in vain. As Ambrose modestly points out, Nixon never does employ "the common slang word for sexual intercourse" so often suggested by the expurgations. "Had Nixon left the words he used in the transcripts, almost no one would have noticed them," argues Ambrose. "Because he took them out, he set off an uproar that matched, and possibly exceeded, the reaction to the Saturday Night Massacre."[175]

"Expletive deleted" swiftly became a comic catchphrase, serving as another punchline used to ridicule the president as bumper stickers, buttons, and banners declared "IMPEACH THE (Expletive Deleted)." Though on one level just a humorous bit of trivia, on another the phrase was symbolic of what had frightened Americans the most about Watergate. Since so much corruption and criminality had been successfully hidden for so long, once it did come to light the imagination could not help but picture even *worse* horrors, especially when so strongly suggested.

Please Change the Subject (9:57)

The graveyard visit is brief, and soon the group is back in the van where Sally reassures Franklin their grandfather's grave was undisturbed. Their destination is uncertain, not explicitly described in the film. In the screenplay, Sally tells Jerry even before they reach the cemetery how their grandfather's house is nearby and that she and Franklin would like to visit it afterwards. In the film this exchange is omitted, making the group's later inquiries about the location of the house and the decision to seek it out seem more spontaneous.

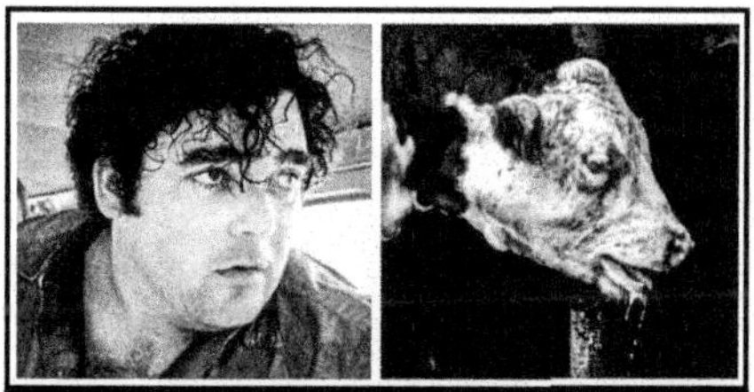

A suggestive match cut of Franklin and a cow being led to slaughter.

The travelers soon become aware of a foul odor, which after some initial confusion is identified as emanating from a slaughterhouse located near the highway. As Franklin explains, it is the same site where their grandfather used to sell his cattle. He adds how their uncle currently works at a similar facility near Ft. Worth. Sweating and with his shirt open, Franklin grows more animated and even chuckles as he describes how "they bash 'em in the head with a big sledgehammer" before he delves into more gruesome details. "They usually wouldn't kill 'em on the first lick," he says. "I mean they'd start squealing and freaking out and everything, and they'd have to come up and bash 'em two or three times. And *then* sometimes it wouldn't kill 'em. I mean they'd skin 'em sometimes even before they were even dead!" A wide-eyed Pam reacts with disgust, calling the process "horrible" and declaring "people shouldn't kill animals for food." As though to assuage her, Franklin continues his monologue by explaining the new, modern killing technique, again doing so with enough glee to increase others' discomfort. "Oh, they don't do it like that anymore," he says. "Now they got this big air gun that shoots a bolt into their skull, then retracts it. It's just boom! It goes boom! Boom! Boom! Boom!"

"That's terrible," says Pam. "It's still going on." Sally objects as well. "Franklin, I *like* meat," she says. "Please change the subject."

The short scene provides ample evidence to inform pro-vegetarian readings of *The Texas Chain Saw Massacre*, with Hooper's claims that he himself gave up eating meat while making the film supplying further support. Making the point more explicit, shots of cows ostensibly being readied for slaughter and backed by sounds of mooing are intercut throughout the conversation, further illustrating the subject that meat-eating Sally wishes not to explore. Those cutaways also make more clear the impression that they, too, are unwittingly being led to a kind of slaughter, such as in the match cut juxtaposing

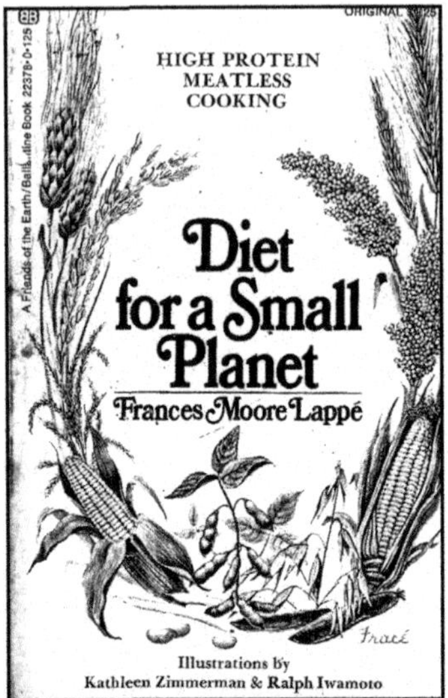

Diet for a Small Planet (1971) by Frances Moore Lappé.

sweaty Franklin and a drooling cow, or the long shot of the van traveling right to left across the screen in the same direction toward which the line of cattle are facing.

At the time *Chain Saw* appeared in theaters, Americans were eating more beef per capita than ever before in the country's history. A new record was set in 1974, and the total would increase each of the next two years to peak at 94.1 pounds per year before declining steadily to the 57-pound range where it has recently settled.[176] (During the 1990s, chicken surpassed beef as the most-consumed meat in the U.S.) Meanwhile the country's cattle inventory was also peaking, in 1975 reaching just over 132 million head before similarly declining over the decades since to the 90-95 million range.[177] For Richard Nixon, the increase in Americans' meat-eating habits during his time in office was something to celebrate. "Beef consumption per person has gone up by one-third in the last 10 years," Nixon remarked in a "Salute to Agriculture" radio address in early May 1971, finding reason to cheer the fact "that for every three pounds of beef [each American] consumed in 1960, the average American is consuming four pounds in 1971."[178]

Not unrelatedly, the early 1970s also saw the first rise of vegetarianism in the U.S., with Frances Moore Lappé's *Diet for a Small Planet*, published in September 1971, often credited as a catalyst. Part recipe book, part call for environmental activism, the book sold three million copies and went through seven editions in less than two years. Lappé describes in detail the grim logistics of meat production, focusing primarily on the damaging ecological impact and waste caused by "The Great American Steak Religion" (a phrase told to her by a European acquaintance to describe the country's meat obsession).[179] Lappé does not foreground Pam's position and take an overtly ethical stance advocating for animal rights, although in a later, revised edition she would clarify her hope that the book would nonetheless "be of value to the growing numbers of people who refuse to eat meat in order to discourage the needless suffering of animals."[180]

Nixon's predecessor Lyndon B. Johnson had been associated closely with the beef production industry both before and during his time in office, often hosting large barbecues for foreign leaders and other political figures at his 2,700-acre "LBJ Ranch" where he regularly kept up to 400 head of Hereford cattle. As it happened, the sale and consumption of meat also came up time and again during Nixon's life and career in conspicuous ways. During his childhood Nixon and his brothers helped run their father's general store where beef was one of the items sold ("I used to grind hamburger as a youngster and was pretty good, too, not too much fat and no pork in it, real good ground beef," he'd explain.[181]) When serving in the Navy during the latter part of the Second World War, Nixon was assigned to the *U.S.S. Bougainville*, a stop-off for pilots to and from battle missions, spending time as well on nearby Nissan Island (a.k.a. Green Island) as Officer in Charge of the South Pacific Combat Air Transport Command. In between loading and unloading cargo planes, preparing manifests, and playing poker with fellow officers, Nixon additionally took it upon himself to procure provisions for the fighter pilots and crews passing through, serving beer and food to them at what came to be known as "Nick's Hamburger Stand." Later when Nixon was Vice President, his brother Don opened a five-restaurant hamburger chain in California known as Nixon's Family Restaurant where the featured menu item was the 20-cent Nixon Burger (with cheese). The business ultimately failed and was sold in 1957, though years later would still cause Nixon headaches thanks to his brother having obtained a $205,000 loan from Howard Hughes to fund the business.

As president Nixon also readily identified as a meat-eater. According to White House Executive Chef Henry Haller, First Lady Pat Nixon's special meat loaf dish was served once a month and became nationally known, with copies of "Family-Style Meat Loaf" featuring two pounds of lean ground beef sent out on White House stationery in order to satisfy "thousands of requests."[182] Another recipe for "The White House All-American Burger" featuring 5-6 ounces of freshly ground lean chuck became associated with Nixon as well after it was served to a gathering of 4,000 at a large staff picnic following a performance by Sammy Davis Jr.[183]

All of which is to say, if we were to associate Nixon with either side of the burgeoning debate surrounding the cattle industry and alluded to here in *Chain Saw*, the president was unambiguously pro-meat.

The CREEPs (10:27)

The Hitchhiker.

"The true monster itself is death," explained Tobe Hooper in an early 1974 interview, speaking authoritatively at a time when he was still making the final edits on his first feature-length horror film. "All the classic horror flicks—*Dracula, Frankenstein, Psycho*—have this in common. They have a unique way of getting inside you by setting up symbols that represent death: a graveyard, bones, flowers. If you put them in the proper order then you create the most important aura known as the creeps."[184]

Having successfully assembled many symbols during the first 10 minutes to establish just such an uneasy "aura," *Chain Saw* then places its five young adults in uncomfortably close proximity to a bona fide creep, the "Hitchhiker."

Sally first spots him on the roadside. After a brief debate the group decides to pick him up over Pam's objections. "Ohhh, he's *weird* looking," she says with a worried expression. "Noooo!"

The tense, impulsive, almost child-like character portrayed by Edwin Neal goes unnamed in the film, only identified as the misspelled "Hitchiker" in both the credits and screenplay. After climbing in he sits in the back of the van as the others eye him warily. He is thin and unshaven, has long, stringy and unwashed black hair, and has on a scruffy dark t-shirt with stains. Around his wrist he wears a thin charm bracelet from which dangle what appear to be teeth. He carries a sack, a Polaroid instant film accordion-style camera, and a small pouch made from animal pelt. There is what appears to be a large birthmark streaking down one half of his face that at first glance resembles blood, and his default expression seems a permanent grimace. He speaks quickly and nervously. At first his voice seems affected from being out of breath after having run alongside the van, though his unsteady gasping continues throughout the ride. When he speaks it sounds as though it requires great effort, whether physical or mental or both.

Coinciding with the construction of the Interstate Highway System begun in 1956, hitchhiking peaked in popularity in America during the 1960s, but by the early 1970s had started to attract negative attention on a national scale thanks in part to sensational stories such as the one of Edmund Kemper, the California-based "Co-ed Killer" who murdered a number of female hitchhikers before his arrest in April 1973. Even so, the group's decision to pick up a hitchhiker would seem to contemporary audiences neither unusual nor especially indicative of idealism or naïveté. They show sympathy ("He'll asphyxiate out there," says Kirk during the discussion over whether to pick him up), but also trepidation, and are immediately on their guard once the Hitchhiker enters the van and starts demonstrating his social awkwardness. Only Franklin, already marked as an outsider of sorts for tagging along with the two couples and because of his handicap, attempts to engage the Hitchhiker. That said, he begins by remarking openly on their guest's odd appearance and demeanor.

"Well, I think we just picked up Dracula," says Franklin, a comment the Hitchhiker seems not to notice. The Hitchhiker explains he had been at the slaughterhouse. He offers no reason for his visit, but mentions his brother and grandfather both used to work there. "My family's always been in meat," he says, to which Franklin responds, "A whole family of Draculas." Later on when the group arrives at Sally and Franklin's grandfather's house, Kirk will again allude to classic horror when he says "it looks like the birthplace of Bela Lugosi," the iconic actor who famously portrayed Dracula in Tod Browning's 1931 film. Besides serving to acknowledge Hooper's cinematic influences, the references are like the graveyard, corpses, and other elements helping to build an atmosphere suitable to a horror film. They indicate in a self-reflexive way how the world inhabited by the group is like a horror movie populated by other horror characters and horror settings.

It becomes clear the Hitchhiker had no particular business at the slaughterhouse other than perhaps to sneak around and take photographs of butchered cattle, some of which he eventually shows to the others. Later evidence in the film helps the viewer piece together that the Hitchhiker likely had been the one disturbing graves at the cemetery in Newt, particularly when the Old Man angrily yells at him "I told you to stay away from that graveyard!" The screenplay includes more dialogue in the van, with the Hitchhiker sounding a great deal more coherent as he explains to the others "I'm an artist" and "I work with leather. I'm a sculptor too." Such lines would link the character back to the radio announcer's reference to the arrangement of corpses as "a grisly work of art." The scene is much more effective as filmed, however, pared down with uncomfortable silences replacing such expository exchanges.

With no job or means of transportation, then, the Hitchhiker seems primarily to occupy his time creeping around, and assuredly creeping out those he encounters as he does.

The story of Watergate also involved a remarkable number of individuals creeping around while committing clandestine and in some cases criminal operations that were directed and even funded by the White House. Thanks largely to the televised hearings of the Senate Watergate Committee during which 65 witnesses testified from May to November 1973, the American public learned and was alarmed by testimony describing these many disreputable activities. Among the earliest was an action perpetrated by the secret "Special Investigations Unit" established in June 1971 shortly after the publication of the *Pentagon Papers*. Ostensibly created to suss out and stop leaks of information emanating from those within the administration, a purpose that earned the group the nickname the "White House Plumbers," the unit engaged in other activities as well sometimes designated (and rationalized) as "political intelligence" work. The unproductive break-in to Daniel Ellsberg's psychiatrist's office in early September 1971, a failed attempt to find dirt on the outspoken leaker of the *Pentagon Papers*, was the first notable mission for the Plumbers. As later revealed at Ellsberg's trial in late April 1973, the break-in had been planned by G. Gordon Liddy and E. Howard Hunt, and two of the other three men involved were also among those later caught and arrested at the Watergate on June 17, 1972 (Bernard Barker and Eugenio Martinez). Meanwhile the

The original "Watergate Seven" arrested for the June 1972 DNC break-in: James McCord, Virgilio Gonzalez, Frank Sturgis, Eugenio Martinez, Bernard Barker, E. Howard Hunt, and G. Gordon Liddy.

Senate Watergate Committee's hearings would spell out how John Ehrlichman, White House Domestic Affairs Advisor, had authorized the operation, as did the men he had charged to direct the Special Investigations Unit, Egil "Bud" Krogh and David Young. (In fact, Ehrlichman himself testified and surprisingly—though unconvincingly—tried to justify the break-in.) Also revealed over the course of those months were details of the continued employment of both Hunt and Liddy for the rest of 1971 and first half of 1972. While Hunt kept busy working on other projects including researching Ted Kennedy and Chappaquiddick, Liddy was hired to work for Nixon's re-election committee. Though nominally given the role of finance counsel to the committee, Liddy was again tasked with gathering "political intelligence," this time in the service of the President's re-election campaign.

During the first weeks of 1972, Liddy hatched a complicated plan he called "Operation Gemstone" that involved wire tappings, kidnappings, black bag operations, the use of prostitutes for the purpose of blackmail, and other nefarious actions designed to damage Democrat leaders and their supporters. He presented his ideas in meetings with then Attorney General John Mitchell who at the beginning of March 1972 would step down from that position in order to chair the re-election committee and manage Nixon's campaign as he had done before in 1968. Though Operation Gemstone was rejected, Liddy nonetheless later received the go-ahead from Mitchell to pursue a scaled-down version of his plan, one that included breaking into the DNC at the Watergate to photograph materials and plant listening devices. (Mitchell testified before the Senate Watergate Committee, too, denying full knowledge of what he had authorized.) Liddy once more recruited Hunt to assist with the management of the operation, Barker and Martinez again to help execute it, and also called upon James W. McCord Jr. who was then employed as security coordinator for the re-election committee. Like the break-in at Ellsberg's psychiatrist's office, the mission was almost entirely unfruitful, producing essentially no "intelligence" of any value. Unlike the earlier break-in, though, this time the perpetrators were caught.

As former White House Counsel John Dean helped clarify during his week of testimony at the end of June 1973, following the Watergate arrests the White House scrambled to cover up its multiple connections to the crime. Not only had authorization for the break-ins at the DNC come directly from the President's re-election committee, but Liddy and Hunt's earlier work with the White House Plumbers (conspicuously involving a similar, criminal act) additionally linked them to those closest to the President, if not to the President himself. The White House's desperation to hide its connection to the Watergate break-in was therefore further heightened by a desire to prevent the earlier break-in from ever becoming public. Meanwhile the re-election committee became heavily involved in the cover-up effort—after all, its chairman had sanctioned the operation (when still Attorney General, no less), its finance counsel had planned and directed it, and others connected to the committee had helped manage a secret "slush fund" used to finance the operation and then also afterwards to pay off the suspects in order to ensure their silence.

Other witnesses filled in details of how those payments were delivered, the most memorable being the primary "bag man" Anthony "Tony" Ulasewicz, the ex-New York City cop and private investigator who had been employed by the committee to help distribute the funds to the seven arrested men from July to September 1972. Originally hired by Ehrlichman back in 1969 to pose as a news reporter in order to gather information about the investigation into the Chappaquiddick incident, Ulasewicz's new job in the summer of 1972 required similar discretion. For the Senate Watergate Committee he described secret meetings, code names, untraceable calls using public phones, using laundry bags and unmarked brown envelopes to transport large quantities of $100 bills, scheduled drops involving hidden keys and airport lockers, and other intrigue as he handled what amounted to more than $200,000 in payoffs. Employing colorful, Damon Runyonesque language to describe the jobs he performed, Ulasewicz frequently provoked laughter from those in attendance as well as delighted responses from committee members ("Who thought you up?" asked a half-serious, half-incredulous Howard Baker.[185]). Ulasewicz explained how even though he originally believed his work to be legal and endorsed by the re-election committee which he understood presumably acted on the White House's behalf, he decided it was prudent to step away from the enterprise once he realized the suspects were blackmailing their benefactors for ever increasing sums. As Ulasewicz put it, he understood that "something here is not kosher."[186]

Still more examples of surreptitious sneaking around by those employed by the campaign were revealed at the hearings. Among them were other "dirty tricks" successfully performed to sabotage Democratic presidential candidates' campaigns, most notoriously by Donald Segretti (another operative paid by the re-election committee who testified in October), as well as other examples of corruption and criminality sometimes collected under the heading of "the White House horrors." Televised all day and rebroadcast all night, the hearings helped bring all of these shadowy dealings out into the light, demonstrating how what happened at the Watergate had hardly been an isolated act, but part of a larger, disturbing pattern of stealthy offenses unsettling enough to make America's collective skin crawl.

Nixon's re-election committee thus became notorious, and like "Watergate" emerged as yet another handy metonym for the administration's depravity. Initially called the Citizens Committee to Re-Elect the President, by the start of 1972 the name had been changed to the Committee for the Re-Election of the President and took as its official abbreviation CRP. But once committee members' involvement in what had happened at the Watergate became widely known, reporters could not resist referring to it by a different and more suitable acronym. The rebranding perfectly evoked not only the covert nature of so many of the crimes that were being revealed, but also the genuine horror enveloping the American public as it came to grips with what Dean in his testimony had described as a lawless "atmosphere at the White House"[187]—CREEP.

The Southern Strategy (10:52)

"Where you headed man?" asks Kirk of the van's new occupant. The Hitchhiker points in the direction they are driving. "South," he says.

Many have observed the way *The Texas Chain Saw Massacre* exploits fears and prejudices regarding the American South. The film is frequently referenced as one of the more influential cinematic depictions of horrors endured by those unfortunate enough to have taken wrong turns into backwoods hellscapes populated by uninviting locals inhabiting states forming the so-called Bible Belt. In this respect *Chain Saw* often appears in lists that include earlier titles like the race-hate parable *The Intruder* (1961), Herschell Gordon Lewis's gorefest *Two Thousand Maniacs!* (1964), and the popular vigilante dramas *Walking Tall* (1973) and *Macon County Line* (1974), as well as subsequent exploitation fare starting with *The Town That Dreaded Sundown* (1976), *The Hills Have Eyes* (1977), and *I Spit on Your Grave* (1978). The rough, unfriendly treatment by Southerners in Dennis Hopper and Peter Fonda's *Easy Rider* (1969) provided another touchstone, in particular the shocking finale in which a pair of hayseeds suddenly drive their pickup truck into the story to shoot dead the two main characters on a Louisiana highway in a random act of violence. Meanwhile John Boorman's adaptation of James Dickey's *Deliverance* (1972) depicting a canoe trip in the northern Georgia wilderness that goes tragically wrong for four Atlanta businessmen represented the most conspicuous mainstream example of what has been described as the "redneck nightmare" genre of film. Indeed, in certain ways *Deliverance* functions as a close antecedent to *Chain Saw*, a film in which the villainous rustics terrorizing the "city boys" are presented as primitive, deviant, and perhaps even mentally stunted due to inbreeding.

Hooper was an Austin native, and Henkel was born in Virginia before moving to Texas as a child. Both were well acquainted with the American South and its perceived image, as well as its suitability as a setting for a particular type of disorienting, nightmarish horror film, a topic the pair directly address in the 2000 documentary *Texas Chain Saw Massacre: The Shocking Truth*. "The significance of Texas... it's kind of the place where something like the Bloody Benders could have happened," explains Hooper.[188] The reference is to the notorious Bender family who during the early 1870s operated a modest store and inn on a farm near Cherryvale, Kansas not far from the Oklahoma border where they murdered and robbed a series of guests over a two-year span. As the number of missing travelers increased so, too, did suspicions about the Benders, finally reaching a point where the family chose to abandon their homestead and flee to parts unknown. A search of the property ultimately revealed 10 buried bodies plus additional dismembered parts of other victims. Word of the crimes as well as accounts of the family's history prior to having settled near Cherryvale and of their possible future travels (and additional murders) began circulating throughout the country, as did later unconfirmed reports of their eventual lynching by vigilantes. Details including a trap door leading to a blood-soaked cellar, corpses recovered with skulls crushed and throats cut, and evidence of mutilation and even live burials added to the story's horror, as did sensational speculation about family members' diminished mental faculties, possible false identities, and incest. Despite the tale being a century old, echoes of the Benders' story can still be discerned in the Old Man's repeated suggestions to the group of young travelers later in *Chain Saw* that they "don't want to go messing around no old house" and would be much better off continuing down the road.

A poster advertising *Deliverance* (1972).

Henkel likewise describes the choice of setting as foregrounding what he calls the "city boy-country boy thing" in *Chain Saw*. "We're all afraid that out there in those kind of dark kernels of rural America or wherever it may be that there are these inbred types that are doing terrible and dastardly things," explains Henkel.[189] Stories like that of the Bloody Benders inspire such anxieties in the way they not only present individuals committing atrocities most of us cannot imagine performing, but also suggest something about the surrounding environment as having somehow nurtured such monsters into being. In the context of a horror film, such stories and the predispositions (or prejudices) they engender provide a means to identify the villain or villains to be feared—that is, to establish that oft-employed category of the Other (with a capital "O") that does not adhere to the same set of societal norms followed by the rest of us who are often represented by the story's victims. Speaking in particular of the urban-rural divide, Hooper employs that very sort of abstraction when pointing out how during his childhood growing up in Texas he "always lived in the city... and 'out there' got kind of scary."[190]

In one respect, Hooper and Henkel simply chose a setting for their film with which they had familiarity and about which they possessed practical knowledge. They had made a similar choice before with *Eggshells,* and would do so again with their next collaboration *Eaten Alive* (1976) that Hooper directed and Henkel co-wrote. The latter presents another horror story set in rural Texas centered on a murderous hotel owner who summarily kills his guests, in some cases feeding them to a pet crocodile kept in the swamp that surrounds the property. The story and circumstance even more closely evokes the Bloody Benders than does *Chain Saw*, and was in fact loosely inspired by another gruesome tale from Southern folklore, that of the serial killer Joe Ball or the "Bluebeard of South Texas." That said, the pair also consciously made use of the image of the South as a readymade source of dread for a significant percentage of their audience, relying upon preconceptions fostered by other cultural depictions of the region and its inhabitants. For filmmakers working on a shoestring budget, the choice of setting represented a practical convenience in more ways than one.

For Nixon the campaigner and the Republican Party, the "Southern strategy" was also exploitative, and also involved manipulating people's fears of others who were not like themselves. The tactic emerged in earnest amid the civil rights movement and in particular following Lyndon B. Johnson's signing of the 1964 Civil Rights Act that outlawed racial segregation in schools and public places, protected voting rights for all races, and prohibited discrimination in employment and federally assisted programs on the basis of race, color, religion, sex, or national origin. Republican senator Barry Goldwater of Arizona had voted against the bill on what he insisted were con-

Nixon campaigning in Georgia in 1968.

stitutional grounds, viewing the law as empowering the federal government to overstep states' rights and improperly interfere with the conduct of private businesses. After winning the nomination as the G.O.P. candidate that year, Goldwater ran a campaign that foregrounded his staunch conservatism and willingness to employ extreme measures to fight communism. In the South, however, it was Goldwater's vote against the Civil Rights Act that particularly won him favor among segregationist whites who had opposed the bill for less defensible reasons, and the campaign welcomed the support. The approach, termed "Operation Dixie" after a program earlier initiated by Dwight D. Eisenhower in the 1950s to try to bolster Republican support in the South, helped Goldwater secure Deep South states that in previous elections had gone Democrat, but it hurt him elsewhere, resulting in a landslide victory for Johnson.

Going forward, Republicans found other means to exploit racial polarization in order to appeal to disaffected Southern whites, often doing so indirectly by arguing for states' rights or by highlighting "wedge" issues like forced busing or urban unrest. In the 1968 presidential election, the pro-segregationist George Wallace won five of those states as a third-party candidate, but Nixon's victories in North and South Carolina, Tennessee, and Florida helped him clinch victory by a slim margin over Democrat Hubert Humphrey. The strategy continued to be employed subsequently, enabling the Republicans to keep making significant in-roads and helping Nixon to sweep the South in the 1972 election. As president Nixon oversaw significant school desegregation in the South as mandated by a 1969 Supreme Court ruling that it must be implemented, although he managed to placate Southern segregationists by making it clear it was the judicial branch of government bearing responsibility. Nixon also courted the South with his choice of Supreme Court nominees, even though both

Clement Haynsworth of South Carolina and Harold Carswell of Florida were rejected by the Senate in part because both had previously voiced pro-segregationist positions (to differing degrees). Even so, the attempt was well received and made Nixon "a hero in the South" according to political strategist Harry Dent who advised Nixon and is often credited as a chief architect of the Southern strategy.[191]

Such efforts also won Nixon the support of Southern lawmakers, a group that later proved significant to him during the final stages of the Watergate scandal. Following the Saturday Night Massacre, the House Judiciary Committee opened an impeachment inquiry at the end of October 1973, though it would take until May 1974 to begin formal hearings and almost three more months more before committee members voted on three articles of impeachment for obstruction of justice, abuse of power, and contempt of Congress. As that vote neared in late July 1974, Nixon and his lawyers contemplated whether or not the 38-member committee would have the votes to support the articles. The Democrats held the House majority and thus a 21-17 advantage in the Judiciary Committee, yet it was thought three Southern Democrats from districts that had heavily favored Nixon in 1972 might potentially vote against the articles. But when a small group of moderate Republicans dramatically broke from those still supporting Nixon, the Southern Democrats followed suit, all but ensuring the committee would vote in favor of the articles and send them to the full House which would likely vote in favor of them as well. At that point Nixon recalled how George Wallace, then Alabama governor, had earlier made an offer of help to Nixon should the situation become especially dire. However when Nixon phoned the governor, Wallace explained he would be unable to persuade the Southern Democrats to change their minds. Speaking to his Chief of Staff Alexander Haig after the call, Nixon recognized at that moment that his remaining days in office were numbered.

"Well, Al, there goes the presidency," said Nixon, his last-ditch attempt to employ a different sort of "Southern strategy" having failed him.

It should be noted that in *Chain Saw* the group is *not* marked as non-Southerners, although only Sally and Franklin are explicitly connected to the Texas setting via family ties. In fact, the original *Chain Saw* screenplay includes dialogue specifying that all five are from

Houston, suggesting a *Deliverance*-like city-versus-country dynamic that in the finished film is mostly implied. Among other dialogue not making it into the film, when the Hitchhiker says he is heading south, the screenplay has Franklin responding, "You could have fooled me. I thought we were headed due north," indicating that one of them is confused. By omitting Franklin's response in the film, we are led to understand the group is driving further south and (as we soon learn) to where the Hitchhiker lives and desires to go.

In other words, the direction they are heading is a treacherous one, carrying them away from security and comfort and toward uncertainty and endangerment.

The Old Way and the New Way (11:37)

The Hitchhiker wants everyone to know he has a knife.

Both the villains and victims might be Southerners in this redneck nightmare, but the two groups could not be more distinct, and it is the Hitchhiker's van ride that begins to introduce the contrast. The six-minute scene also parallels the other most significant instance of a representative of one group interacting with the other, the lengthy "dinner scene" near the end of the film in which Sally and the Hitchhiker's family similarly fail to communicate (and in which blood is also shed). Sally's later interactions with the family will build upon a theme first presented by the Hitchhiker here, namely, an association of the family with the past and its antagonism toward the present and future as represented by the young group of travelers.

As noted, Franklin does make an attempt to connect with their passenger. When the Hitchhiker volunteers that members of his family once worked at the slaughterhouse, Franklin sees an opening. "Hey man, did you go in that slaughter room or whatever they call it... the place where they shoot the cattle in the head with that big air gun thing?" he asks. Franklin adds how he and Sally's uncle, currently employed at another slaughterhouse, once invited him into such a room to witness the weapon being used. Franklin's earlier description of the air gun to others suggests what he had seen was a penetrating type of captive bolt pistol that employs compressed air to shoot a pointed bolt into the cattle's skull before retracting, thereby concussing the animal and damaging the brain enough to render it unconscious before it is slaughtered.

"Oh, that that that gun's no good," stutters the Hitchhiker. "The old way with the sledge, see, that was better. They died better that way." With a confused look, Franklin counters that he understood the air gun to be preferable, implying it to be a more humane and/ or efficient means of killing. "Oh, no, no," the Hitchhiker says while shaking his head. "With the new way, people put out of jobs."

When *The Texas Chain Saw Massacre* premiered on October 1, 1974, the United States had been mired in a severe economic recession for nearly a year, one that would continue for several months more. During that period the unemployment rate rose dramatically from about five percent when Nixon began his second term of office in January 1973 to about nine percent in May 1975.[192] Numerous factors contributed to the loss of jobs, among them an abrupt increase in the inflation rate from 3.65 percent to start 1973 to nearly 11.8 percent to start 1975,[193] the oil crisis caused by the debilitating oil embargo imposed by the Organization of Arab Petroleum Exporting Countries from October 1973 to March 1974, and a group of new economic policies begun in August 1971 that among other ramifications led to the devaluation of the dollar and removal of the gold standard. In all, approximately 2.3 million Americans lost payroll jobs during the 1973-1975 recession, the most significant job loss since the Second World War.[194] During the 1960s those employed by the meatpacking industry in many cases enjoyed competitive pay, good benefits, and safe working conditions thanks largely to the efforts of relatively strong unions, all of which translated to especially low turnover rates when compared to other industrial jobs. Those conditions would swiftly change, however, as increasing numbers of plants were opened in rural areas and the extensive use of immigrant labor helped to drive wages down. The introduction of new technology and mechanization also reshaped how slaughterhouses functioned, speeding up production lines and in many cases lessening worker safety while reducing both available jobs and the need for specialized skills.[195]

The feeble-minded Hitchhiker hardly seems aware of such larger trends when complaining about "the new way" and its effect on employment at the local slaughterhouse. As he continues it appears he, too, once worked there, and perhaps like his family members lost his position due to the introduction of the air gun. "I was the killer!" he giggles with unnerving excitement when sharing his Polaroids of slaughtered cattle, giving the impression that rather than having taken them that afternoon the pictures might be morbid souvenirs from his former occupation. Proving his intimate knowledge of the industry's methods, the Hitchhiker then builds upon Franklin's earlier dissertation by describing in detail how every part of the animal is used, dwelling in particular on the process by which pâté-like head cheese is made. "They take the head and they boil it, except for the tongue, and they scrape all the flesh away from the bone," he explains. "They use everything! They don't throw *nothing* away. They use the jowls and the muscles and the eyes and ligaments and everything. And the nose and the gums and all the flesh, and they boil it all down into a big jelly of fat."

As the women renew their objections to the subject having been revived, Franklin tries to placate the Hitchhiker by agreeing that like him, he also likes head cheese. Pam continues to complain, and with a grumble Franklin tells her "you'd probably like it if you didn't know what was in it" before the group settles into silence. Franklin idly picks at his nails with a pocket knife while Roger Bartlett & Friends' incongruously cheerful "Fool for a Blonde" plays over the radio. Suddenly the Hitchhiker impulsively reaches forward and takes the knife away, then after examining the blade lets out a laugh before deliberately cutting his own palm with it over the others' cries. Exhaling with apparent pleasure as blood drips down his arm, the Hitchhiker hands the knife back to a wide-eyed Franklin.

From there the ride continues to go south (in more ways than one), with the Hitchhiker performing still more disturbing and inexplicable acts. First he pulls a straight razor from his boot and opens it, chuckling and commenting proudly "it's a good knife!" He is instructed to put it away and does, then after catching a glimpse of Franklin's worried look decides to open up his Polaroid camera. He spends some time laughing and pointing it at the others, each frozen with anxiety wondering what the Hitchhiker will do next. Finally he snaps a picture of Franklin, the flash recalling the film's opening sequence during which the photographer's subjects had been corpses. As he waits for the photo to develop, he asks to be dropped off at his house located just off the highway. Kirk objects that they are in a hurry, but the Hitchhiker insists the house is close. "Well, couldn't you just walk, I mean, if it's so close?" asks Sally, but he persists, and even invites them to dinner. "*You* like head cheese," he says, pointing to Franklin. "My brother makes it real good. You'll like it!" Kirk apologetically turns down the invitation, and with a look of dejection the Hitchhiker turns his attention back to the photograph. Slowly he unpeels it and upon seeing the picture his expression turns to childlike joy. He hands it to Franklin who judges it a poor photograph, but the Hitchhiker disagrees and asks for a payment of two dollars. Again he is turned down. After being handed back the photo he meticulously smooths out a sheet of aluminum foil and places the photo on it, carefully dumps a small amount of gunpowder over it from his sack, then lights a match and sets it ablaze. While the others start to yell he lets the photo burn a few seconds before closing it up in the foil and jamming the mess into his sack. Amid the rising chaos the Hitchhiker swiftly produces his knife again and with a forward lunge grabs Franklin's forearm, then slices it as Wayne Bell's "stinger" sound cuts through the screams, again recalling the film's opening. Finally Jerry pulls to the side of the road and the Hitchhiker is ejected from the vehicle. He runs alongside the van as it pulls away, kicking it and then smearing blood on its side. As they drive off, the Hitchhiker holds his arms wide as though in triumph. In a final shot he sticks out his tongue and delivers a parting raspberry salute from the side of the road.

There is no obvious or logical explanation for the Hitchhiker's odd conduct. A danger to others and possibly also to himself, he impresses us as not "normal," or at least not so in the world of the film as it has been presented to this point. Eventually we will encounter the family members to whom he refers, and we will come to realize the Hitchhiker is in fact a fitting representative for the seeming craziness they exemplify. Edwin Neal's bravura performance during the scene further helps distance us from the character, ensuring we identify squarely with the others in the van. Like them we are bewildered by the Hitchhiker, and perhaps additionally rattled by thoughts of what else the filmmakers might have in store. Unlike them, however, we can also find humor in his outrageousness, even if our initial shock might prevent us from appreciating the absurd comedy of his jester-like behavior the first time through.

In any event, hostility is established. Not only is the Hitchhiker ungrateful for the ride, but by the time he chooses to lash out, the group appears to have offended him in multiple ways—by not taking him to his house, by not accepting his invitation to dinner, and by not agreeing to purchase the photograph of Franklin. Initiating all of this strife is his disagreement with Franklin over slaughterhouse killing methods, with the Hitchhiker's stubborn insistence that the "old way" is preferable to the "new way" linking him to a backward-looking, reactionary perspective intolerant of modernization or other forms of change. In a similar way, his strange hobby of disturbing corpses and fashioning the decaying remains into "grisly" art pieces as though to reanimate them appears a symbolic refusal to let the past remain buried. Even his interest in photography could be linked to a fascination with the past and a desire to preserve it. As we will find out, the rest of his family shares such a point of view, even if only one other character, appropriately named the "Old Man," has the means to articulate it. Meanwhile the group of travelers is unwittingly heading directly into one of those scary "dark kernels" Henkel mentions, a place where the Hitchhiker lives and the group to which he belongs is in power. He may look "weird" or seem abnormal elsewhere, but that is not the case where they are headed, and where most of the rest of the story will be taking place. There the Hitchhiker and his family are the authority, the ones who govern the fate of anyone who happens to intrude upon them or threaten their well-being. (The distinction between the two groups is even emphasized in the end credits where extra spaces segregate the story's victims from its villains.)

The film's commentary on the Nixon administration's corruption and criminality rests in part on the way *Chain Saw* establishes its two distinct groups of victims and villains, both of which satirize the opposing factions in the real-life "nightmare" of Watergate. The family represents a grotesque, exaggerated version of the government whose actions serve to terrorize the American public, here represented by the "five youths" with whom the audience identifies.

The association of Nixon and those in power with the "old way" and those who opposed them with the "new way" was well established during his first term, with the continued engagement in Vietnam justifiably driving the wedge between the two groups especially deep. As Senator Frank Church famously stated in May 1970 a week after the shootings at Kent State, "This war has already stretched the generation gap so wide that it threatens to pull the country apart."[196] For Nixon the association was in some respects a vestige of his earlier 1960 presidential campaign against John F. Kennedy when Nixon represented the familiar old guard of an incumbent administration and his challenger something new and inspiring. In that campaign, both parties highlighted Kennedy's youth as a relevant issue for voters, albeit for different reasons. For the Democrats, Kennedy's age meant new energy and positive change, while for the Republicans it indicated immaturity and inexperience, all despite the fact that Nixon was only four-and-a-half years older and both men had begun their political careers in Congress in the same year of 1946. It should be noted, however, that throughout his career, including while president, Nixon's support was not strictly limited to older voters. In 1972, the first election following the ratification of the 26th Amendment that lowered the voting age from 21 to 18, Nixon defied predictions that younger voters would overwhelmingly favor his opponent, George McGovern, and in fact 52 percent of the under-thirty "youth vote" went Nixon's way.[197] Even so, the Vietnam War in particular had emphasized a generational divide, with the White House responding to the protests and dissent of younger Americans with repeated appeals to a so-called "silent majority" of supporters largely comprised of an older demographic.

One dramatic illustration of Nixon's association with the "old" and his antagonism toward the "new" came at a White House event on January 28, 1972 honoring the publishers of *Reader's Digest* occasioned by the magazine's 50th anniversary. The Ray Conniff Singers performed, the Grammy-winning vocal group whose repertoire of "easy listening" pop standards especially appealed to older listeners. In the same East Room where he would deliver a tearful farewell to his staff a little over two-and-a-half years later, Nixon introduced the performance, and earned a laugh from the crowd after proclaiming his appreciation of the group's traditional sound. "Ray Conniff and his very famous choral group will now entertain us," said Nixon with a wry grin, "and if the music is square, it's because I *like* it square." Alas for the president, the jovial atmosphere would swiftly sour. Before the first song began, one of the singers, Carole Feraci, stepped forward and held up a small homemade banner that read "Stop the Killing." She then delivered a short statement asking Nixon to "stop bombing human beings, animals, and vegetation," adding how "if Jesus Christ were here tonight, you would not drop another bomb," and then blessing the peace activist priests Daniel and Philip Berrigan and *Pentagon Papers* leaker Daniel Ellsberg. Feraci's protest was met with scorn among those in attendance, and after performing one song she was asked to leave, although not before enduring a thorough interrogation from the Secret Service. Response to news coverage of the episode was divided, with Nixon supporters citing how Feraci was a Canadian and not a regular member of the group as reasons to dismiss her protest. Her youth additionally made her a target of censure, and an emblem of sorts for the conflict between the younger and older generations. Talking to reporters afterwards, Feraci evoked both her age and her modest status relative to the politically powerful whom she was protesting. "If an oobie-doobie girl like me has courage, the rest of the people will, too," she said.[198] Such optimism appears as though it might have subsequently waned, however, as a couple of months later in early April 1972, an Associated Press item about Feraci titled "She Has Nightmares" was published in the nation's newspapers, including in the *Austin American*. "Carole Feraci describes the night-

SHE HAS NIGHTMARES — Carole Feraci describes the nightmares she says she's had since she displayed a cloth banner that said "Stop the Killing" while performing before President Nixon and others in the White House with the Ray Coniff Singers. "I just know they're going to come get me," she says.
(AP Wirephoto)

Carole Feraci, a.k.a. the "oobie-doobie girl."

mares she says she's had" since staging her protest, reads the copy. The text appears beneath a photo of her with a distressed look, her hands reaching up toward her face making her appear not unlike a horror movie actress in peril. The caption concludes: "'I just know they're going to come get me,' she says."[199]

The frequency of protests like Feraci's diminished following the signing of the Paris Peace Accords in late January 1973, and as already noted for a brief period Nixon enjoyed his highest-ever approval ratings. But such domestic calm was short-lived. Soon the Watergate scandal emerged as a serious and very public crisis, following Vietnam as a new reason for many Americans, young *and* old, to distrust the government and regard Nixon as a villainous, out-of-control character dangerously abetted by his circle of co-conspirators. The office itself as it had evolved under recent presidents was viewed by many as having become too powerful, even unconstitutionally so as the executive branch assumed ever greater authority. Arthur M. Schlesinger Jr. famously described this process in his 1973 book *Imperial Presidency* and its climaxing with the Nixon administration's systematic efforts to wrest from Congress control over both foreign and domestic agendas. In order to expand the conduct of wartime military operations, authority over budgetary decisions, and oversight powers, Nixon respectively evoked "national security," "presidential impoundment," and "executive privilege" in order to resist being constrained.[200] When Watergate then threatened to weaken Nixon, those efforts were heightened even further, with such actions provoking more criticism for the damage they appeared to cause. Every American president had been an object of scorn among some percentage of the electorate, but for Nixon during Watergate that gradually became the prevailing view. But it was more than that. For many, the president had become more than just a representative of positions with which they disagreed. He was trying to *hurt* them.

Such was the "us-versus-them" dynamic in play when *Chain Saw* was written and produced, one which led those who created the film's two groups of victims and villains to say that Watergate had in many ways inspired them.

Law and Order (17:42)

A Nixon-Agnew 1968 campaign button.

"Ohhhh... I'm about half-ready to call a cop," says Kirk with a shudder as Sally and Pam attend to the injured Franklin. Besides the cemetery investigation it is the film's only reference to the police who are otherwise absent from the world of *The Texas Chain Saw Massacre*. The declaration sounds facetious, suggesting cynicism about the usefulness of calling upon law enforcement for help. It also reinforces the younger generation's distrust of authority figures.

As Watergate played out and the extent of corruption and criminality in the Nixon administration became increasingly evident, many noticed a certain, conspicuous irony produced by Nixon's very effective self-branding as the "law and order" president.

Nixon's initial ascent through the political ranks had been remarkably swift. It began with a decisive victory over five-time incumbent Jerry Voorhis in a Congressional race in which the Nixon campaign successfully deceived voters into believing the longtime anti-communist Voorhis enjoyed communist support. Over the next six years Nixon won by large margins re-election to the House and a Senate race, then secured a place on the Republican ticket as Dwight D. Eisenhower's Vice President before even having reached the age of 40. While a freshman Congressman and member of the House Un-American Activities Committee, Nixon increased his national profile significantly when he played a leading role in the Alger Hiss case that resulted in the former advisor to Franklin D. Roosevelt being found guilty of two perjury counts for denying he had been a Soviet spy. As a vice-presidential candidate, Nixon faced a serious accusation of his own concerning a secret campaign fund. But after boldly defending himself on national television in what came to be known as the "Checkers" speech, Nixon quelled that crisis and remained on the ticket, ultimately winning two more elections and serving eight years as Ike's VP.

Nixon's upward momentum was thwarted, however, by a close

loss to John F. Kennedy in the 1960 presidential election. An ill-begotten run for governor of California by Nixon followed two years later, resulting in a resounding defeat. When concluding his concession speech, Nixon was unable to resist delivering a final parting shot to reporters for what he perceived as prejudice against him during their coverage of the campaign. "As I leave you, I want you to know, just think how much you're going to be missing," he said with a smirk. "You don't have Nixon to kick around any more, because, gentleman, this is my last press conference."[201] Taking him at his word, political pundits unanimously estimated Nixon's career finished. After days' worth of editorials echoing that judgment, the following Sunday evening an ABC half-hour news special aired that was literally titled "The Political Obituary of Richard Nixon." Adding insult to injury, among the panelists chosen to dance on Nixon's grave on television that night were Jerry Voorhis and Alger Hiss.

"By the beginning of 1963, Richard M. Nixon was dead," explains historian Theodore H. White in *The Making of the President 1968*, who then paraphrases Charles Dickens describing the death of Scrooge's boss Marley in *A Christmas Carol* as a way of reiterating Nixon's political prospects: "No doubt whatever about that. Political clerks, clergymen, undertakers and mourners had all signed the register. Nixon was dead as a doornail."[202] Seemingly done with politics, Nixon joined a New York law firm whose members included John Mitchell, his future campaign director and Attorney General. But soon a series of events took place that created favorable conditions for a possible Nixon return. Kennedy's assassination was the first, prompting immediate conjecture that it could perhaps compel Nixon to challenge for president once again in 1964. Reporting on CBS the following afternoon from outside Nixon's Manhattan apartment, correspondent Bill Leonard explained how "the conversation here frankly, unofficially, cannot help but speculate that these unfortunate events have suddenly projected Mr. Nixon once again and very firmly into the presidential picture."[203] Nixon understandably avoided making any statements about his own political future on that day, and once Barry Goldwater locked up the Republican nomination Nixon deliberately stepped back to assume a supporting role, avoiding becoming collateral damage during Goldwater's disastrous campaign and overwhelming defeat to Lyndon B. Johnson. After biding his time for another year, Nixon led a "Congress '66" committee to campaign vigorously for Republicans. He continued to maintain a relatively low profile until Johnson thrust Nixon back into the national conversation in early November just days before that year's elections. Johnson had issued an update on the situation in Vietnam and Nixon penned a critical response that was published in the *New York Times*. During a press conference the next day, Johnson responded negatively to Nixon's op-ed, surprisingly name-checking Nixon in a manner that seemed personal. Reporter and political historian Jules Witcover later described Johnson as having delivered an extraordinary "verbal bludgeoning" to Nixon, one made even more remarkable given the fact that Nixon was not actively running for any office. "Intentionally or not, the President's words immediately swung the national spotlight on Nixon," explained Witcover, the effect being that "the President's attack bestowed at once upon Nixon the image of *the* leader of the opposition."[204]

The Republicans performed well in 1966, with a big gain in the House, a small one in the Senate, and other key victories including Ronald Reagan ending Nixon foe Pat Brown's run as governor in California in a landslide win. The following year it was clear Nixon would be a leading contender in the next presidential election, and after Republican rivals George Romney, Nelson Rockefeller, Reagan, and others fell away Nixon gained the party's nomination. Meanwhile the first months of 1968 saw the Democrats splitting into multiple opposing factions as Johnson's hold upon the party continued to weaken amid the mishandling of Vietnam. The wave of surprise attacks on South Vietnamese begun in late January by the North Vietnamese and Viet Cong known as the Tet Offensive caused massive casualties, including nearly 4,000 American soldiers killed by the end of March when the first phase concluded. It also turned public opinion against the war, a moment famously signaled by CBS news anchor Walter Cronkite judging in late February that "it seems now more certain than ever, the bloody experience of Vietnam is to end in stalemate."[205] Having recognized "if I have lost Cronkite, I've lost middle America" (the story goes), on March 31 Johnson surprisingly announced he would not seek re-election.[206] That left Eugene McCarthy and late campaign entrant Robert F. Kennedy to battle each other for the anti-war vote while also vying with Hubert Humphrey, Johnson's vice president, and third-party candidate George Wallace who was busy marshaling support in the South. Four days later civil rights leader Martin Luther King Jr. was assassinated, prompting riots in over a hundred U.S. cities. Then in early June, Robert F. Kennedy was shot moments after declaring victory in the California primary and would die the next day. Ultimately Hubert Humphrey received the party's nomination at the Democratic National Convention in Chicago in late August after withstanding McCarthy's challenge and a late push for Ted Kennedy to step forward as a possible contender. However, the Democrats were far from unified. Humphrey's identification with LBJ's position coupled with the party's failure to pass an anti-war peace plank to include in its platform at the convention helped heighten tensions inside the International Amphitheatre. Meanwhile dramatic protests took place outside the venue, in nearby parks, and at the Conrad Hilton where candidates and many delegates were staying. Violent clashes involving police and national guardsmen shown on national television shocked the nation, evoking comparisons with news coverage of race riots and Vietnam. "The whole world is watching!" chanted demonstrators as they were beaten and arrested. For a significant number of Americans, what they were watching was the country frighteningly descend into what appeared unruly chaos.

Such developments were obviously all encouraging to Nixon's presidential aspirations. It was against such a backdrop the Nixon campaign carefully honed his "law and order" image designed to assure the nation their candidate was the best choice to restore calm and take America back to the relatively less tumultuous past of the Eisenhower years. As White recalls, Nixon's failed gubernatorial campaign in 1962 had included "the early invocation of his later law-and-order theme" via repeated references to increases in the crime rate, though the strategy then failed to land with California voters.[207] Such would not be the case in 1968, in large part because Nixon's return to the national political stage was accompanied by a carefully orchestrated public relations strategy powered by the hiring of advertising executives and consultants. The group was tasked with accentuating Nixon's qualifications and gravitas while minimizing both his most recent ignominious exit from politics and memories of the angle-shooting, dirty campaigner of his early political career. As shared in

Joe McGinniss's behind-the-scenes exposé *The Selling of the President 1968* (the title of which parodies White), a memo from consultant Harry Treleaven describes the need to promote Nixon positives like experience, toughness, integrity, and conscientiousness while downplaying negatives such as his lack of newness, glamour, humor, and warmth. Other aspects of the candidate in need of diminishing included "the 'tricky Dick' image, the reputation for meanness and ruthlessness, for putting politics ahead of principle," as well as another "negative that does seem to hang on" for him, "the loser image."[208] The "law and order" theme served all of these purposes succinctly and efficiently. It emphasized Nixon's readiness to lead and the current administration's lack of control. It recalled the "Cold Warrior" Nixon who like an attack dog rooted out communism wherever it was found, suggesting the candidate would similarly handle crime and other disturbances as he strove to protect the innocent and punish the guilty. The messaging also evoked consistently positive response from supporters. As Treleaven observed in another memo from May 1968, "The biggest hand RN's been getting has been when he talks about people having more respect for law and order."[209] When accepting the Republicans' nomination at their convention in early August, Nixon deliberately foregrounded how "the nation with the greatest tradition of the rule of law is plagued by unprecedented lawlessness" as well as "the problem of order in the United States." And while McGinniss's book at times suggests the contrary, Nixon also denied the charge that his campaign's theme included a covert message favoring whites. "To those who say that law and order is the code word for racism, here is a reply: Our goal is justice—justice for every American. If we are to have respect for law in America, we must have laws that deserve respect. Just as we cannot have progress without order, we cannot have order without progress."[210]

As election day drew closer, a series of innovative television commercial "spots" created by documentarian Gene Jones continued to blast the law and order message. Some juxtaposed in montage fashion violent images from the fighting abroad and protests at home, often backed by Nixon's cool and even narration outlining the necessity to defend "decent and law-abiding citizens" and "to take the offensive against the criminal forces that threaten their peace and security." The most controversial of the spots, internally titled "Convention," zeroed in on the DNC disaster with a series of cross-cut stills juxtaposing Humphrey accepting the nomination, blood being spilled on the Chicago streets, casualties being tended to in Southeast Asia, and poverty-stricken Americans. In this case no narration is employed, the soundtrack entirely consisting of the jaunty Dixieland standard "A Hot Time in the Old Town" being repeatedly interrupted by jarring, echo-filled reverb as the images flash past, making it appear as though the open-mouthed and grinning Humphrey is responding to the nation's trouble with gleeful laughter. In fact, the commercial both visually and aurally resembles the end-credit sequence of *Night of the Living Dead*, a film that coincidentally premiered a few weeks before the ad was shown during the October 28, 1968 episode of *Laugh-In*. The spot sparked so much consternation and backlash, it only aired a single time before being pulled.[211]

All of it worked. Back from the dead, Nixon won the presidency in a close election, capping a remarkable comeback. No major party's presidential candidate since the late 19th century had lost a general election and then run again and won, and no one has done it since.

After assuming office, "law and order" remained a mantra consistently evoked by Nixon in remarks, statements, and addresses throughout his first term and into his second. At a news conference on March 15, 1973—held just a week before dramatic suggestions of a more extensive cover-up of White House criminality became public at the Watergate suspects' trial—Nixon contrasted his administration's toughness on crime with the corresponding failures of his predecessors. "During the sixties, the United States went far down the road of the permissive approach to those charged with crime," said Nixon. "And we reaped a terrible harvest, the greatest increase in crime that this country has ever had, explosive to the point that law and order, so-called, became a great issue in '68. It was still a great issue in '72."[212] Most often the phrase appeared in the context of discussing the need to reduce crime, although the emphasis on "order" often also suggested indirect justification for responding forcefully to dissent and public protests. The latter issue most emphatically gripped the nation during the month of May 1970 after the killing of four student protesters at Kent State University by members of the Ohio National Guard, followed 11 days later by the shooting deaths of two protesting students by police at Jackson State College in Mississippi. In between came the "Hard Hat Riot" in New York City where two hundred construction workers mobilized by the state's AFL-CIO labor union attacked protesting students. Nixon's response throughout was to resist any public show of grief for protestors' deaths or injuries and to side with order-maintaining authorities, and the month ended with a White House meeting between Nixon and NYC union officials at which the president was presented a hard hat "as a symbol, along with our great flag, for freedom and patriotism to our beloved country."[213]

Nixon at the famous "I am not a crook" press conference, November 17, 1973.

These events and others might all be cited as informing Kirk's reluctance to call the police. Of course, by Saturday, August 18, 1973—the date on which *Chain Saw* takes place—the Nixon administration's own lack of respect for law and order was commonly understood, perhaps providing yet another incentive not to trust the authorities. Even Vice President Spiro Agnew, who spoke of "law and order" more often and more vociferously than even Nixon did, had become an accused criminal. When campaigning during the midterms in 1970, Agnew characterized student demonstrators as "misfits" and "garbage" while encouraging voters to support Republicans "who favor a tough stance on law and order, who favor strong campus administrations that will not tolerate this kind of outrageous conduct."[214] Cut forward to early August 1973 when news broke of an investigation into Agnew having accepted kickbacks from public works contractors when he had been a county executive and governor of Maryland, and even continued to accept bribes after becoming Vice President. Within weeks, Agnew would precede Nixon into historical infamy by resigning on October 10.

A little over a month later came one of the most remembered moments from Watergate, one that perhaps more than any other highlighted the irony of Nixon's self-identification as the "law and order" president. With calls for impeachment growing louder in the wake of the Saturday Night Massacre, Nixon held a press conference among the nation's newspaper editors in the early evening of Saturday, November 17, 1973 at Walt Disney World in Orlando, Florida. Lasting an hour and broadcast live on national television and radio, much of the press conference was taken up by questions surrounding the ongoing battle over the tapes, with Nixon at times appearing uncharacteristically tense and even manic when stumbling over his words and misspeaking (e.g., of Haldeman and Ehrlichman, "I hold that both men and others who have been charged are guilty until I have evidence that they are not guilty"). Questions on other topics were asked, however, including one about a wholly separate controversy concerning Nixon's apparent underpayment of federal income taxes. After defending himself against that charge once, Nixon subsequently circled back to the issue to talk more broadly about his finances and the need for a president to be transparent when it came to his investments. In a way, Nixon's references to audits and sources of income sounded like a distant reprise of his famous "Checkers" speech in 1952 in which he successfully defended himself against accusations of financial improprieties when a vice-presidential candidate. Here, though, the backdrop of Watergate caused Nixon's professions to have "never profited from public service" to sound as though he were being more earnest than necessary when defending himself, especially when he added somewhat tangentially that "in all my years of public life, I have never obstructed justice." Winding up his comments on the issue, Nixon took an even broader view of the question of presidential conduct and the need for transparency. "I welcome this kind of examination," he said, "because people have got to know whether or not their president is a crook. Well, I am not a crook. I have earned everything I have got."[215]

By denying something of which he had not been accused, the president who stood for law and order had supplied the nations' newspapers an unmistakably damning headline: "Nixon Tells Editors, 'I'm Not a Crook.'"[216]

It goes without saying, the group will be continuing their trip without consulting the authorities. "That's the last goddamn hitchhiker I ever pick up," says Jerry from the driver's seat.

The Events of the World Are Not Doing Much, Either, to Cheer One Up (18:09)

Protestors calling for Nixon's impeachment on October 22, 1973, two days after the Saturday Night Massacre.

"Hey, listen to Franklin's horoscope," says Pam as Sally attends to her brother. Reading from an astrology magazine, Pam continues. "Travel in the country, long-range plans, and upsetting persons around you could make this a disturbing and unpredictable day," she reads. "The events of the world are not doing much, either, to cheer one up."

The first part of Franklin's horoscope is an obvious and droll reference to the misfortune he has just endured. The second might seem less immediately relevant, aside perhaps from recalling the opening radio reports of a litany of calamities—if, that is, we forget the ubiquitous coverage of Watergate then filling the headlines and the increasing dread they tended to cause.

Indeed, newspapers across the country that Saturday morning included op-eds written in response to Nixon's second Watergate speech from Wednesday night with titles like "Questions Unanswered," "Decline of Authority," and "Nixon Strikes Low Chord."[217] Meanwhile other events filling front page headlines in that morning's papers were hardly any more encouraging. Those included a successful Soviet test of missiles with multiple warheads, a pledge-slash-warning by the U.S. to provide air support to South Vietnam should the North show overt aggression, and an update on the Agnew case and whether or not indictments would be sought.[218]

American Astrology (18:18)

Pam reads from *American Astrology*, a magazine contemporary audiences might well have recognized from newsstands or supermarket checkout lanes. (It is in fact the April 1973 issue, a negligible detail.)

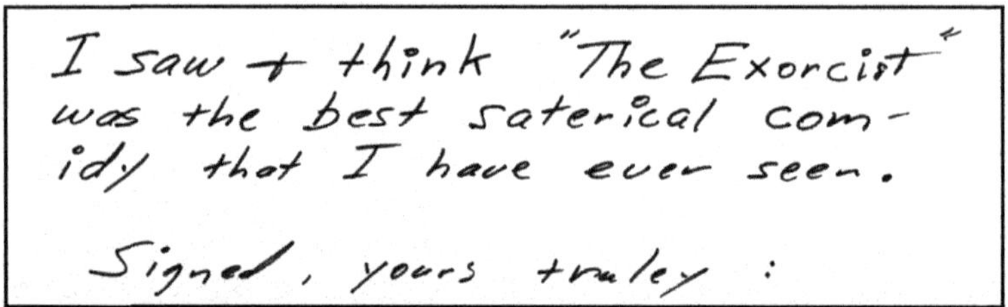
I saw + think "The Exorcist" was the best saterical comidy that I have ever seen.

Signed, yours truley :

An excerpt from what is thought to be the last letter from the "Zodiac Killer," mailed to the *San Francisco Chronicle* on January 29, 1974.

Started by Clancy Publications in 1933, it was one of the most popular astrology magazines in America during the early 1970s, along with *Dell Horoscope* having a circulation of approximately half a million.[219] Historically speaking, *American Astrology* was also the first publication to popularize the standard horoscope columns organized by zodiac signs from which Pam ostensibly reads.[220]

"Hey Pam, read Sally's... she's Capricorn," says Jerry. Pam furrows her brow as she finds Sally's horoscope, then reacts with dismay. "Oh no, Capricorn's ruled by Saturn," she begins. "There are moments when we cannot believe that what is happening is really true. Pinch yourself and you may find out that it is."

It is another unsubtle bit of foreshadowing of the nightmare to come. (Another negligible detail—Richard Nixon was a Capricorn.)

Speaking of both astrology and other events of the world not doing much to cheer one up, the period during which the so-called "Zodiac Killer" was active almost exactly coincided with Nixon's presidency. In December 1968, just after Nixon's election and prior to his taking office, the never caught or identified suspect killed his first two victims in Nixon's home state of California, then in July 1969 attacked another couple, killing one more. A month later he began sending letters and cryptograms to California newspapers claiming credit for the killings and identifying himself as "the Zodiac," then came two more attacks resulting in two more deaths and an injury. From there continued a nearly five-year period of letters and cards being received by various newspapers and individuals, many of which are believed to have come from the same source. Ultimately the letter writer would boast of 37 killings.

The final letter considered legitimate was sent to the *San Fran-*

cisco Chronicle and postmarked January 29, 1974. It was a short note that started with a one-sentence review of what was at the time the most popular horror movie in America. While the spelling was uncertain, the appraisal nonetheless acknowledged the satirical potential of horror.

"I saw + think 'The Exorcist' was the best saterical comidy that I have ever seen."[221]

The Old Man (19:31)

The Old Man has no gas, but he'll sell you some good barbecue.

There is a lengthy shot of a balding man on a stool looking up at the hot sun beating down on him. The camera pulls back to reveal he is sitting at a gas station, with a storefront sign above him indicating they sell barbecue. Though only shown briefly, the sign somewhat ominously appears to read "WE SLAUGHTER BARBECUE."

We see it is a Gulf station as the van pulls up beside the two gasoline pumps, and Sally and Pam exit the van to visit the restroom. Another older man, the apparent proprietor, approaches the van on the passenger's side. Following his lead, the bald man wheels a bucket forward, draws a soaked rag from it, and begins to wash the windshield.

As Gunnar Hansen explains, the sign actually reads "W.E. SLAUGHTER," suggesting a name for the owner and a less than delicate pun.[222] The name is not mentioned in the screenplay and does not come up again in the film, and in the 1986 sequel directed by Hooper the family is given a different surname, also a pun—Sawyer. (In the 1995 installment *Texas Chainsaw Massacre: The Next Generation* written and directed by Henkel, the Slaughter family name returns with one character named Walter Edward Slaughter.)

It is the first appearance in the film of Jim Siedow's character, described in the screenplay as "a man somewhat past his middle years." When he speaks the character is generically referred to as "Old Man," which as has been noted is also how Siedow is listed in the credits. At the time, Siedow was 54.

"The Old Man" was a name frequently used by Nixon's aides and advisors when they spoke to one another about the president. Doing so drew attention to the fact that many of them were considerably younger than Nixon who was in his late 50s and early 60s while in office. Among those closest to Nixon, his National Security Advisor and later Secretary of State Henry Kissinger was 10 years younger and one of his closest contemporaries. Both Haldeman and Ehrlichman were in their 40s, Dean was in his 30s, Ron Ziegler turned 30 shortly after becoming White House Press Secretary, and Dwight Chapin began as Deputy Assistant in his late 20s. Nixon's primary speechwriters Raymond Price, Bill Gavin, and Patrick Buchanan were also all in their 30s when Nixon first took office.

The term is often used to refer to one's father, and indeed, in his farewell speech to staff Nixon would reminisce about his parents, referring to his father as his "old man."[223] When used by Nixon's aides, it was mostly a term of endearment indicating the president's father-figure status among those closest to him, although perhaps sometimes used ironically given Nixon's social reticence. Buchanan, later a presidential candidate himself, conspicuously continued to use the term whenever speaking of Nixon, such as in his recent memoir chronicling the period, *Nixon's White House Wars*. Writing of the intense period in April 1973 after Dean had broken from the inner circle, Buchanan notes how Haldeman would probably have to resign as well and be replaced by a new Chief of Staff, and whoever took the role, "the Old Man would need someone he trusted and was comfortable with to get him through the days ahead."[224]

No Gas (19:39)

The Old Man greets Kirk and Jerry, and in the era of full-service gas stations they call out the window for him to "fill 'er up."

"I got no gas," he says plaintively. "*You're* out of gas?" says Jerry, sounding incredulous. "My tank's empty," comes the reply. "Transport won't be here until late this afternoon, maybe not even until tomorrow morning." The Old Man raps the front of the van twice and turns to walk away.

In June 1973, a gas station owner in Perkasie, Pennsylvania lets his customers know the pumps are empty.

Seekers of *Chain Saw* subtexts are understandably eager to highlight this plot point in which the group find themselves low on fuel in a rural area, ostensibly requiring gas in order to return home safely and failing to find any. Such readings often link the empty tank at this particular station not just to the general economic stressors discussed above, but more particularly to the national gas shortage caused by the Organization of Arab Petroleum Exporting Countries' oil embargo imposed in retaliation for the United States' having delivered aid to Israel during the Yom Kippur War. In truth the embargo did not begin until mid-October 1973, a couple of months *after* the film is set and when the scene was shot, and at least six months or more after the plot turn had been written into the screenplay. Even so, gas shortages had been irregularly affecting some stations throughout the country for many months leading up to the embargo, making the scene both realistic and relatable for initial audiences.

Prior to the embargo, OAPEC had been applying pressure to foreign oil corporations to raise their prices at a time when America's reliance on imported oil was increasing. During his first term Nixon removed previous prohibitions on oil imports and from 1970 to 1973 they more than doubled to a point where they comprised about a third of what America was using.[225] Recognizing a looming energy crisis, in April 1973 Nixon announced multiple strategies designed both to increase domestic production of various energy sources and to reduce the country's reliance on foreign imports. However, the focus in the short term was to satisfy immediate demand, and thus Nixon ended the Mandatory Oil Import Program that had placed quotas on how much the nation's oil companies could import. In some cases independent gas stations in particular were made vulnerable by these measures, especially when competing against major oil companies who thanks to a more secure supply chain were able to undercut the independents with lower pricing, a situation that led multiple federal agencies to begin looking into possible improprieties.[226] In any case, the administration's efforts more or less helped carry America through the spring and summer months, but made the country even more vulnerable by October when the embargo began.

What happens in the film would have been entirely probable in mid-August 1973, a time when anyone traveling in the east Texas panhandle would have been likely to encounter some stations without gas, but others with a ready supply. It makes sense, then, for Kirk and Jerry to express surprise that the station is out of gas and to respond by asking the Old Man about other stations nearby. Post-embargo, when the gas shortage was widespread enough to affect nearly everyone, their response would have been different. They would have been neither surprised nor would they have been encouraged to find the situation better elsewhere.

By the time *Chain Saw* was released in October 1974, the OAPEC embargo had come and gone, having ended in mid-March. Even so gas prices remained elevated, and the experience of waiting in long lines, carpooling, rationing, price controls, and encountering gas stations with empty tanks was fresh in viewers' minds, thereby encouraging the link between the events of the film and the contemporary context. Hooper's repeated endorsements of the connection in interviews further informed such readings, giving sanction to those wishing to interpret the specific adversity forced upon the group as a kind of microcosm of a more general hardship being endured by Americans at around the same time. The parallel is therefore suggestive, further supporting the notion that what happens to the group is not merely inflicted upon them by a peculiar family of madmen, but is somehow a consequence of the nation's dysfunction.

You Think You Could Do That to Yourself? (22:05)

As the Old Man walks away from the van, Franklin calls him back with a question about "where the old Franklin place is." The Old Man returns to the van's side, and the bald man humorously follows him back as well and begins to wash the windshield a second time as though not aware he had done it before. Franklin provides a short description of the house, explaining how he thinks it is located nearby but is not sure exactly where.

The Old Man is evasive, saying he might have seen the house before though he does not recommend the group seek it out. "You boys don't want to go messing around no old house," he says. "Those things is dangerous. You're liable to get hurt." Jerry quietly says they will be careful, but the Old Man continues making the point about the hazards of trespassing on "other folks' property." Franklin responds by saying his father owns the house (which therefore should, it would seem, be called the *Hardesty* place, not the Franklin place). The Old Man nonetheless repeats his caution to the group not to investigate, inviting them instead to stay and have some "good barbecue" while revising his previous estimate to say the transport will in fact probably be arriving soon. He raps the front of the van twice as he did before and starts to walk away, then after spotting Sally and Pam at the Coke machine returns to add how "them girls now, they... they don't want to go messing around an old house" before going back inside.

At Kirk's suggestion, Jerry follows the Old Man inside to ask him about another gas station and to get some barbecue, leaving Kirk and Franklin in the van. Franklin has his pocket knife out again, and uses it to pick destructively at the van's interior before Kirk stops him. "Franklin, you maniac, you're tearing up the van," says Kirk. "Um, yeah, I just start doing that," says Franklin who stops and studies his knife, discovering some of the Hitchhiker's blood still on it. "That guy cut the hell out of himself," Franklin marvels. "You think you could do that to yourself?" Kirk exhales dismissively, declaring "I'm not crazy."

"It takes something, though," says Franklin. "Just to do that to yourself like he did." Franklin asks Kirk if he thinks he might have said something to have provoked the Hitchhiker, and Kirk laughs out loud. "Franklin, you're crazier than he was," he exclaims.

The pair's reflection on the Hitchhiker's apparent madness prompts idle though peculiarly literal discussion of their own, with Kirk explicitly confirming his sanity while jokingly questioning Franklin's. Much as Franklin had been the only member of the group curious to interact with the Hitchhiker during his ride, he also appears to be the only one inquisitive enough to want to explore the Hitchhiker's mental state afterwards. For demonstrating such curiosity, Franklin becomes identified with the Hitchhiker, accused (albeit in jest) of having a mental handicap to go along with his physical one.

One of the most extraordinary aspects of the Watergate scandal—extraordinary, at least, at the time it occurred—was how it revealed not merely that the White House had been overtaken by corruption and even criminality, but by a kind of unsettling "craziness" or seeming irrationality as well. As the country came to understand in full during the Senate Watergate Hearings over the summer of 1973, the break-in and bugging of the Democratic National Committee headquarters had not been an isolated incident, but one of several cloak-and-dagger operations planned and perpetrated by individuals acting at the White House's behest and dating back well into Nixon's first term. As the White House tapes and others' accounts would confirm, Nixon's own personal insecurities and distrust built up over a lengthy career in the public eye in fact provided a primary motive for such efforts. When asked in a 1983 interview about criticisms that he and his administration were overly "obsessed with secrecy," Nixon freely accepted the charge. "As a matter of fact, you're being too kind," he said in answer to the question. "I was paranoiac, or almost a basket case with regard to secrecy."[227]

Earnest discussion of such schemes began soon after Nixon took office as he contemplated how best to manage increasing protests spurred by the United States' continued military engagement in Southeast Asia. In June 1970, Nixon directed Special Assistant Tom Charles Huston to act as a liaison with the nation's intelligence agencies to investigate "foreign communist support of revolutionary protest movements in the United States."[228] Judging "the 'present' intelligence collection capabilities in the area were inadequate," Nixon ordered the creation of an interagency committee to be headed by longtime FBI Director J. Edgar Hoover, and at an initial meeting of a subcommittee Huston presented a detailed outline endorsed by Nixon listing the committee's purpose, procedures, and objectives. A 43-page "Special Report Interagency Committee on Intelligence (Ad Hoc)" was soon produced that subsequently came to be known as the "Huston Plan," and after Nixon's review and approval the plan was forwarded to the heads of the FBI, the Central Intelligence Agency, the National Security Agency, and the Defense Intelligence Agency

Charles Colson, Nixon's "hatchet man."

for implementation. Hoover objected to several elements of the plan, however, in particular the called-for removal of various restrictions on wiretapping, mail intercepts, and even illegal break-ins and burglaries of surveilling protestors and their alleged sponsors. While the Huston Plan was officially revoked, elements of it nonetheless were later enacted surreptitiously by the White House's own in-house intelligence team, the Special Investigations Unit or "White House Plumbers" later created in the wake of the June 1971 publication of the *Pentagon Papers*. (It was while defending the Huston Plan in his post-resignation series of interviews with David Frost that Nixon would infamously declare "When the president does it, that means it is not illegal."[229])

As it happened, the Huston Plan would prove one of the less startling examples of extreme, seemingly crazy measures pursued by Nixon and his men that constantly filled headlines just before and during the filming of *Chain Saw*. Nixon aide Charles Colson, formerly the president's Special Counsel and described by many as the president's "hatchet man," figured prominently in several of these stories. In early June 1973, the *Washington Post* published an article describing another aborted plan proposed by Colson to firebomb the Brookings Institution, a Washington, D.C. think tank where he suspected a former aide to Henry Kissinger had squirreled away classified State Department documents. The firebombing would create a diversion, apparently, in order to cover a burglary of the aide's office. (Colson initially denied the story, then admitted to Bob Woodward "there is always a possibility that I might have said it."[230]) Another sensational story that summer involved Watergate co-conspirator E. Howard Hunt having been instructed by Colson to forge cables to suggest John F. Kennedy had ordered the assassination of South Vietnam president Ngo Dinh Diem three weeks before Kennedy was killed. Hunt described the forgeries and Colson's directive to the grand jury in May and to the Senate Watergate Committee in September. (Colson denied this accusation as well, though admitted Hunt might have "misunderstood something I said to him."[231]) Yet another Colson project involved his having directed his assistant George Bell to compile an "enemies list" of Nixon critics and adversaries known internally as the "Opponents List and Political Enemies Project." Described by Dean to the Senate Watergate Committee during the last week of June 1973, the list initially included a core group of 20 names plus more than 200 other businessmen, celebrities, reporters and other media, members of the House and Senate, and organizations, with a later list made public in December including no less than 576 individuals. Dean's testimony included sharing a memo he had written addressing the list and outlining ways to "use the available federal machinery to screw our political enemies" such as by "grant availability, federal contracts, litigation, prosecution," and other means.[232] (Colson unconvincingly denied involvement in this, too, although later testified to the House Judiciary Committee that his office had maintained "a list of people we would not invite to White House official functions."[233])

Such tales only represented the most sensational of many similarly outlandish plots shown to have predated the Watergate arrests. As Dean explained by way of summary, "the Watergate matter was the inevitable outgrowth of a climate of excessive concern over the political impact of demonstrators, excessive concern over leaks, an insatiable appetite for political intelligence, all coupled with a do-it-yourself White House staff regardless of the law."[234] Meanwhile the DNC break-in itself was judged by many at the time as a kind of unnervingly outlandish venture in its own right, a high-risk, low-reward endeavor that made so little sense as to suggest horror film-like insanity.

During testimony before the Senate Watergate Committee, multiple witnesses characterized the "Gemstone" plan originally presented to CREEP by G. Gordon Liddy as a kind of lunacy produced by a fevered, unhinged imagination. "I think it can best be described as a complete horror story," said John Mitchell when describing what Liddy had presented to him in late January and early February 1972 when Mitchell was still Attorney General though about to step down to head the re-election committee. "A mish-mash of code names and lines of authority, electronic surveillance, the ability to intercept aircraft communications, the call girl bit and all the rest of it," Mitchell continued. "The matter was of such striking content and concept that it was just beyond the pale." When asked by Sam Dash, chief counsel to the committee, why he didn't order Liddy from his office, Mitchell humorously answered "in hindsight I not only should have thrown him out of the office, I should have thrown him out of the window." That line drew a big laugh, but Dash drew an even bigger one when he continued, "Well, since you did neither...."[235] During later questioning, Mitchell would jokingly suggest of those involved in the Watergate break-ins "that it might even have been better... [to] take them out on the White House lawn; it would have been simpler to have shot them all and that would have been less of a problem than has developed in the meantime."[236] Mitchell was kidding, although from Liddy's manic perspective such a preposterous solution apparently would not have been questioned. As Dean testified, on the Monday following the Watergate arrests, Liddy made it clear to him that "he was a soldier and would never talk," and should the White House deem it necessary, he was willing to sacrifice his own life in order to protect the presidency. "He said if anyone wished to shoot him on the street, he was ready," Dean explained.[237] Jeb Magruder similarly testified about Liddy's odd "mannerism" (as he called it), describing one instance when he put his hand on Liddy's shoulder and "he asked me to remove it and indicated that if I did not, serious consequences would occur." Dash asked Magruder what those consequences were. "Well, he indicated that he would kill me," said Magruder.[238]

Robert Conrad portrays G. Gordon Liddy performing the candle "trick" in the 1982 TV movie *Will: G. Gordon Liddy*.

The best remembered Liddy story, one that uncannily resembles the Hitchhiker's outlandish feat with Franklin's knife, would not become more generally known until after the hearings and Nixon's resignation while Liddy was serving four-and-a-half years in federal prison for his crimes and steadfast refusal to testify either before the Senate or the grand jury. Dean alludes to the Liddy "candle story" in his 1976 memoir *Blind Ambition*, and Liddy himself highlights performing the act repeatedly in his 1980 memoir *Will* as evidence of a lifetime of effort "to bring my will to maximum power."[239] The story is also told in the 1976 film adaptation of *All the President's Men*, supplied by Bob Woodward to screenwriter William Goldman after not having included it in his 1974 book with Carl Bernstein. In the film, Woodward's informant "Deep Throat" (portrayed by Hal Holbrook) describes how he once witnessed Liddy deliberately hold his hand over a candle at a party. "He kept it right in the flame until his flesh was burned. Somebody said, 'What's the trick?' and Liddy said, 'The trick is not minding.'" While that version is no doubt embellished with a borrowing from a very similar scene and dialogue in the 1962 film *Lawrence of Arabia*, Liddy most certainly performed the "trick" many times, including when recruiting men to fill out his "political intelligence" team in early 1972 in order "to prove myself to them," as he told Dean, by showing them "that I could stand any amount of physical pain."[240]

As the Watergate drama unfolded, it became increasingly clear how an extreme character like Liddy not only had a place in the intensely suspicious "atmosphere at the White House" (as Dean described it in his testimony), but was entrusted with enough responsibility to orchestrate a predictably catastrophic operation like breaking into the DNC. Such audacity both disturbed and captivated Americans in a manner akin to Franklin's fascination with the Hitchhiker.

Political commentator Irving Kristol, a Republican and Nixon supporter, well represented this point of view in May 1973 just before the Senate Watergate Committee hearings began. Getting personal, Kristol tells how the "only comparable experience I have had to Watergate—and I am reminded of it more acutely every day—was when an editorial colleague on a magazine suffered a nervous breakdown, but without his or my realizing it." For him, Watergate similarly presented others acting according to an alternate "unreal reality" prompted by an apparent "wave of collective delusion, suspicion and paranoia engulfing high White House circles and overwhelming all the barriers that common sense erects against such a possibility."

Kristol believed there was only one way to summarize the "lengthy conspiratorial chain" behind "so complicated a criminal enterprise" being revealed to the American public in tantalizing fashion.

"This is not cynical malpractice," judged Kristol. "It is a kind of madness."[241]

Looks Like He Was Trying to Write Something (23:40)

Franklin believes the Hitchhiker's smear has meaning, while Kirk is less convinced.

The girls and Jerry return to the van. Jerry has picked up a to-go bag of barbecue. He has also picked up information that the nearest gas station is in Newt, the town where the cemetery they had earlier visited is located. Before getting into the van, Sally lingers as she notices the blood the Hitchhiker smeared on its side, which she then reports to the others. "Looks like he was trying to write something," she says.

The group is taking a risk by deciding to seek out the old Franklin place, although as far as they are aware the risk has nothing to do with the Old Man's warnings, but merely concerns their limited fuel. Kirk clarifies this point with a joke. "Franklin, if we run out of gas before we get back to that service station, you're towing us back in your chair," he grins.

They find the isolated house and park, and after getting out Sally remarks "I wish they hadn't let the place fall apart." There is a lengthy, slow-moving panning shot moving right to left as though spying on the group through the unmowed grass from a hidden location. Their distant voices can be heard faintly over the soundtrack's low, portentous drone.

Once all are out, they take a closer look at the smear. "Oh, that's weird," says Kirk. "I wonder if that means something." "It's the Mark of Zorro... he's going to get you," Jerry says to Franklin who looks up from his chair worriedly. As the others go inside the house Kirk starts to try to clean the van with a cloth, but Franklin stops him, wishing to study the mark a bit more and wondering aloud whether "that guy will try and follow us."

The blood smear only vaguely suggests the trademark "Z" of the swashbuckling masked hero of pulp stories, early cinema, TV and radio. Some have interpreted it as the Hitchhiker having more generally marked the van's occupants for murder, a reading unsupported by subsequent events in the film. Meanwhile the original screenplay does include some effort to assign the mark added significance that did not make it into the finished film. While studying the smear, Franklin suggests "this real witch, Sybil Leek, that lives in Houston" would "know what that symbol means."[242] Originally from the U.K., Leek became a minor celebrity in America during the 1960s and 1970s thanks to frequent television appearances and a long list of publications about witchcraft, the occult, and the supernatural. In fact, when the unused reference to her was included by Hooper and Henkel, the self-proclaimed "Queen of Witches" was conspicuously associated with politics, having in April 1972 published an *Astrological Guide to the Presidential Candidates*. Leek's book earned national notoriety for having included among many inaccurate predictions about the upcoming race the following forewarning: "There is one menace to the career and potential of George Wallace. The nearer he gets to his goal, the greater the danger of political assassination."[243] A month after the book's publication, Arthur Bremer shot Wallace four times at a campaign rally, leaving the candidate paralyzed and forcing an end to his campaign two months later. Leek's correct guess, given extra notice by *Time* magazine and elsewhere, perhaps encouraged Franklin's idea that she could be of use to help crack the code.

More pointedly, there is an explicit callback to the "symbol" later in the screenplay that is also omitted from the film. During the dinner scene, a stage direction describes the Hitchhiker moving Grandpa's chair to put him in closer proximity to the bound Sally. "On the back of the grandfather's chair is painted the symbol the hitchiker [*sic*] scrawled on the van," goes the description, suggesting a cultish signifier that might be used to impose some kind of external order onto the chaotic narrative.[244] (Connections between the family and an Illuminati-like secret society would resurface in the sequels, in particular the Henkel scripted and directed *Texas Chainsaw Massacre: The Next Generation*.)

In the world of the film, the smear is essentially a cipher, only meaningful to the extent that it bothers Franklin. Even so, like the many other portents populating the first third of the film, Franklin's worry signals the possibility there is *something* nefarious going on, perhaps accessible if only we could piece together the available clues.

Messing Around an Old House (26:09)

The Old Man offering some friendly advice.

The group explores the old Franklin place, and as they do Sally shares her memories of the house with Jerry, Kirk, and Pam.

The two couples playfully walk about upstairs, their merriment contrasting with Franklin's frustration below as he struggles to maneuver his wheelchair into the house. Once inside he appears to experience a mini-breakdown, mocking their laughter and facetiously quoting something Sally ostensibly said to him earlier in the day regarding their outing: "Come on, Franklin. It's gonna be a fun trip." Much as we last saw the Hitchhiker doing from the side of the road, Franklin looks up and angrily blows raspberries in a petulant display. He then recklessly rolls his chair and bangs his knee, causing him to cry out in pain.

Kirk and Pam descend the stairs and ask Franklin about a swimming hole he had mentioned before, and he directs them to follow a trail between two old sheds behind the house. Left alone once more, Franklin wheels back toward the front door and sees on the porch what appears the remnants of a dead animal sitting atop a gathered blanket with bones visible and feathers added as though for decoration. The arrangement recalls the "grisly work of art" in the cemetery at Newt. Franklin then looks up to see another bit of morbid craftwork hanging down from above, described in the screenplay as "a crude wind chime or mobile of some sort made of sun bleached bones."[245]

Even without the bones, the abandoned house keeps reminders of death firmly in the foreground. Torn screens, detritus on the floors, and peeling paint and wallpaper coupled with Sally's earlier remark indicate the grandfather whose grave they had earlier visited was likely the house's final occupant. Among her musings, Sally mentions how the only time she ever stayed at the house was when a child "right after my grandmother died." (Presumably the grandmother would have also been buried in the Newt cemetery, an omitted detail.) The jokey banter of the young, lively visitors as they mill about the old neglected house introduces an obvious incongruity as well, making it seem as though while they are not technically trespassing, they are in a place where they do not belong.

The Old Man's warning against "messing around an old house" suggests the same idea. The film's first half-hour has established different thematic terms through which impending conflict can be understood—the city disturbing the country, the young disturbing the old, the living disturbing the dead. Each of these oppositions references classic horror tropes mindfully pursued here. The house that Kirk says resembles "the birthplace of Bela Lugosi" also deliberately evokes the horror cliché of the haunted house, although as it will turn out the actual danger doesn't exist at the old Franklin place but at a neighboring one to which members of the group are about to wander.

It is the large white house nearby that harbors secrets, a criminal conspiracy, and more direct relevance to contemporary political events.

Uncovering a Pattern (32:19)

Kirk and Pam discover old, abandoned cars hidden under camouflage.

We follow Kirk and Pam as they happily escape the house and Franklin's bad vibe. The cut catches Kirk mid-thought saying "zero in the world" and "just shoot him and put us out of our misery" while they are running, casting non-serious though cruel judgment on their disagreeable traveling companion. Carrying towels, the couple runs over a hill and down into a valley where they surmise the now dry creek bed to have once been the site of the swimming hole remembered by Franklin. A motor can be heard in the distance, and the camera pans up to show on the other side of the valley a horizontal windmill and the rooftop of a large house peeking up over the next hill.

"Gasoline," says Kirk.

As they proceed toward the house and the sound of the running motor, a low angle dolly shot features the sun shining brightly (and ominously) to fill the top half of the frame. Along the way we are shown yet another example of "found art" involving a number of items affixed to the limbs of a small tree, including rusted pots, pans, kettles, and cups and a stopwatch with a spike through it twisting in the wind. While walking Kirk outlines a plan to buy a couple of dollars' worth of gas from whoever lives at the house, leaving his guitar as collateral while they go get more gas elsewhere, then returning to replace the gas they bought and retrieve his guitar. "They don't want your guitar," says Pam. "They're not gonna want to sell us some gas... let's just go back now." Kirk's idea again makes the local gas shortage the group is experiencing a central plot point, with the need for gas again indirectly carrying them into harm's way.

Despite Pam's objection, they nonetheless continue onward toward the house, circling around a barn surrounded by wild sunflowers, one of several ramshackle outer buildings scattered about the property. The screenplay pointedly highlights how "no power lines run to the house and no automobiles or stock are visible."[246] Kirk notices some camouflage netting next to the barn and jogs ahead to inspect. He lifts up the covering and peers underneath to discover around a half-dozen apparently out-of-service automobiles concealed from view. Here the screenplay indicates a slightly different intention to have shown many more cars hidden inside the building ("The interior of the barn is packed with automobiles of every sort and age"), and according to Hooper budgetary constraints kept the filmmakers from being able "to show that a lot of these cars had been buried and the radio antennas sticking up out of the ground."[247] Kirk calls Pam over to take a closer look at the vehicles before they continue.

The cars indicate a pattern, the significance of which is difficult for Kirk or Pam to discern. Its meaning is also likely not immediately obvious to first-time viewers and perhaps even escapes those rewatching the film, namely, that the previous owners of the abandoned cars—like the previous owner of the abandoned house the group was just exploring—are all dead. The manner of their deaths becomes clearer soon, after some of the youths themselves are made victims to extend another, related pattern. We are even shown clues

The Watergate arrests at the DNC led to the uncovering of a larger pattern of crime and corruption.

later hinting at the subsequent fate of their bodies, suggesting along with the absence of livestock they have supplied a primary ingredient for W.E. Slaughter's barbecue.

The film as a whole exhibits several of these patterns, a consequence of how the "structural puzzle pieces" of *Chain Saw* are ordered and, as Hooper once described, "the way it folds continuously back in on itself, and no matter where you're going it's the wrong place"—what Henkel otherwise calls the film's "nightmare syntax."[248] The significance of these patterns is largely obscured from the group, with only Sally surviving long enough to be allowed to draw any meaningful connections between the discrete pieces of information. The viewer is in a relatively favorable position in this respect, being able to appreciate (for instance) how the deliberately positioned corpses in the cemetery, the dead animal display and bone mobile at the old Franklin place, and the objects tied to the tree all form a pattern indicating the Hitchhiker's handiwork, linked together like the teeth hanging off the symbolic-seeming charm bracelet he wears. Even so, such connections are often subtle, only indirectly suggesting an underlying logic to explain the murderous family's mayhem.

The Watergate scandal was experienced similarly by most, its elements emerging piecemeal and requiring interpretive effort to recognize how they related to each other and what their significance was within a larger narrative. Initial reports of an apparently isolated incident over time came to be understood as part of a larger pattern of corruption and criminal behavior stretching well before and continuing long after. For just over two years, the various "structural puzzle pieces" comprising the greater part of the story of the scandal were gradually revealed, though even during the late spring and early summer of 1974 when the final edits to *Chain Saw* were being made, a satisfactory resolution to Watergate remained uncertain. Testimony before the Senate Watergate Committee and grand jury helped reveal behavioral patterns that explained the "bizarre" break-in and bugging of the DNC. It also revealed subsequent efforts to cover up the White House's connections both to that crime and to others, with some of those charges later corroborated by the discovery and revelation of what had been said on the secret White House tapes. But such patterns were slow to emerge, and once they did were still challenging to compile into a clear and convincing narrative.

Meanwhile as increasing numbers of staff and others linked to the White House were removed, resigned, and/or were indicted, the president persevered as Watergate's central antagonist, with the story's remaining suspense primarily generated by the question of his ultimate fate. Indeed, while supporters continued to defend Nixon as the victim of unwarranted censure, the press-influenced public conversation relentlessly vilified the president, fully resurrecting the caricature of "Tricky Dick" that had for years been suppressed at least well enough for Nixon to win two elections and retain high approval ratings even with the disaster of Vietnam. Summarizing the daily condemnation of Nixon in newspapers and on television that saturated popular culture in particular from May 1973 onwards, Stephen Ambrose notes how the criticism did not always limit itself to observable evidence. "They printed or broadcast rumors and gross exaggerations of the nature and extent of the criminal acts of the Nixon White House," writes Ambrose. "The Democrats, justifiably outraged by the actions of Richard Nixon and his friends, made unjustified comparisons of Nixon with Hitler, talked darkly about the coming of fascism to America, and denounced the Imperial Presidency they had done so much to create."[249]

Amid all the complicated patterns of Watergate, Nixon was the most obvious and central target, and the most eminently satirizable villain.

Killer in a Tie (35:24)

Leatherface dressed for work.

Approaching the film's midpoint, the next sequence completes the transition from "idyllic summer afternoon drive" to full blown "nightmare." Aside from the

Hitchhiker's death by eighteen-wheeler in the mad finale, all four of the onscreen killings take place over the next 17 minutes of screen time. Each of the murders occurs quite suddenly, and all are committed by the frightening man-child, Leatherface.

In January 1973, just when Henkel and Hooper had begun to write the screenplay for *The Texas Chain Saw Massacre*, a 29-year-old filmmaker named George Lucas started compiling notes for the first draft of an elaborate "space opera" that eventually became the blockbuster science fiction epic *Star Wars*. The film harkened back to adventure serials to present a distant galaxy in which a group called the Rebel Alliance valiantly battles the autocratic Galactic Empire. While the characters Lucas created and themes he introduced would evolve considerably over subsequent films, Lucas found inspiration in contemporary American politics much as the similarly-aged makers of *Chain Saw* did. In fact, Lucas would later maintain that the character of the malevolent Emperor Palpatine was directly suggested by a certain president he believed was trying to turn a democracy into a dictatorship.

During a July 1981 story conference with collaborators on the third film in the franchise, *Return of the Jedi*, Lucas explained his characters' backstories, including how Darth Vader—a.k.a. Luke Skywalker's treacherous father, Anakin—had fallen under the influence of Palpatine. "Anakin Skywalker started hanging out with the Emperor, who at that point nobody knew was bad, because he was an elected official," explained Lucas. "Was he a Jedi?" asked *Jedi* co-screenwriter Lawrence Kasden. "No, he was a politician. Richard M. Nixon was his name," answered Lucas. "He subverted the senate and finally took over and became an imperial guy and he was really evil. But he pretended to be a really nice guy. He sucked Luke's father into the dark side."[250] Lucas literally calling his villainous sci-fi sovereign "Richard M. Nixon" might sound unexpected, particularly from the perspective of decades later, well after the plots of both the Star Wars franchise and American politics have taken so many circuitous twists and turns. But in truth many popular films conceived and produced during the Watergate era conspicuously demonstrated the influence of the scandal and contemporary politics in their characters and plots, almost regardless of the films' subject matter and/or their makers' expressions of intention.

For example, Francis Ford Coppola's first two *Godfather* films bookended Watergate with the first part premiering March 1972 and the sequel December 1974, meaning that analogies between the Corleone crime family and Nixon's White House were consistently evoked by political op-ed writers and film critics alike. A *New York Times* editorial from May 1974 was typical when criticizing the "pervading tone" of the discussions of blackmail and burglary on the White House tapes as not just unbecoming of a president, but more closely resembling conversations between the film's criminal characters: "The language is the language of 'The Godfather.'"[251] Even the participants in those conversations were aware of the parallel. John Dean recounts how when discussing the cover-up with his lawyer Charles Shaffer in May 1973, Shaffer referenced the character when responding to the story of Nixon ("the P") boasting it was "no problem to get a million bucks" in hush money to keep defendants quiet: "The P sounds like the Godfather, for Christ's sake."[252] (Incidentally, as Mark Feeney details in his book *Nixon at the Movies*, Nixon watched *The Godfather* in a private showing at Camp David in April 1972 shortly after its premiere. It was one of over 500 feature films the president screened during his five-and-a-half years in office, although he was much more apt to select titles from the late '40s, '50s, and early '60s to view than ones currently playing in theaters.[253])

In a contemporary response to the first *Godfather*, academic Norman Silverstein pursues a similar comparison. He remarks of the film that "it seems to glorify the Nixon Administration" in the way it appears to legitimize the need for leaders to make moral compromises in order to retain power, comparing Michael Corleone taking over the family business to Nixon winning a second term and reading the film's ending as looking favorably on the future prospects of both. Silverstein then surmises that "given the Watergate scandals and publication of the tapes," the about-to-be-released sequel "will be successful only if it can show the illusion behind those failed hopes."[254] In her review of *Part II*, film critic Judith Crist affirms that Coppola had achieved exactly that by "adapting his themes to the changing times" and successfully reflecting how "the post-Watergate mood requires a little less adulation of immoral men."[255] Satirists made the connection as well, including David Frye whose comedy LP *Richard Nixon: A Fantasy* from late 1973 imagines the president as the leader of a mob-like crime ring whose story begins with a secret meeting in which Nixon asks Don Corleone to help him "get out of the Watergate mess quickly." Art Buchwald likewise mused how "Watergate Is Like 'Godfather,'" although the humorist could not resist concluding the mob family fared better by the comparison given how "the Don Corleones were so much smarter than the Don Watergates."[256]

Discussing *The Godfather* sequel and other notable titles released in 1974, film historian David Cook remarks how the "most striking feature of the year's films is their acknowledgment of trauma in the American body politic" caused in large part by the particular and prolonged ordeal of Watergate. While the political messaging of films like *The Godfather Part II*, Alan J. Pakula's paranoid conspiracy thriller *The Parallax View*, Roman Polanski's corruption-themed neo-noir *Chinatown*, Coppola's surveillance mystery *The Conversation*, and activist Tom Laughlin's anti-establishment harangue *The Trial of Billy Jack* was conspicuous enough, even seemingly non-political fare like the big box-office disaster films *The Towering Inferno*, *Earthquake*, and *Airport 1975* can be seen as delivering clear (if unsophisticated) criticisms of "political/corporate corruption at the top," explains Cook.[257] Meanwhile the following year's highest-grossing film *Jaws* was similarly linked to Watergate for its critique of authority figures valuing their own political power over the safety and welfare of citizens, even if director Steven Spielberg denied such a purpose, insisting rather "It's a film about a shark."[258] The line recalls Hooper's cheekily reductive claim about *Chain Saw* that "it's a film about meat," although both he and Henkel were eager to endorse political subtexts, especially with regard to Watergate. Unlike Lucas and his assertion about his evil Emperor, neither Hooper nor Henkel ever went so far as to insist Leatherface *is* Richard M. Nixon. Even so, from the moment Leatherface arrives to commence his carnage, the film provides multiple reasons for viewers to think of the Antagonist-in-Chief.

After a cursory inspection of the hidden cars, Kirk and Pam circle around to the front entrance of the house, stopping along the way to observe a noisy gas-powered generator supplying electricity to the property. Pam sits on the porch steps while Kirk knocks on the screen door and calls out repeatedly, getting no response. Stepping away he kicks something, and after looking down realizes it is a tooth, clearly human as it has a metal filling (yet another puzzle piece that if understood correctly would serve as a warning not to proceed). Kirk picks it up and after draping the towel over the bannister jokingly presents the tooth to Pam as a gift, earning himself a chuckle and indignation from Pam who storms off to sit on the swing in the front yard.

Regardless of the activity, Nixon almost always wore a tie. "It isn't a case of trying to be more formal... I'm more comfortable that way," he explained.

Undeterred, Kirk knocks again forcefully enough to push the door open. After calling out a few more times he becomes intrigued by both the sight of a carefully arranged collection of animal skulls hanging inside a doorway at the far end of the foyer and what sounds like a pig squealing inside. Kirk looks back at Pam, steps inside, then hastily rushes forward, nearly losing his footing on the short ramp leading up to the far doorway as he does. A figure suddenly appears from within, and the perspective shifts so that we look up at him along with Kirk. In a shot that lasts less than one second, an upward pan shows a large man wearing an apron, a buttoned-up shirt, and a necktie, his face covered by a strangely stitched-together mask with crude holes cut out for the eyes and mouth. His arm is raised, and after a cut back to a long shot we see him forcefully strike Kirk on the head with a sledgehammer. Kirk collapses to the ground instantly, then shakes violently for a few seconds before the man hits him a second time, killing him. The man grunts as he drags Kirk's body inside, then he pulls a sliding metal door shut with a loud slam, the soundtrack responding with a frightening low rumble.

It is a rapid, shocking sequence. The very brief shot of the killer's mask is perplexing and off-putting, and only later are we allowed a less hurried view to consider it further. By contrast the shirt and tie give the uncanny impression of a man dressed for work, even if the pink short-sleeved button-up appears rumpled and dirty and the necktie features a strange, art deco-like image resembling an elongated cloud—"a goofy blue tie with a scalloped silver curve painted on it," as Hansen describes it.[259] Meanwhile the yellow apron made of what appears rubber vinyl has dark splotches on it, soon to be confirmed as blood. Leatherface will continue the odd-seeming formality later when he discards the apron in favor of a heavy suit jacket for the dinner scene. But here, as we are first introduced to him, we learn he wears a tie even when working alone at home.

If Leatherface were intended to parody Richard Nixon, having him wear a tie would be essential. Whether he was delivering a televised address, greeting heads of state, going for a morning walk, throwing out the first pitch at a baseball game, relaxing with his dogs, or bowling in the special alley he had installed in the White House basement, the president invariably wore a necktie, and usually a suit jacket as well. Journalist and historian Bob Greene once described interviewing Nixon many years after his resignation, and being surprised to learn Nixon never took off his suit jacket and tie even while working at home. "It isn't a case of trying to be formal," Nixon explained. "But I'm more comfortable that way. I've done it all my life.... It's hard for people to realize, but when I'm writing a speech or working on a book or dictating or so forth, I'm always wearing a coat and tie. Even when I'm alone."[260]

The image of the invariably formally-dressed president underscored the contrast between Nixon and the younger, fashion-forward generation. It also became a required detail of practically all satirical portraits of him along with his heavy eyebrows, large ski-slope nose, and drooping jowls. Comedian and political commentator Mort Sahl confirmed as much at the start of his 1973 LP *Sing a Song of Watergate* when introducing the subject of his monologue, biographer-style: "He was born 61 years ago in a log cabin in Whittier, California... in a blue suit, as I understand it," says Sahl. "A medical miracle at the time."

The White House Horrors (35:51)

While the film remains realistic, with the death of Kirk the manner of storytelling transitions from detailed, dialogue-filled scenes to a series of high-stress set pieces that sometimes edge over into more impressionistic horror. Whereas during the first half of *The Texas Chain Saw Massacre* the viewer experiences a constant though manageable state of dread punctuated by occasional moments of anxiety, from here forward unsettling tension mixed with out-and-out terror becomes the norm with hardly any respite.

A tracking shot of Pam approaching the white house.

We had caught glimpses of the side of the house when Kirk and Pam first approached it, then again from the front as the moving camera followed them from a distance, voyeur-like, before stopping behind a porch swing sitting in the front yard about 50–60 feet away. In that shot the wooden frame and chains of the swing framed the steps and front door as the pair walked onto the porch and Kirk knocked, although intervening foliage mostly obscured a view of the house itself. After Kirk is killed, there is a cut back outside to an annoyed Pam calling his name while sitting on the swing, a bright shot contrasting sharply with the darkness of indoors. Pam then stands and steadily walks toward the house. Starting behind the swing then moving underneath it, the camera trails behind her from below in what evolves into a magnificent wide angle tracking shot incorporating the bright blue sky above, the emerald green trees to the sides, and in the foreground Pam's cherry red shorts and the pink skin of her bare back and legs. Looking upwards at Pam from behind, her body initially takes up most of the screen and thus hides the house, but as she gets closer, the house (with, as we now know, a killer inside) ominously fills the frame as though surrounding her.

This is the haunted house, the one no one should be messing around.

It is a large white house. The screenplay describes it as "a huge, old and weathered mansion,"[261] although in the film it appears well maintained, even stately. Built in the 1890s, it was designed by the famous American architect George Franklin Barber who was nationally known for his late Victorian residential designs. With its complex roof, curved entry hall, transom window above the front door and columns along the front, at least from the outside it contrasts sharply with the dilapidated old Franklin place. Located on Quick Hill in the rural city of Round Rock just outside of Austin, the house was later disassembled and relocated about an hour away in Kingsland in 1998 where it reopened as a restaurant. It was chosen out of convenience, being rented at the time by friends of art director Robert Burns. That is to say, while certainly fulfilling the traditional Gothic horror trope as the site where the monsters hide, any similarity to the residence often used as a metonym for American government and the presidency is likely a product of happenstance.

The so-called "White House horrors" have already been discussed, a phrase added to Watergate's colorful lexicon after John Mitchell's July 1973 testimony before the Senate Watergate Committee. "It is a most appropriate label, not merely for the Watergate break-in and cover-up, but for the entire list of White House-sponsored illegal acts of political espionage and even broader violations of constitutionally guaranteed rights and liberties," wrote the *New York Times* in an opinion piece responding to Mitchell's testimony.[262] As Mitchell clarifies, his use of the phrase referred not so much to the already public spectacle of the Watergate break-in, but more specifically to what prior to the 1972 election had been the still-hidden catalogue of pre-Watergate machinations carried out by the White House's Special Investigations Unit and others during the year leading up to the break-in and bugging of the DNC. These included the break-in at Daniel Ellsberg's psychiatrist's office, the attempt to manage the "Dita Beard matter" in which a memo authored by Beard, a lobbyist for International Telephone and Telegraph, had leaked to reveal a huge ITT donation to the Republican National Convention in return for a favorable settlement of an antitrust suit, the Diem cables forged by E. Howard Hunt, the Brookings Institution firebombing plan, other "extracurricular activities in the bugging area," and "miscellaneous matters with respect to Chappaquiddick."[263] Preventing the disclosure of the White House's involvement in those nefarious activities was a primary motive for covering up its connection to those arrested at the DNC, given how investigation of that crime could well lead to the others. When asked by the committee's chief counsel Sam

Dash whether he and others were concerned that stories comprising the "White House horrors" would come to light prior to November as a result of the Watergate investigation, Mitchell answered affirmatively. "I think that we all had an innate fear that during the campaign that they might be revealed," said Mitchell.

Even so, as the *New York Times* editorial indicates, from July 1973 onward the phrase was used more generally to refer to *all* of the illegalities committed by Nixon's White House, providing convenient shorthand for those likening the scandal to a horror show taking place at the president's residence, a forbidding mansion concealing sinister and dark secrets. By then it had also become clear that if not for the botched operation at the DNC, the administration's villainous behavior would likely have persisted unchecked. "There is increasingly persuasive evidence that, except for the Watergate bungle, the White House horrors would have continued to haunt the nation." Highlighting Nixon's own complicity with the cover-up, the *NYT* implores readers therefore not to dismiss Watergate "as a tale of bungling political spies" with connections to the president. "It contains instead all the elements of a horror story about a narrow escape from the kind of governmental power that must never again be allowed to emanate from the White House."

Two days after that editorial appeared, shooting began on *The Texas Chain Saw Massacre*, a horror story ending with a narrow escape.

The Madman Theory (37:43)

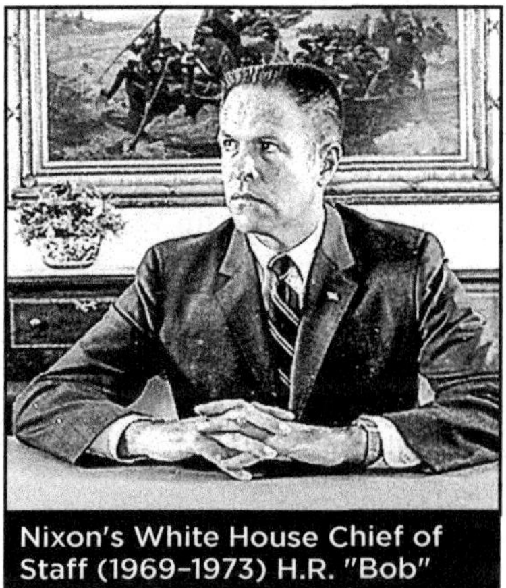

Nixon's White House Chief of Staff (1969–1973) H.R. "Bob" Haldeman, January 1971.

The camera stops moving behind Pam, allowing her to walk ahead and onto the porch where she peers through the screen door into the darkness inside.

The viewer is unaware as yet that a whole family of crazies lives in the big white house, never mind that the Hitchhiker and the Old Man are among them. We have only briefly seen the hulking man in a strange mask who killed Kirk, with such knowledge adding considerable consternation as we watch Pam uncertainly enter the house searching for him. She looks about worriedly, and like Kirk she takes a tumble, losing her footing as she falls into a side room filled with feathers and a squawking chicken in a birdcage as though kept as a pet. That alone is unnerving to Pam, then we look along with her at the rest of the room to discover it filled with bones, teeth, and skulls, both animal and human. Recalling the Hitchhiker's handiwork, some of the items are arranged artistically, either hanging from the ceiling by pieces of string or affixed to chairs and tables as macabre ornamentation. It is a set design inspired by those tales told to a young Hooper by his Wisconsin relatives of a killer and grave robber (likely Ed Gein) who filled his house with furniture made of bones and lampshades made of human skin. Through her disorientation Pam recognizes she has unwittingly stumbled onto something she was not meant see, a "skeletons in the closet" secret here made terrifyingly literal. She begins coughing and retching as though nauseated, crying out Kirk's name as she staggers back out of the room and into the hallway.

Suddenly the metal door slides open to reveal the masked figure who at the sight of Pam lets out a hoarse, animal-like shriek—a madman, clearly, a fact now seemingly further confirmed by the weird museum-like room full of gruesome objects.

There was no shortage of speculation about Richard Nixon's mental health during the Watergate crisis. Especially after the obviously self-harming Saturday Night Massacre and his frantic "I am not a crook" press conference (in October and November 1973) through to the U.S. Supreme Court ruling on the tapes and release of the "smoking gun" transcript (in July and early August 1974), many in the press and behind the scenes wondered about the president's emotional stability. Not long after the resignation, stories of Nixon's erratic behavior and comments (and heavy drinking) during those final months emerged to contribute to the portrait of an alarmingly out-of-control leader whose fitness for office was in doubt even without considering the specific charges against him listed in the articles of impeachment. Days before Nixon resigned, his son-in-law, Edward Cox, expressed concern about his mental health to Senator Robert Griffin, telling him how "The President was up walking the halls last night, talking to pictures of former presidents—giving speeches and talking to the pictures on the wall."[264] Some worried Nixon could somehow try to use the military to prevent his removal from office, with his Secretary of Defense James Schlesinger asking General George S. Brown, head of the Joint Chiefs of Staff, to consult with him first should he receive any orders from the White House.[265] Meanwhile Nixon's Chief of Staff Alexander Haig, essentially forced to lead day-to-day operations at the White House during those final weeks, had even developed genuine concern the president could be contemplating suicide thanks to Nixon's own repeated allusions to the subject. (Cox had confided in Griffin a similar worry.) Such references culminated with a maudlin exchange between the pair on August 7, the day before the resignation announcement. "You fellows in your business, you have a way of handling problems like this," Nixon said to Haig, a decorated Army veteran who the year before had left his position as Vice Chief of Staff to work in the White House. "Somebody leaves a pistol in the drawer," Nixon continued. Then, after pausing long enough for Haig's agitation to mount, the president added, "I don't have a pistol."[266]

Even before those final months, Nixon's many idiosyncrasies and quirks had inspired an entire subgenre of writing about him, the "psychobiography." Such studies delved back into his Quaker upbringing and impoverished childhood as source material to provide various psychological explanations for the president's actions and decisions. Reviewing some of these works, historian Iwan Morgan allows that "as a genre, psychobiographies offer insights" into Nixon's personality although often involve a great deal more conjecture and "inferential" analysis than more conventional historians tend to tolerate. "There is also a tendency to exaggerate Nixon the individual without full consideration of the historical and institutional contexts in which he operated," adds Morgan, an observation that also explains why Nixon was such a frequent object of satire.[267] Adding fuel to that fire, not long after Nixon left office something called "the madman theory" emerged as a frequently referenced explanation for some of his irrational-seeming decisions and overall villainy. The theory was in truth a somewhat specific political stratagem connected to one of several methods employed by Nixon in negotiations with both the Soviets and North Vietnamese during the Vietnam War. However once it became known it was applied more widely (and less accurately) to the general maneuvering and deceit of Tricky Dick.

One indirect inspiration for the approach was Nixon's background as a poker player and his understanding of how a player's image at the table can affect his ability to be successful when bluffing opponents. Another, as Haldeman later shared in his 1978 book *The Ends of Power*, was Dwight D. Eisenhower's handling of the end of the Korean War shortly after he took office in 1953 with Nixon as his Vice President. Eisenhower managed to convince North Korea of his intention to use nuclear bombs to end that conflict, thereby precipitating a hasty conclusion to that war. Nixon tried something similar with North Vietnam after taking office in 1969. "Nixon coined a phrase for his theory which I'm sure will bring smiles of delight to Nixon-haters everywhere," explains Haldeman. "He said, 'I call it the Madman Theory, Bob. I want the North Vietnamese to believe I've reached the point where I might do *anything* to stop the war. We'll just slip the word to them that, "for God's sake, you know Nixon is obsessed about Communism. We can't restrain him when he's angry—and he has his hand on the nuclear button"—and Ho Chi Minh himself will be in Paris in two days begging for peace.'"[268] Much as the idea of madness helps heighten dramatic suspense in *Chain Saw* by introducing uncertainty in the viewer regarding what additional horrors are to come, so, too, did Nixon believe fashioning himself as unpredictably dangerous would helpfully unsettle his opponent. Even so, despite actively cultivating an image as a crazed maniac incapable of being controlled in order to attempt such "bluffs" several times over subsequent years, Nixon was never truly able to achieve the purpose of forcing the North Vietnamese to "fold" in response to his overweening threats.

Haldeman was right about "Nixon-haters" being more than eager to brand Nixon a madman or worse. Throughout the war critics and protestors assailed Nixon as a murderer as the numbers of casualties steadily rose. The accusation was most frequently lobbed following significant episodes such as the Cambodian incursion begun in April 1970, the gradual and increasingly alarming reports of ongoing secret CIA operations and bombings in Laos, the mining of North Vietnamese harbors in May 1972 and the renewed bombing campaign that followed, and the "Christmas bombing" of Hanoi and

Nixon brooding in the Oval Office, February 1970.

Haiphong in December 1972. Such a charge is delivered to devastating effect in the Peter Davis documentary *Hearts and Minds* begun in the fall of 1972 and completed in 1974, a film that thoroughly details how America's fatal misapprehension of its goals and what was achievable in Southeast Asia itself represented a kind of shared madness. Near the end of the Oscar-winning film, Davis chronicles the Christmas bombing by first showing Nixon later celebrating it at an elaborate banquet for returning POWs in May 1973, then cutting back to images of Bach Mai Hospital, destroyed by errant bombs during the campaign, and a woman weeping over two dead children. Next a mourning father cries at the site of his destroyed farmhouse as he explains how his eight-year-old daughter and three-year old son and other family members were killed. "Nixon, murderer of civilians!" he says through an interpreter. "What have I done to Nixon so that he comes here to bomb my country?"

With regard to Watergate, one occasional defense of Nixon, evoked both then and now, was "at least no one died." Even so, that did not prevent his actions from sometimes being compared to and judged as though they were morally akin to those of a murderer. The idea even arose during the Senate Watergate Hearings when Nixon's ex-Domestic Affairs Advisor John Ehrlichman disingenuously argued in favor of the president's authority to break laws in the service of national security. In one of several exasperating exchanges between Ehrlichman and questioning senators, Ehrlichman stubbornly refused to move away from the position that illegal break-ins such as the one conducted at Daniel Ellsberg's psychiatrist's office were allowable should the president deem them necessary. Responding to that, Senator Herman Talmadge posed a hypothetical to Ehrlichman. "Now if the President could authorize a covert break-in and you do not know exactly where that power would be limited, you do not think it could include murder, do you?" asked Talmadge. "I do not know where the line is, Senator," replied Ehrlichman.[269]

Satirists went there more often, and with much less hesitation. Novelist Philip Roth's scathing, absurdist takedown of Nixon, the short *Our Gang (Starring Tricky and His Friends)* published prior to Watergate in November 1971, presents an especially severe caricature of the president as a frighteningly soulless speechifier named "Trick E. Dixon." In Roth's story the president becomes the victim of an assassination, an event for which *everyone* tries to claim credit. But the narrative does not end there, as an epilogue describes Tricky running against Satan for the presidency of hell. "My fellow Fallen," says Dixon in his opening statement in a debate against the Prince of Darkness, "the Sons and Daughters of Disobedience deserve a Devil of consummate depravity, a Devil who will devote himself not to old and worn-out iniquities, but to bold new programs in Evil that will overturn God's kingdom and plunge men into eternal death."[270] The strange and obscure horror comedy *The Werewolf of Washington* from October 1973 presents a similarly farcical scenario involving a White House not unlike Nixon's in which the president's press secretary Jack Whittier (named after Nixon's birthplace) who lives at the Watergate goes on a murderous spree after being bitten by a werewolf. The film concludes with Whittier being killed, but not until after he has bitten the president who while giving a Nixon-like address transforms into a werewolf himself over the closing credits.

In one of the funnier jabs, the National Lampoon likened Nixon to the central character of a horror movie in a *National Lampoon Radio Hour* segment from February 1974. While delivering a FDR-style "fireside chat," Nixon confesses to having lied to the American public from the beginning about Watergate, confirming that he himself erased the tape containing the eighteen-and-a-half minute gap, that he "conveniently lost the tapes with more conversations that might have brought forth accusations," and that "everything John Dean has told you is not only true, but there are far worse things John does not even know." What made him decide to reveal all? Recently he watched *The Exorcist* (at the time the country's top box office attraction), and while doing so "came to realize that it was not at all the real

Richard Nixon [who was] responsible for Watergate." He consulted an exorcist to examine himself, and "sure enough, he did discover the presence of a demon... the ghost of an old corrupt politician whose name I shall withhold for his family's sake." The demon safely driven out, Nixon declares his readiness to resume working for the American people by serving out his second term.

Political cartoonist David Levine picked up on the same idea in one of his many frightening caricatures of Nixon, one portraying the president as Linda Blair's character, "tied to his bed, foully screaming as a figure is expelled from his mouth; the figure is a spooky mini-Nixon."[271] Mark L. Lester's little seen 1975 farce *White House Madness* also includes the same riff among a string of outlandish sketches satirizing Nixon, thrusting Billy Graham into the role of the one having to perform an exorcism on the president. Demonizing Nixon via comic portrayals of him as a horror villain continued thereafter, such as in a *Saturday Night Live* sketch from early 1978 occasioned by horror icon Christopher Lee appearing as guest host and the impending publication of Nixon's autobiography. Lee plays a vampire hunter who seeks out Nixon in order to destroy his memoirs with a wooden stake before they can be published. "If we don't put an end to it now, it will only be a matter of weeks before it spreads to libraries and bookstores in every city, town, and mall in America," says Lee. "We can't allow the undead to continue haunting us! We must put the soul of Watergate to rest... now!" he cries before plunging the stake into the manuscript.

Likening Nixon's actions during Watergate to that of a madman, murderer, or monster was hardly unusual. Carrying such comparisons to extreme or absurd conclusions was instinctive among many of Nixon's contemporaneous satirists, the makers of *Chain Saw* among them. However others both then and later would be less jovial when making such comparisons. For example, following Nixon's death in 1994 when the memory of Watergate and other failings had faded enough to inspire unironic tributes hailing his achievements, Hunter S. Thompson instead shared his "own bloody relationship with Nixon over the years" in a way that recalled without pity just how brutal a figure the president had cut twenty years before.

"He was the real thing—a political monster straight out of Grendel and a very dangerous enemy," said Thompson. "He could shake your hand and stab you in the back at the same time."[272]

The Hook (39:30)

Pam on the hook: "That was always the number one 'walker' scene," said Kim Henkel.

As earlier noted, references to *Chain Saw*'s resemblance to a documentary are sometimes overstated, no doubt influenced in part by the film's truth conceit. The fact is, the frequent use of stylized elements and careful editing perhaps not obvious on a first watch more than verify the filmmakers' painstaking and consistent efforts to manipulate the audience. As Sallye Richardson who co-edited the film with Hooper over the last several months of post-production observes, "*Chain Saw* was made in editing."[273] Leatherface's shocking though essentially bloodless attack of Pam that ends with her being hung on a meat hook is the film's best example of such manipulation.

Less than 30 seconds elapse from the moment Leatherface sees Pam in the hallway to his placement of her on the hook. As with the killing of Kirk, he works quickly and efficiently, the only delay coming when Pam runs back out of the house onto the porch. Leatherface races out after her, lifting her off the ground like a ragdoll by her bare torso so forcefully that her sandals fly off, then carries her back through the hallway and into the kitchen. We watch them enter from the hook's perspective, in a sense, the shot angled from above with the menacing implement in the foreground as they pass by a large freezer unit positioned along the wall by the door. (There are two hooks, in fact, hanging from a homemade wooden apparatus resembling a gallows.) As Leatherface hoists Pam up toward the hook there is a cut to a brief, wide shot that reveals a dead Kirk sprawled on the table before them. Without hesitation Leatherface drops her onto the hook and turns away, leaving us with a disturbing close-up of an open-mouthed Pam in agony.

During that half-minute there appear 13 different shots (some static, some moving), which along with both characters' screeching and non-diegetic rumbling on the soundtrack produce a visceral reaction from the viewer. "Those shots cut together smooth and fast," observes Gunnar Hansen, referring to the final few, thereby causing some to be "convinced they have just seen the hook penetrate Pam's back" when in fact they have not. "Many remember the scene as filled with gore," Hansen adds, pointing out another common misapprehension.[274] The viewer is understandably influenced by that earlier, lingering shot of Pam's exposed back as she approached the house, its memory greatly increasing our unease as she dangles helplessly as though livestock. First-timers unavoidably recoil in their seats as they watch. Even veteran viewers find it difficult not to wince.

For a storyteller, "the hook" represents a moment that undeniably captures the attention, making the audience want to learn and discover more. Advertisers similarly speak of the concept as an important marketing strategy, that promotional element that successfully arouses interest and encourages further interaction. In *The Texas Chain Saw Massacre*, the moment Pam goes on the hook has an opposite effect for some, signaling the end of their desire to pursue the film any further. When *Chain Saw* first began to be shown in theaters at the end of 1974, there were several sensational accounts of audiences reacting negatively, including one frequently told of a near-riot during a sneak preview at the Empire Theater in San Francisco in November. Having arrived to see the action thriller *The Taking of Pelham One Two Three*, the audience was shown *Chain Saw* first without knowing anything of the film beforehand. According to film critic Danny Peary, "viewers threw up; others stormed the lobby to protest what they (and their children) were being subjected to," and "when no money was refunded, punches were thrown."[275] Talking to Joseph Lanza for his recent book about *Chain Saw*, one in attendance at the Empire reports how he and his wife left the screening early, joining about 80 others in the lobby to complain. "I thought at the time someone might have a good lawsuit for intentional infliction of emotional distress," he remembers.[276] John Dugan, who portrays Grandpa, recalls more specifically how when he first saw the film in Chicago, the attack on Pam was the moment that most dramatically winnowed the audience. "We had a lot of walkers out of that theater," says Dugan. "When Teri McMinn gets hung on the meat hook, I'd say 25 percent of the theater got up and walked out. Just like, *Okay, that's enough of that.*"[277] "That was always the number one 'walker' scene," Henkel similarly recollects. "If the audience was gonna walk, that's when they walked."[278]

That said, for those who *do* choose to continue watching, the sequence is especially affecting, residing in the memory not just for the remainder of the film but long afterwards. No review or summary omits it, with most highlighting it as emblematic of the viewing experience as a whole. The scene also utterly establishes *Chain Saw*'s exploitation bona fides, finally piercing any veneer of trust (so to speak) between viewer and filmmaker that may still have lingered after everything that had gone before. As appalling as it is, for many viewers the scene is transfixing, keeping them in their seats wondering what could possibly come next.

For many Americans, the day filming began on *Chain Saw* nearly coincided with the moment those following the story of Watergate became well and truly "hooked." It was the very next day, July 16, 1973, that former Deputy Assistant Alexander Butterfield confirmed to the Senate Watergate Committee and the American public the existence of the Nixon administration's secret taping system and a comprehensive library of recordings of conversations dating back two-and-a-half years. A year-long battle over access to the tapes soon commenced, providing a dramatic counterpoint to all Watergate discussion going forward as there suddenly existed potential support or refutation of every claim made by Nixon and others regarding the cover-up. Everything was in doubt, turning the ongoing televised hearings, daily reports of new revelations, and official denials and obfuscations into dramatic twists and turns in a sensational soap opera.

Author and frequent public commentator Gore Vidal, who just prior to Watergate penned a satirical play that judged Nixon negatively, summed up the country's mood during an early November appearance on *The Dick Cavett Show* where the scandal was frequently discussed. "One of the sad things that has happened to the country is that the 'empty men' and now... some of the 'empty *bad* men' have taken over. But I wouldn't live in any other time than now. I have to have my Watergate fix every single morning!" said Vidal, earning laughter from the studio audience. "There are Watergate junkies all over the place," confirmed Cavett in response. "It's become an important part of people's lives."

Hearing Is Believing (39:39)

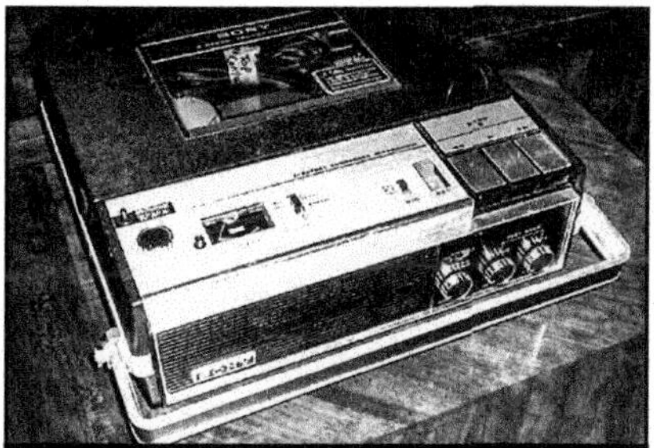

One of the Sony reel-to-reel tape recorders used to record conversations in the Oval Office from early 1971 to July 1973.

The scene does not end with Pam's placement on the hook. It gets worse.

Leatherface turns around and picks up a long two-pronged carving fork from the table on which Kirk rests. He then walks over to the counter and after tossing the fork aside grabs a chainsaw that rests beside the sink along with coffee cups and other items as though it were a common kitchen appliance, belonging there just as much as a toaster. He pull starts it before lifting it high and wiggling his head as though in triumph. As he does a very quick shot of Pam is inserted, a rapid upward pan that starts with her feet hanging limply over a wide metal bucket on the floor below her to catch dripping blood, then swiftly raises up to show her face still frozen in open-mouthed terror. At just three seconds, the shot of Pam is a bit like a magician's flourish in the way it hides how the "trick" is done (the actress hangs from an unseen harness while the second unused hook appears suggestively beside her within the frame) while seemingly proving its actuality. For a moment it appears Leatherface might be about to carve up Pam, but after we return to the wide shot we see him move over to the lifeless Kirk and begin to carve him up as she watches. There is a slow zoom past Leatherface to a final close-up of Pam, the loud, whirring sound of the chainsaw overwhelming her screams.

It is the debut of the titular power tool. It is also the first time we hear the chainsaw, and its menacing roar will become something of a constant for much of the remainder of the film. While Pam can see what Leatherface is doing to Kirk, the angle obscures his work from the viewer. That said, it appears he is dismembering the body mere minutes after Kirk's death, with the apron, hooks, freezer, and carving fork all suggesting a butcher's workspace. Similarly Leatherface's instinctive, methodical handling of the pair implies he has experience dealing with and storing away evidence of the horrors that routinely happen in the white house. As critic Donald C. Willis explains, "The director trusts to his title and his hardware: you don't *see* what the awful chain saw does. You don't need to—all you need to know is how one works. *Hearing* is believing *here*."[279]

For Nixon, the existence of the secret White House recordings and the fact that certain of those tapes provided concrete evidence of his knowledge and involvement in the Watergate cover-up from the very beginning proved his undoing. The saga of the tapes and key moments in the battle over which of them would ultimately be heard by the House Judiciary Committee as part of its deliberation of impeachment articles or by the Watergate Special Prosecutor (first Archibald Cox, then Leon Jaworski) to help with its investigation has already been covered. So has the fact that it was not until the final two weeks of Nixon's presidency that the Supreme Court ruled the White House finally had to turn over 64 tapes to Jaworski, with the "smoking gun" tape confirming Nixon's culpability among them. Worth adding, however, is the fact that during the whole of Watergate the American public was not actually able to *listen* to any of the recordings for themselves. There were transcripts, including the infamously edited ones released by the White House in April 1974 as a desperate, ultimately failed attempt to prevent the actual recordings from having to be submitted. But the tapes themselves were not being played on radio or television. In other words, the actual sound of Nixon's gravelly baritone, so familiar to Americans, cutting through all ambiguity while agreeing with and building upon Haldeman's idea to encourage the CIA to halt the FBI's investigation into the Watergate break-in ("just say… 'the president believes… they should call the FBI in and say that we wish for the country, don't go any further into the case'"), or describing the desire to compile a list of targets for revenge ("I want the most comprehensive notes on all of those that that tried to do us in… they are asking for it, and they are going to get it"), or blithely confirming his ability to acquire an astonishing amount of untraceable funds to be used for hush money ("you could get a million dollars, and you could get it in cash. I, I know where it could be gotten") was withheld from the public throughout the crisis.[280]

After Nixon left office, the federal government took control of the tapes, and for the last two decades of his life, Nixon and his lawyers were able to prevent the great majority of the recordings from being made public. During that time only those involved in court cases and a select few researchers were able to obtain access to a small number of them. Over the years since, most of the 3,700 hours' worth of recordings have been made available by the National Archives and Records Administration, with the last large batch released in August 2013. Thus while today it is trivially easy to listen to the tapes, it was not until after the resignation and even after Gerald Ford's pardon of Nixon that any members of the general public were able to do so. The very first public playing of a Watergate-related recording took place at the obstruction of justice trial of Bob Haldeman, John Ehrlichman, John Mitchell, Robert Mardian, and Kenneth Parkinson on October 17, 1974, a "premiere" of sorts that came not long after *Chain Saw's*. Around 180 people were in attendance, including the judge and jury, the defendants and their counsel, and spectators including Associated Press reporter Harry F. Rosenthal. Together they heard what Rosenthal described as "the deep, distinctive sound of Richard M. Nixon saying things in the privacy of the Oval Office in a way he would not have dreamed of doing it in public." At one point when Nixon confidently declared the cover-up would succeed and the Watergate issue would disappear, "the entire courtroom seemed to gasp."

Actually listening to the words being uttered rather than merely reading them had a profound effect, as indicated by the headline appearing over the report Rosenthal filed: "The chief electronic witness: Hearing is believing."[281]

Everything Means Something, I Guess (42:45)

"Everything means something, I guess," says Sally.

The buzzing chainsaw and screams fade following a cross-cut from inside the house to the nearby windmill rotating rapidly, an image that visually mimics the menacing drone. Franklin is inspecting the blood smear again, once more wondering about its significance while Jerry teases him.

"He's gonna get you... he's gonna kill you, Franklin," says Jerry of the Hitchhiker while Sally insists Franklin is worrying needlessly. (The screenplay describes fretful Franklin as a "Chaplinesque figure" during the scene.[282]) Franklin and Sally fuss for a moment over the whereabouts of his missing pocket knife, then Jerry decides to go look for Kirk and Pam before it gets dark, leaving the siblings to wait at the van. While they do, Franklin revives the earlier conversation about horoscopes, this time seemingly in the context of curiosity about the Hitchhiker's mark.

"Did you believe all that stuff Pam was telling about Saturn and retrograde and all that?" asks Franklin. "I don't know," says Sally. "Everything means something, I guess."

On the surface, their small talk sounds both innocuous and a little redundant, perhaps seeming even less significant thanks to the real danger surrounding them and toward which Jerry purposefully walks. Yet Franklin's repeated musings about signs and symbols, especially when put together with the film's conspicuous attention to detail and the filmmakers' many statements about subtexts and nonliteral meanings, give Sally's line added significance, as though she were addressing the viewer not to take everything at face value.

A Theory of Containment (46:46)

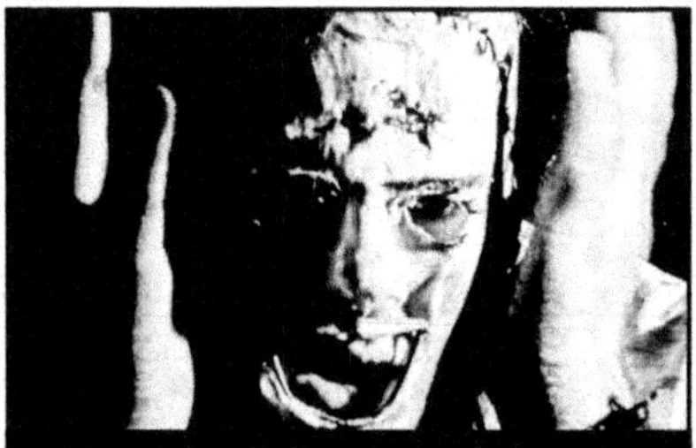

"*Where* do all these people keep coming from?" wonders Leatherface.

"We have a cancer—within—*close* to the presidency, that's growing. It's growing daily. It's compounding. It grows geometrically now, because it compounds itself."[283]

That's how White House Counsel John Dean began his detailed description of nine months' worth of cover-up activities and their impending unraveling in a meeting in the Oval Office with his boss on March 21, 1973. A little over three months later a no-longer employed Dean would share all he could remember about the conversation in his Senate Watergate Committee testimony, and the phrase "a cancer growing on the presidency" became another widely cited Watergate slogan. The metaphor was doubly apt, some observed, describing both the rapid deterioration of the White House's haphazardly pursued scheme to hide its connection to the DNC break-in, as well as the more general malignancy the administration represented within the republic at large. The presidency itself *was* the cancer, in a way, threatening to annihilate the country from within.

Once the Nixon administration's secret taping system became public, a few of the recordings sought by investigators became especially intriguing to those following the story. The June 20, 1972 conversation between Nixon and Haldeman was a frequent topic of speculation, particularly following the tantalizing discovery of its eighteen-and-a-half minute gap. So, too, was the September 15, 1972 conversation conducted shortly after the original indictments of the burglars in which Nixon complimented Dean for having managed the cover-up so well up to then. The recording of that March 21, 1973 conversation between Dean and the president was also the focus of a great deal of scrutiny, thanks to Dean's Senate Watergate Committee testimony and Nixon's repeated claim that it was only during that late morning conversation that he first learned about the cover-up.

Interestingly, it was Dean's late June testimony that set the investigation on a course that led to the discovery of the taping system. Wishing to cast doubt on Dean's credibility and otherwise shield the president, the White House supplied informational memoranda to the committee's ranking member, Republican Howard Baker, as well as to minority counsel Fred Thompson. Delivered by the new White House Counsel, Fred Buzhardt Jr., these memos contained various information designed to guide the Republicans' questioning of witnesses, providing details of meetings between Dean and Nixon including the "cancer on the presidency" one of March 21. During his testimony Dean shared a feeling he had about the possibility that another of his conversations with the president might have been recorded. A couple of weeks after that, a stenographer working for the committee gave staff member Scott Armstrong a copy of notes taken from conversations in which Buzhardt had supplied Thompson with "lengthy quotations from Mr. Nixon's one-on-one meetings with Mr. Dean" (as Armstrong later recalled).[284] The detail and precision of the quoted passages raised Armstrong's suspicions, prompting him to ask former Deputy Assistant Alexander Butterfield if he could offer any explanation. Butterfield could not, but when Armstrong's assistant Don Sanders asked Butterfield point blank if he knew if any of the president's conversations had been recorded, Butterfield confirmed the existence of the taping system. The following Monday Thompson would ask Butterfield the same question in the televised hearing, thereby earning public credit for the revelation even if in truth others had been responsible for uncovering it. In fact, the taping system might not have been discovered at all if not for the White House's behind-the-scenes dealings with Thompson.

Nixon could not avoid including a transcript of the much-discussed March 21, 1973 meeting in *The White House Transcripts* published in April 1974, thereby corroborating the dire assessment Dean had described himself making in his testimony. Also confirmed was Dean's explanation to Nixon that from the very start it was obvious to all how damning it would be were the White House's connections to the burglars to become known. "This was something that just could have been disastrous on the election if it had... [if] all hell had broken loose," Dean says to the president. As a result, his actions from that point forward had been entirely directed toward preventing that eventuality. "I worked on a theory of containment," says Dean. "Sure," answers Nixon, who as later evidence would show understood the situation in much greater detail than he was letting on.[285]

When Jerry follows Kirk and Pamela into the house, it is not surprising he soon suffers the same sad fate of his friends. Veterans of decades' worth of "and then there were none"-style slashers inspired by *Chain Saw* foresee Jerry's demise, as would contemporary audiences for whom the narrative trajectory was less common though still predictable. Even so, despite having twice witnessed Leatherface's efficient brutality with those wandering into his house uninvited, the scene still shocks. Meanwhile the killer's reaction afterwards is perhaps more intriguing, and more evocative of the idea of a growing, compounding situation in need of covering up.

As Sally and Franklin continue their listless conversation, a long wide shot of Jerry walking into the setting (crazy-making?) sun fades into another of him circling around to the front of the white house, the perspective causing the house to appear even larger than it did before. He unhesitatingly skips up the porch steps and begins to knock while calling through the screen door, explaining that he is searching for his friends. Upon noticing Kirk's towel still draped over the bannister nearby, Jerry turns back to the door to call some more, then after hearing strange animal-like noises coming from inside he is encouraged to enter. He walks straight back through the doorway at the end of the hall, then a thumping sound draws him into the kitchen. There is no sign of Kirk or Pam, although Jerry does notice the hooks and sees blood on the table and walls. He then realizes the sound he hears is coming from the freezer along the wall. After a short struggle made even more tense by a series of rapid cuts, he opens the lid.

White House counsel John Dean, March 1973.

In a true horror show moment, Jerry sees Pam tucked inside the freezer appearing dead as though in a coffin. Then suddenly she springs to life for just a moment, her eyes wide open, mouth agape, and arms flailing before she immediately collapses back into a comatose state with her upper half hanging outside of the freezer. A frightened Jerry backpedals away from the freezer, then spins around to see Leatherface with sledgehammer raised. Jerry only has time to let out a short scream before Leatherface strikes him with full force, a crushing blow to the head. Like the others, Jerry's death comes especially quickly after his having entered the house—less than a minute.

Wordless, worried moans escape from Leatherface as he violently forces Pam back inside the freezer and slams it shut, then with great distress looks around the kitchen before darting back to the cluttered front room. We watch from behind as he spies out the front window as though expecting to find still more home invaders approaching, then with continued agitation he inspects the room as well for anyone else hiding. Finally he sits down heavily in a chair by the window, drops the sledgehammer onto the floor, and hunches forward while tapping the sides of his head in harried fashion. "*Where* are they coming from? *Where* do all these people keep coming from?" says Hooper on the DVD commentary, articulating Leatherface's fretful thoughts in a humorously high-pitched voice. Finally the killer calms down, and a zoom to an extreme close-up provides a first detailed look at the human skin mask and its crude stitching. Contrasting with the weapon-wielding murderer we have been watching, Leatherface here appears almost like a child in trouble, an impression furthered by his apparent inability to form words. Through the mask's irregular holes appear anxious eyes and crooked teeth (in fact filed down baby teeth in a mold supplied by Hansen's dentist[286]), suggesting the mask literally provides an adult face behind which a juvenile hides.

Whatever might be the intellectual capacity of this butcher of humans, he instinctively works according to a theory of containment. He has successfully rid the white house of all unwanted investigators, so far at least. He appears to have swiftly broken down Kirk as though he were a cattle carcass, ostensibly having stored his remains in the freezer along with Pam, and there is little doubt he will soon be taking care of Jerry's corpse in a similar fashion. While he may not comprehend the moral or legal significances of his actions, he well understands the need to clean up and conceal.

He looks out the window. Like Nixon, he worries over whether he has done all he needs to, and what trouble might await him if he has not.

The Nixon Shock (52:11)

The next cut reveals the passage of time. The sun is down, night has fallen, and a shot of clouds passing reveals a full moon illuminating the evening sky. (There was an actual full moon the night of August 14, 1973, four nights before the story is set.) Sally and Franklin are still waiting by the van, and with Franklin sitting in his chair before it, Sally honks the horn. She also turns on the headlights, indicating it has only just become dark enough for them to need the light. They argue pros and cons of going to search for the others or returning to the gas station for help, though discover the latter is not an option as Jerry has taken the keys. Sally finally resolves to go look for them, intending to leave Franklin to wait at the van. They fight over the flashlight which Franklin refuses to relinquish, then Sally storms off with Franklin desperately trying to wheel himself behind her. Eventually and with great effort she has to push him, and the pair appear increasingly vulnerable moving slowly through woods while continu-

Leatherface suddenly attacks Franklin.

ing to call out after Jerry. As they struggle forward, the dimness of the scene makes it difficult at times to see them. Occasionally the entire screen is black, then the reflection of Franklin's chair or the flashlight's beam appears to help us track them once more. Sally mentions seeing a light, then a house in the distance, while Franklin says he thinks he hears something nearby. The sequence stretches more than five minutes, a significant lull in terms of its relative lack of sensory input for the viewer when compared to the rest of the film. Even so, the tension remains high throughout thanks to what came before. Franklin calls out to Sally to stop pushing. Again, he thinks he hears something.

Suddenly the image of Leatherface fills the screen, brightly lit by Franklin's flashlight as the killer starts his chainsaw and raises it high in the film's most intense jump scare. He attacks Franklin in his wheelchair, alternating between vertical and horizontal slices. Viewing the attack from behind the chair, we do not actually see the chainsaw connect with Franklin's body (even if some viewers mistakenly report that they do). We do see blood spattering onto Leatherface's yellow apron while Sally stands screaming nearby with her arms raised. After witnessing this horror for close to twenty seconds, Sally runs away through the woods. We follow her, as will Leatherface.

Before becoming president, Nixon well established a predilection for unexpected and showy gestures or announcements delivered without warning and often with an intention to surprise and unsettle political opponents. One early encouragement to use the technique was the success Nixon enjoyed when employing it as a member of the debate team at Whittier College. As the team manager later recounted, Nixon possessed a unique "ability to keep his opponent off-balance," upsetting his foe with a "steady attack" of information that often would cause the other side to "become emotional and stop thinking clearly." A teammate also recalled how Nixon "would always have a surprise" with which to unnerve others.[287] Poker similarly taught

"Unpredictability is the greatest asset or weapon that a leader can have," said Nixon.

Nixon the usefulness of keeping opponents off their guard and unable to anticipate his next move. In a 1983 interview Nixon outlined various ways he believed "many of the things you do in poker are very useful in politics," highlighting in particular the need to play "close to the vest" and conceal as much information about yourself and your intentions as possible. "One of the problems, you see, in foreign affairs particularly, in dealing with great leaders abroad, particularly those that are adversaries, is the almost insatiable tendency of American politicians to want to put everything out on the table," explained Nixon. "Their inability to know when to bluff, when to call, and above everything else, how to be unpredictable" he saw to be a great deficit in others. "Unpredictability is the greatest asset or weapon that a leader can have... and unless he is unpredictable, he's going to find that he loses a great deal of his power."[288]

Nixon took such an approach often during his political career, especially early on when he consistently enjoyed success by making startling, unanticipated "moves" that increased his figurative chip stack while depleting his opponents'. For example, a key moment in his very first Congressional race in 1946 came during a joint appearance in South Pasadena involving Nixon and his Democratic opponent, the incumbent Jerry Voorhis. Among the many dubious and false claims made about Voorhis by the Nixon camp during that campaign was the charge that Voorhis had been endorsed by a "Communist-dominated" political group, the Congress of Industrial Organizations' Political Action Committee (CIO-PAC). Not only did the claim run counter to Voorhis's own anti-Communist record and ignore his signal legislative achievement, the passage of the Voorhis Act of 1940 that forced political organizations controlled by anti-American foreign powers to register with the Justice Department, but it was also patently untrue. The CIO-PAC had *not* endorsed Voorhis, and in fact in the spring had published reasons why the group opposed his candidacy. Meanwhile a different though affiliated group, the National Citizens' Political Action Committee (NCPAC) based in Southern California, had debated internally whether or not to endorse Voorhis and had also chosen not to, although some members committee at one point considered doing so. Even though Voorhis had not accepted any endorsement from either organization, Nixon ads nonetheless blithely insisted that a "vote for Nixon is a vote against the Communist-dominated PAC," an inaccuracy that purposely conflated the two groups.[289] It was at the event in South Pasadena that Voorhis demanded that Nixon supply "proof" of his campaign's accusations against him. As one of the event's organizers Paul Bullock later recalled, Nixon had obtained a copy of an internal memo from the NCPAC committee discussing the possibility of endorsing Voorhis. "Walking up to Voorhis, in a dramatic gesture... Nixon shoved the piece of paper at his opponent and identified it as documentary evidence of the truth of his allegations," writes Bullock. "Voorhis was completely taken by surprise," wholly unequipped to counter such seeming evidence in public in this way. "Unprepared for this move and confused by it, he mumbled that this seemed to be a different organization," writes Bullock.[290] The Voorhis campaign would later produce a response clarifying that he had not been endorsed by either committee, but the damage had been done and Nixon defeated his opponent handily.

Bullock compares Nixon's bold gesture to later ones made frequently by Joseph McCarthy during the years of his "red scare" campaign. It also prefigured other moments from battles taken up by Nixon during his early career, each of which seemed to include strange, headline-grabbing twists made all the more effective thanks to their novelty. The Alger Hiss spy case in 1948 swung on the stunning revelation of microfilm hidden in a pumpkin patch. The bitter 1950 senate campaign versus Helen Gahagan Douglas was marked by the publication of a circular falsely painting Nixon's opponent as a Communist sympathizer, the color of the infamous "pink sheet" chosen to connote both Douglas's sex and her allegedly "red" leanings. A nationally-televised address in 1952 made to defend himself against accusations involving misuse of a private campaign fund when vice-presidential candidate ended with an unexpected, pathos-filled reference to a cocker spaniel named Checkers.

Like a maker of exploitation films, Nixon instinctively understood the usefulness of surprise when manipulating an audience and how such a strategy required him not to "tip his hand" too early. He was particularly enamored with the prime time televised address, delivering more of them than any other president before or since (only Ronald Reagan who served two full terms comes close). Nixon viewed such speeches as opportunities to speak directly to the American public without having to allow any filtering of his message by the press. As he later noted regarding the "Checkers" speech, after the media had (in his view) "gone overboard in predicting that I would be forced off the ticket, they naturally found it very difficult to accept that by going over their heads to the country on TV, I had proved them wrong."[291] Having such control allowed Nixon to manage exactly when and how the most important information in a given announcement would be conveyed, thereby potentially maximizing its effect including by heightening its surprise. Even prior to his resignation speech the night of August 8, 1974 when over the course of the day and early evening all news outlets were confirming that Nixon would announce his intention to leave office, there was great uncertainty regarding just what he would say or possibly admit to, and even a small few who believed he could still change his mind and *not* resign.

One instance of Nixon making an announcement deliberately staged so as to produce a heightened response came during a Sunday night televised address delivered August 15, 1971. Pre-empting *Bonanza* and other popular prime time shows, Nixon began his presentation by listing a series of notable though undistinguished measures soon to be implemented as part of an overall effort to halt inflation and stimulate the economy. He then punctuated the speech with a short volley of bombshells—a 90-day freeze on all prices and wages in the United States, a suspension of the convertibility of the U.S. dollar into gold (i.e., the end of the "gold standard"), and a new 10 percent tax to be levied on all goods imported from other countries. These measures were immediately described both at home and abroad as "the Nixon shock," so named due to their being introduced to produce an economic jolt and because of the lack of forewarning

Nixon employed surprise whenever it was politically advantageous to do so, often via televised addresses delivered during prime time.

preceding them. The speech earned favorable reviews and the stock market responded positively upon its opening the next day, even if the measures' actual effects were considered by many observers to be negligible and of uncertain value long term.

Nixon's unpredictability and penchant for big, showy surprises made him even more of an objectionable figure to those who opposed him. About six weeks after the "Nixon shock" address, New York City Mayor John Lindsay decried how Nixon seemed always poised "to create the greatest amount of doubt about what we intend to do and when we intend to do it" in both domestic and foreign affairs. Such an apparent "doctrine of unpredictability, with its dazzling array of ever-opening options, has great attraction for the power-holders of this world," Lindsay complained. "But it has little charm for peaceseekers. If we are to have peace then the less ambivalence, the more balance, continuity and consistency the better."[292] While Lindsay's attacks on Nixon were a precursor to his own brief though unsuccessful presidential campaign the following year, they nonetheless resounded with others frustrated by the administration's lack of candor and seeming impulsiveness.

Much later, following the many unsettling surprises of Watergate, Stephen Ambrose described in broader terms how damaging such a leadership strategy could be in the epilogue to his three-volume biography of Nixon. "In a free, open, and democratic society, politics is above all an education process," explains Ambrose. "The leader leads through persuasion and consent. Nixon tried to lead through surprise and manipulation." That approach not only made Nixon a less effective president, but special kind of American villain. After all, "Secrecy and surprise are the enemies of democracy."

Ambrose judges that Nixon's insistence upon hiding information from others in order to achieve greater personal benefit from its revelation meant that even his successes were much less significant than they might have been otherwise. "The three actions for which he was the proudest—ending the war in Vietnam, opening to China, establishing détente with the Soviets—were achieved through secret, closed discussions," Ambrose observes, adding how each of these accomplishments would have been more lasting and meaningful "had he involved the people and their representatives in the policy-making process." Nixon's covert strategies in Southeast Asia have been discussed. His diplomatic visit to the People's Republic of China to meet with leaders and Chairman Mao in February 1972 was secretly planned for years, since shortly after Nixon took office. That made the announcement of the China trip in July 1971 genuinely stunning not just to Americans but also around the world (including in Russia where behind-the-scenes negotiations for a U.S.–U.S.S.R. summit had reached a temporary impasse). The trip proved a media spectacle and provided Nixon maximum political benefit to begin an election year. Meanwhile the China announcement pressured the Soviets to agree to a meeting as well, making Nixon's October 1971 disclosure that a first summit would take place in Moscow the following May less bombshell-like though still astonishing coming from the career Cold Warrior. However, as historian Iwan Morgan notes, "Nixon's secrecy and deception in the conduct of foreign policy did not build stable domestic foundations for détente." Indeed, operating in such a fashion ensured that once Watergate erupted Nixon was destined to lose whatever credit he had gained thanks to the country having been largely shut out of the conducting of his "personal foreign policy."[293]

With Nixon in the White House there was no relaxing. Like Leatherface, he was full of surprises, and fully capable of the occasional Saturday Night Massacre.

Who Will Survive and What Will Be Left of Them? (58:35)

Speaking of "and then there were none"-style slashers, as the story of Watergate developed it began to exhibit just that sort of narrative structure, especially once the indictments, resignations, and firings of White House staff began piling up. A common quip was to embellish the number of casualties the scandal caused among members of the administration and staff, upping the already large "body count" to

With all the indictments, resignations, and firings, the Nixon White House resembled the cast of an "and then there were none"-style slasher.

absurd heights. For example, the National Lampoon's *The Missing White House Tapes* LP includes a skit "The Constitution Game" in which hundreds have been drawn from the long line of succession to the presidency in a vain effort to find at least one person in the administration who has not committed a disqualifying crime. They are up to contestant number 435, the Deputy Assistant Under Secretary of Agriculture for Soil Affairs. On his blistering spoken word piece "H_2Ogate Blues" with Brian Jackson, Gil Scott-Heron alludes to another well-known version of the joke when he references "bumper stickers that say 'Free the Watergate 500.'" Meanwhile on his *Richard Nixon: A Fantasy* comedy LP, David Frye satirized Nixon's first Watergate speech in which he announced the resignations of Haldeman, Ehrlichman, and Kleindienst and the firing of Dean. "Today I have regretfully been forced to accept the resignations of 1,541 of the finest public servants it has been my privilege to know," growls the impersonating Frye.

Even Nixon was ultimately unable to survive the figurative slaughter, of course, although in the reporting he was often cast as the primary cause for all the carnage. Like Leatherface, Nixon was the one responsible for others' "sacrifice." The number of Nixon's victims was considerable, including those who suffered punishment for crimes they committed to protect the presidency as well as those hurt and embarrassed by Nixon's lies after they had vigorously defended him. "He has wounded others often," said Dan Rather in a report delivered the week Nixon resigned, "but never so many, so deeply, so often as now."[294] The American public likewise were victimized by Nixon, and it is their abuse *Chain Saw* comments upon in exaggerated fashion.

Sally's abrupt flight through the woods begins what will become a nearly half-hour long ordeal that concludes the film. The sequence is in fact its own three-act mini-drama that begins and ends with two spectacular, harrowing chase scenes bookending an interim period involving Sally's capture and torture. As the prototypical "Final Girl," Carol Clover's term to describe the formula-fulfilling last female standing in a slasher,[295] the question of whether or not Sally, the last of the "five youths," will survive (and if so, what will be left of her) provides the film's primary remaining suspense. Meanwhile the remainder of the film additionally supplies intriguing information about other characters we have met before, in particular filling in details of the strange group of men who inhabit the white house, colluding in secret as they wreak havoc upon others whose fate they govern.

The first part of the chase is through the woods, with Sally frequently seeming trapped by the surrounding branches while Leatherface cuts through them with his whirring chainsaw. Finally she emerges into a clearing where she sees the back of a house with its lights on, and screaming "Somebody help me!" she unhesitatingly races to the back door which she finds locked. As her assailant closes in she circles around to the front where we recognize it is Leatherface's house, and upon entering she closes and locks the door behind her. Still crying out for help she races upstairs as Leatherface begins to slice up the front door in a very inefficient criss-cross pattern. Once upstairs Sally sees a light coming from a room and runs into it. The room appears mostly empty with trash on the floor and scant furniture. At the far end are two chairs in which sit elderly figures, and beside one of them on the floor is the skeleton of what looks like a dog with fur attached to it. Sally runs to the old, withered man whose chair is positioned so that he faces the door and implores him to help her, but he is unresponsive and perhaps not even alive. She then turns to the other figure to see the mummified, rotting corpse of a woman with no eyes, and Sally's mounting fright is underscored by multiple instances of Wayne Bell's "stinger" sound.

Sally runs out of the room and starts back down the stairs, but Leatherface has finally made his way through the front door. She screams and turns around, running back up the stairs with him close behind, then without pausing runs straight through the dormer window, crashing heavily to the ground two stories below. Leatherface looks down at her through the broken window, then runs back downstairs. Sally recovers and runs away from the back of the house, retracing the path she had previously traveled. The chase is on once more. She runs back through the woods with her eyes wide as though starting to experience some kind of mental collapse. At one point she hits a branch and falls onto her back, barely recovering in time to avoid Leatherface. She exits a different part of the woods to see the back of another lit building and rushes toward it, screaming "Help me!" Like Sally, the viewer is disoriented, wondering if she is perhaps running in circles in accordance with the film's "nightmare syntax."

Leatherface chases Sally.

In fact she *has* traced a long circle, in a sense, having returned to the gas station the group visited before. She dashes around to the front of the building to find the door through which she entered that afternoon is locked. She continues to the door of the adjacent cook shed. Just as she slaps the door with both hands it opens inward, and she falls roughly onto the floor inside. The Old Man is there. Strangely, the chainsaw noise has stopped. Whereas Leatherface chose to saw his way into the locked house, he appears to decide not to continue the pursuit into the cook shed.

The Old Man lifts the trembling, sobbing Sally onto a bench. She is hysterical, telling him "somebody's trying to kill me" and asking him repeatedly to call the police. She mentions how the man chasing her has killed Franklin, then through her gasps wonders as well about Jerry and the others. The Old Man assures her all is well, checking outside once to confirm "there's nobody out there now." He explains there is no phone and says they will need to drive to Childress (an actual small town in the east Texas panhandle, unlike the fictional Newt). He convinces her to wait while he gets his truck, worrisomely leaving the door open after he leaves.

As an authority figure with an expressed willingness to help, the Old Man is initially a welcoming presence to Sally, an apparent means to help her find a way out of this nightmare. Soon, however, he forcibly carries her right back into it, at the same time introducing her and the audience to the criminal conspiracy around which the entire story revolves.

A Large and Well-Organized West Coast Jewel Theft Ring (1:00:06)

The open door signals the Old Man's lack of concern about a killer on the loose, an initial clue that all is not right. Sally nonetheless sits and waits for him to return, still shaking with fear and wide-eyed as though on the verge of going into shock. Marilyn Burns is tremendously affecting and believable here and for the rest of the film. Her performance establishes an especially high standard for all future "Final Girls."

A couple of odd details arise during Sally's wait. Noticing them allows the viewer to make some important connections, though they might be easy to miss thanks to the distraction of that open door.

A radio is playing country music, and after Arkey Blue's mournful crooner "Misty Hours of Daylight" concludes a news broadcast begins. As it does Sally fixates on the brick-encased smoker positioned in the near corner, glowing red with various cuts of meat cooking inside. It is a conspicuous image on which to linger, made more so by the radio announcer's follow-up report on the disturbance of graves at the Newt cemetery. The report, again read by real-life news reporter Levie Isaacks, essentially repeats the one delivered at the start of the film although with some additional detail concerning the status of the corpses. "There were instances in which only the heads and extremities were removed, and others in which only a hand or foot had been removed, the remainder of the cadaver left intact," explains the announcer. The references to body parts while the camera slowly pans over the cooking chunks of meat is overtly suggestive, and when put together with the meat hooks and Leatherface's work station the shot implies a link between what Leatherface stores in the white house freezer and what the Old Man serves at W.E. Slaughter's Barbecue. The association between those two involves the Hitchhiker as well, given his apparent connection to the graves being disturbed at the Muerto County Cemetery.

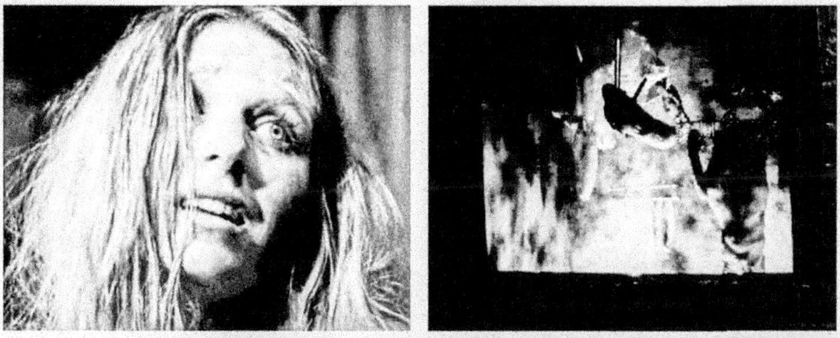

As Sally looks at the meat cooking in the smoker, a radio report tells of body parts being removed from corpses.

The other odd detail concerns a new lead in the case shared by Sheriff Jesus Maldonado, an expansion on the earlier report of "evidence linking the crime to elements outside the state." As the reporter explains, "Maldonado has information linking the robberies to a large and well-organized West Coast jewel theft ring," though the sheriff has no explanation for the missing body parts. It sounds like a complete *non sequitur*, as negligible as the weather forecast delivered just before. Knowing what we know, it seems likely the sheriff has been given a bad tip, making the line seem even less significant.

Then again, the mention of a criminal conspiracy at the very moment the film has started to reveal the central one in the film's story seems potentially apt. The first time we heard Isaacks delivering the news over the radio (his contribution coming late in post-production, likely in early 1974), his reference to indictments and a grand jury unmistakably evoked Watergate. Could a strange reference to a West Coast jewel theft ring have anything to do with the political scandal as well?

In an April 1973 column contemplating "The Riddle of the White House," U.K. journalist Michael Davie remarked on the burgeoning scandal and "strong smell of corruption" present in the Nixon administration. In his commentary Davie drew special attention to the fact that "The character of the White House staff has been determined by the peculiarities of life on the West Coast," wondering if "a generalised explanation of the Watergate conspiracy" might be found in the outsider status Nixon and his "Orange County Boys" necessarily held in D.C.[296] It was a salient observation, inspired by the fact that both the president and many of his men were indeed cross-country transplants.

Nixon was born and raised in Whittier (near Los Angeles), and throughout his political career often identified strongly with California and the West Coast while also developing a complicated, often antagonistic relationship toward "Eastern elites." Soon after taking office in 1969, Nixon purchased a residence in San Clemente, California, La Casa Pacifica, which became known as the "Western White House" thanks to his frequent visits and business conducted there. Meanwhile many on Nixon's staff were similarly associated with California and the West. John Ehrlichman was originally from Washington state, and grew up in Southern California before attending the University of California Los Angeles and Stanford. Bob Haldeman was a Los Angeles native who went to the University of Southern California and UCLA before working at the J. Walter Thompson advertising agency. Among those who worked for Haldeman at the agency in L.A. were several other future Nixon staffers, including Press Secretary Ron Ziegler, Deputy Assistant Dwight Chapin, and Special Assistant Tim Elbourne. Those three, along with Donald Segretti, the operative who engineered several infamous "dirty tricks" during the 1972 campaign, had all been classmates at Southern Cal, with the group later referred to by a former classmate as the "USC Mafia" due to their political activities.[297] Other USC grads of that same circle who were also recruited to work for Nixon included Herbert Porter and Gordon Strachan, both of whom became caught up in Watergate thanks to their work for the '72 re-election committee, a.k.a. CREEP.

It is a greater stretch to speak here of "Operation Gemstone," the label G. Gordon Liddy gave his crazed series of "political intelligence" schemes that ultimately resulted in the break-ins at the Watergate, or of the way Liddy named other operations within the overall plan Diamond, Ruby, Emerald, Quartz, Crystal, Sapphire, Opal, Topaz, Garnet, and Turquoise (plus Coal and Brick).[298] In any case, even if incidental, it is humorous to think how an outwardly innocuous detail from the radio report about a West Coast jewel theft ring could still conceivably evoke a political subtext.

The Instinct to Cover Up (1:02:07)

The Old Man returns with a gunny sack and a toothy grin.

When Sally arrives distraught and screaming that someone has killed Franklin and is now trying to kill her, the Old Man understands immediately what has happened. The viewer also soon understands the Old Man will be no source of comfort for Sally when he returns with the truck and enters the room with a toothy grin holding a gunny sack and rope.

At the sight of the rope Sally's expression hardens, and when she asks him what he is doing he tells her "you just cooperate, young lady, and we'll have no trouble." Now standing, Sally grabs a knife off of a butcher's block and holds it up threateningly, but the Old Man manages to grab a broom from beside the door and uses it to knock the knife from her hands. He begins hitting Sally with the broom as she screams, and with one of the blows the broom handle breaks as she falls to the floor. He continues to beat her with the broken handle until a solid strike to her head knocks her unconscious. He then ties her hands behind her back, prisoner-like, stuffs a dirty rag into her mouth, pulls the sack over the top half of her body, and with some difficulty carries her out and into the passenger side of the truck. The Old Man acts quickly and with purpose, suggesting he has perhaps had to perform a similar duty in the past. It seems impossible that he could not have heard the chainsaw and screaming outside before, but it is clear that even if he did not, he nonetheless knows what has to be done. Sally's distressed state and story signal to him immediately what has happened, who was responsible, and the need for him to prevent the crime from being discovered.

During his attack on Sally, the Old Man appears unable to avoid laughing and grinning, adding to the disturbing nature of the scene. His mood seems to change frequently back and forth between stern seriousness and clownish glee. This "Jekyll and Hyde" quality along with actor Jim Siedow's passing resemblance to Richard Nixon encourages Joseph Lanza to pursue a comparison between the Old Man and the president, or "the cook" and "the crook," as Lanza says. Besides the physical similarities (bushy eyebrows, large nose and lips, drooping jowls), the pair demonstrate a similar "moral ambiguity" here connoted by the Old Man's shifting moods, making Siedow's character into "a Nixon caricature," says Lanza. Later we discover the Old Man's putative position of authority among the family, and Lanza likens his lack of control over others to Nixon's inability to manage his men. The Old Man, Lanza suggests, is "the keeper of a deteriorating household, just as Nixon tried to keep an orderly facade for a threatened White House."[299]

There are certainly ways to view the Old Man as Nixonian. Here, however, when gagging and literally covering up a witness to Leatherface's crime, his action perhaps more closely resembles that of Nixon's protectors who similarly acted instinctively to cover up the White House's connection to Watergate and to other crimes as well as Nixon's own early knowledge and input into the ongoing effort. Speaking of the cover-up before the Senate Watergate Committee, John Dean told how the staff acted without premeditation or planning. As he explained it, the cover-up "just sort of happened." As soon as the first reports of the arrests at the DNC were made, the cover-up "had already... begun and was, in fact, in place and was going."[300] The Old Man's "containment" of Sally can be looked upon similarly, an automatic response to the situation presented to him, enacted to protect the interests and livelihood of himself and those with whom he lives and works.

This Little Moment About Capitalism (1:03:03)

After piling Sally into the truck, the Old Man gets in the driver's seat and is about to leave when he realizes he has left the light on in the cook shed and the door standing wide open. Having taken care of that and gotten back behind the wheel, he speaks to Sally over her muffled cries as though making conversation before beginning a friendly ride. "Had to lock up and get the lights," he says with a chuckle. "Cost of electricity is enough to drive a man out of business."

"This was a goofy moment here," says Hansen on the DVD commentary, alluding to the Old Man's fastidiousness. "Yeah, right... this

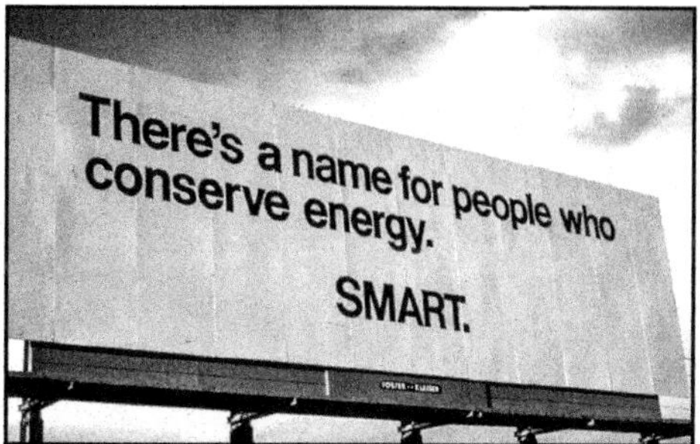

A billboard from 1973 encouraging energy conservation.

little moment about capitalism," Hooper responds with a laugh.[301]

At the time, comments about the always-too-high power bill were as common as talking about the weather, a go-to topic to which all could relate. By late summer 1973, rate increases for electricity associated with inflation had become a common concern, and by the middle of the following year the price of electricity would reach an all-time high, relatively speaking. According to the U.S. Bureau of Labor Statistics' Consumer Price Index, price inflation for electricity peaked at 18.07 percent in 1974, more than three times the levels of previous years and higher than has been the case every year since.[302] Meanwhile among the country's 50 largest utilities, electricity bills increased more than 55 percent during the first half of 1974 as more companies increased rates in response to escalating inflation.[303]

To take Hooper's cue and for a moment consider the Old Man's actions within an economic context, the need for him to turn off the light off and conserve electricity is functionally equivalent to the need for him to kidnap Sally.

Rising power costs is one consequence of the "times" in which the Old Man lives. So, too, have economic factors created problems for his business, including causing the transport to become unreliable and sometimes leaving him without gas to sell to customers. Meanwhile we have now been given enough circumstantial evidence to recognize how production slowing at the nearby slaughterhouse, another result of the nation's current economic hardship, has also impacted the Old Man's business in at least a couple of ways. The conspicuous shot of meat cooking in the smoker during the radio report of corpses missing body parts at the cemetery strongly implies an alternative supply chain for the meat used in his barbecue. Leatherface's scrupulous handling of the bodies of his victims suggests yet another. While we only witness the beginning of his slaughtering Kirk, other elements of the scene imply a more comprehensive process of preparing and storing the meat such as related earlier by the Hitchhiker's informed explanation of how slaughterhouses ready the various parts of the cattle for market ("They don't throw *nothing* away."). Thankfully the viewer is spared specifics, but exsanguination, evisceration, carcass splitting, and cooling are all understood, with Leatherface's mask indicating that skinning and tanning are also being performed. We might recall as well how the Hitchhiker mentioned his brother and grandfather had previously been employed at the slaughterhouse, understanding that his objection to new mechanized methods of killing as having taken away jobs was likely prejudiced by having family members lose their positions.

Leatherface, in other words, has been forced to work from home. There he performs a similar job as the one he held before in order to help the family put food on the table (literally). The Old Man's abduction of Sally serves a similar purpose.

You Damn Fool, You Almost Got Caught (1:05:04)

The mention of capitalism recalls for Hooper the film's political messaging, and as the Old Man drives away with Sally, Hooper is led to emphasize that point. "This film kind of came out of the Watergate times," he says. "It was kind of inspired by it."[304] The scenes that follow illustrate the inspiration most directly, starting with the first exchange between a couple of co-conspirators as they return to the white house.

During the short trip from the gas station, the Old Man again exhibits his unsettling dual personality. With a menacing grin he stabs violently at Sally with the broken broom handle as he drives, and we hear her muffled cries from within the sack. Meanwhile amid what appears uncontrollable laughter come expressions of concern. "I hope you're not too uncomfortable down there," he says, insisting she not worry and that they will "be over this in a bit." As they near the house, the sight of the Hitchhiker waving his arms by the side of the driveway causes the Old Man's grin to fade and he begins to curse. He stops the truck and gets out, berating the Hitchhiker while striking him with the broken broom handle. Eventually he climbs

The public release of the transcript of Nixon and Haldeman's Oval Office conversation of June 23, 1972 provided the "smoking gun" proving the president's knowledge of the cover-up from the outset.

back behind the wheel and drives up to the house with the Hitchhiker riding in the back. Once there the dressing down continues as the Old Man orders the Hitchhiker to carry their captive inside.

Sally's increasingly dire circumstance might distract some from following the details of the Old Man and Hitchhiker's agitated discussion of the family's crimes and the need to conceal them from the authorities. However, going back through the interaction reveals uncanny parallels between their exchange and conversations among White House principals concerning efforts to thwart investigations into the administration's connections to the Watergate break-in. In particular, the conversation between the Old Man and Hitchhiker echoes multiple elements of Nixon and Haldeman's discussions of June 23, 1972, including the "smoking gun" conversation that when finally revealed publicly on August 5, 1974 effectively ended Nixon's presidency. Exact quotes from Nixon and Haldeman's conversation were unknown to the filmmakers at the time of shooting, although the damning transcript was certainly fresh in the minds of *Chain Saw*'s initial audiences in late 1974. The general substance of their discussion was already known and suspected, however, with their scheming also resembling other interactions involving Nixon and his cohorts that had been highlighted during the Senate Watergate Hearings and endlessly scrutinized by the American news media from early 1973 onward. That the Old Man and the Hitchhiker's first conversation corresponds so well to one of the first conversations between the President and his Chief of Staff furthers the notion that the family represents an exaggerated, satirical version of a corrupt administration replete with secrets and beset by paranoia.

When he first spots the Hitchhiker, the Old Man spits out a series of epithets. "Half-wits," he grumbles. "Little coon shits. Come here, you old nap-haired idiot!" The reaction resembles Nixon's own profane, exasperated assessment of the bungling burglars getting caught and their multiple connections to the re-election committee having been so easily uncovered. In particular, Nixon spews vitriol toward G. Gordon Liddy, the operation's leader. "Well, who was the asshole that did [this thing]?" asks Nixon. "Is it Liddy? Is that the fellow? He must be a little nuts." Haldeman answers "he is" and Nixon continues by saying "he just isn't well screwed on, is he?"[305]

The Old Man's frustration with the Hitchhiker has a similar cause, namely, worry over the Hitchhiker's recklessness having placed the family in danger. "You damn fool, you almost got caught over at Newt," he yells, referring to the cemetery. "No, no, they didn't see me," the Hitchhiker insists. "They don't know *nothing*." In the Oval Office conversation, Haldeman likewise attempts to reassure his boss that despite the arrests the investigation will be stymied and the scandal successfully contained. He expresses (unfounded) optimism that the idea to have CIA Deputy Director Vernon Walters tell Acting Director of the FBI L. Patrick Gray "to put the hold on this" will be sufficient. "We're set up beautifully to do it," he adds, claiming the plan "will fit rather well because the FBI agents who are working the case, at this point, feel that's what it is," namely, that "this [the operation that included breaking into the DNC] is CIA."[306] Incidentally, Haldeman was not nearly so sanguine about the plan's prospects in his diary entry for that day, noting there how it was already the case that "[John] Dean feels the investigation is out of control" and that Dean and others "feel the whole thing is at the brink now."[307]

"I told you to stay away from that graveyard!" the Old Man bellows as he continues his rant, confirming what has already been heavily implied regarding the Hitchhiker's responsibility for the goings-on at the Muerto County Cemetery. It is tempting to compare the Old Man's admonition to Nixon's suggestion to Haldeman also warning against unwanted "digging." Building on the plan put forth by Haldeman, Nixon suggests the CIA's story to the FBI could be bolstered by an additional, vague claim that further scrutiny from the FBI would uncover details of an earlier, actual CIA operation, the failed Bay of Pigs invasion in early 1962. It is an idea, it appears, that originates with the common link of E. Howard Hunt, the Watergate participant who a dozen years before had been involved with the Bay of Pigs operation as an intelligence officer in the CIA. The FBI continuing their investigation, Nixon suggests, will make the "CIA look bad, it's going to make Hunt look bad, and it's likely to blow the whole, uh, Bay of Pigs thing which we think would be very unfortunate for CIA and for the country at this time."[308] Figuratively speaking, the message Nixon is trying to impart is to tell the FBI to refrain from digging around the Bay of Pigs "graveyard" and perhaps unearthing secrets better left buried for reasons of national security. (Nixon's elliptical reference here to the "Bay of Pigs thing" has provided significant motivation to explorers of JFK assassination conspiracies thanks in large part to its ambiguity.)

They reach the house. After getting out and while ordering the Hitchhiker to carry Sally inside, the Old Man continues to chastise him for carelessness that has left the family vulnerable. "I told you never to leave your brother alone," the Old Man cries, referring to Leatherface and clarifying that the Hitchhiker and the chainsaw-wielding killer are siblings. "Hopefully your brother didn't let any of those kids get away," he adds, indicating direct knowledge of what has been going on in and around the white house all afternoon and evening. Haldeman similarly pointed to the undesirability of allowing the FBI's investigation to proceed unhindered, given how it "goes in some directions we don't want it to go." Stopping it then and there would be much preferable to taking a chance on trying to convince potential witnesses to cooperate with the growing cover-up, he explains, since otherwise "we're relying on more and more people all the time."[309] Haldeman's fear was eventually realized, of course, although not before Nixon secured re-election in November.

As the Old Man completes his diatribe, he similarly demonstrates an awareness of what the consequence would be should the family fail to work together to keep their criminal activities hidden.

"We'll have the whole county out here!"

Look What Your Brother Did to the Door! (1:06:22)

As they enter the house, the Old Man delivers his funniest line of the film.

"Look what your brother did to the door! He ain't got no... no

The Old Man expresses disappointment at Leatherface's sloppy work.

pride in his home?"

The Old Man's anger at Leatherface for slicing up the door with his chainsaw seems farcical and over-the-top, crazily incongruent with the immediate situation involving Sally. Yet it is weirdly consistent with the Old Man's ever-vacillating personality, making the reaction seem completely in character. The damaged door also recalls various instances of sloppiness exhibited by Nixon's Special Investigations Unit, a.k.a. the Plumbers.

One such example infamously involved a door, namely one leading from the basement garage to the stairwell of the Watergate Office Building. Much as had been done during the first time the group broke into the Democratic National Committee offices three weeks before, in preparation for the second attempt on June 17, 1972, one of the burglars, James McCord, had entered the building during the early evening hours while it was still open and placed pieces of masking tape over the striking plates and bolt holes of several doors leading into the stairwell, both in the basement and on multiple floors. Doing so restrained the spring-loaded bolts, thereby preventing the doors from locking. However when McCord and a couple of the others returned after midnight, the tape on the basement door had been removed and the door locked. Later it would be determined that Frank Wills, a security guard at the Watergate, had noticed the tape during his rounds and removed it. Another of the group, Virgilio Gonzalez who was an experienced locksmith, picked the lock of the basement door and the burglars made their way inside. Once more masking tape was used on the basement garage door to enable the others, including McCord, to enter afterwards, but when the last of them entered the tape was not removed, leaving it to be discovered again by Wills. This time the guard phoned the Washington, D.C. police, leading to the arrests of the five men found inside the DNC. Leaving the tape was a significant blunder leading directly to the burglars' capture, a "look what they did to the door" moment that earned significant notice, especially during the early days of the televised Senate Watergate Hearings.

The filing cabinet of Daniel Ellsberg's psychiatrist following a September 1971 visit by the White House's Special Investigations Unit, a.k.a. the "Plumbers."

Another more analogous example to the ruined door was the damaged filing cabinet the Plumbers left behind in the office of Dr. Lewis Fielding, the Los Angeles psychiatrist whose clients included *Pentagon Papers* leaker Daniel Ellsberg. As discussed before, the risky operation undertaken in September 1971 was authorized by Ehrlichman and involved Hunt, Liddy, and others (including two participants involved in the Watergate break-ins) who broke into Fielding's office in an attempt to locate Ellsberg's file and obtain potentially discrediting information about him. That mission also involved an initial trip designed to unlock a door ahead of time only for the door to be relocked upon the burglars' return. In this case it was decided to break a ground floor window in order to gain entry to the building. That decision led to another to vandalize the office in a thorough and obvious way in order to make it appear that those who had committed the crime were searching for drugs.[310] Accounts differ regarding what information the Plumbers obtained about Ellsberg, although most involved agreed the mission yielded nothing of value. As also noted before, the White House's desire to keep the Fielding break-in under wraps added urgency to the Watergate cover-up, given the likelihood that a thorough investigation of those who participated in the latter crime would lead investigators to learn about the former.

Fielding saved his damaged gray metal filing cabinet, and after his death his widow donated it to the Smithsonian National Museum of National History where it was added to the museum's collection of items related to political history. With its dents and markings showing where the locked drawers had been pried open, the cabinet not only helps chronicle the Watergate story, but additionally stands as a kind of physical symbol of the Nixon administration's corruption and criminality. It also documents the Plumbers' recklessness and ineptitude, qualities that eventually contributed directly to Nixon's fall.

The Old Man declaring that the damaged front door indicates Leatherface's failure to be sufficiently house-proud is humorous in the same way his fretting over the electricity bill was, given how such commonplace concerns seem absurdly out of place when delivered during a violent kidnapping. Even so, his comments clarify the family's priorities. The maintenance of their home and livelihood is of utmost importance, making it necessary that any threats to their current status and well being must be eliminated. The damaged door certainly would appear suspicious should anyone come around in search of the missing travelers, something the Old Man is no doubt aware of as well.

The moment Sally realizes they are all in it together.

Conspiracy (1:06:59)

Once inside, the Old Man stops yelling at the Hitchhiker and turns his anger toward Leatherface, calling him a "fool" and chasing him into the kitchen. The aggressive interrogation that follows further shows how keeping their criminal enterprise hidden is the Old Man's primary concern.

"You better get them damn other kids," he yells, an approximation of the line "You better damn got them other kids" in the screenplay. Leatherface whimpers in response, his gibberish appearing in the text as "A ab e y ob er ewe ober" and the like.[311] Franklin's folded up wheelchair is set against the kitchen wall behind the Old Man, proof that indeed Leatherface has done exactly what the Old Man has demanded of him. Their scene continues with the Old Man asking Leatherface "Where are the kids?" and Leatherface rapping on the freezer to indicate where the bodies have been stored, then pointing to the wheelchair. "None of them get away?" asks the Old Man, and Leatherface makes a "nuh-uh" sound. Satisfied, the Old Man pauses for a moment, then again calls Leatherface a fool for ruining the front door before hitting him with the broken broom handle.

At the same time in the front room the Hitchhiker sets the still screaming Sally on a chair and begins tying her to it. It is a visual pun—an "arm" chair with actual human arms—more evidence of the film's (darkly) humorous intentions. When he removes the sack from over her head, she screams upon recognizing him. His surprised reaction mirrors hers, albeit in a mocking way as for him the emotion being expressed is delight. "I thought *you* was in a hurry," he says gleefully.

Sally is horrified by the revelation. At that moment she realizes all three of the men she has encountered that day (the Hitchhiker, Leatherface, and the Old Man) are related in some fashion, working together as co-conspirators. She also sees she is back inside the same house from which she had fled just a short time before. She is traveling in circles within circles, seemingly unable to escape the nightmare.

Sally began the day seeking information about a crime, the disturbances of graves at the cemetery where her grandfather is buried, a seemingly bizarre, isolated act. Similarly did the story of a break-in at the Watergate first appear a curious trifle to most Americans. But just as Sally's inquiry has led to something much more serious and troubling, so, too, did further probing into Watergate reveal deeper, more extensive corruption and criminality. In both stories, one of the most upsetting twists involves the discovery of a dangerous cabal conspiring with one another to commit horrors in a white house.

Grandpa (1:10:51)

The Old Man gives the orders, but soon we learn another person serves as the true head of household.

After the Hitchhiker finishes tying Sally to the chair, he excitedly runs into the kitchen to tell Leatherface, "you did good, she's a nice girl!" The fact that he tells Leatherface this and not the Old Man indicates his awareness of Leatherface's role in her capture, once more underscoring the collaborative nature of the family's

Grandpa becomes more alive, and Sally faints dead away.

business. The Old Man interrupts them, yelling at the Hitchhiker, "You nitwit, go upstairs and get your Grandpa!" The Old Man then turns his attention to Sally who is writhing within her binds and crying through the gag. "We'll fix you some supper in a few minutes," he says, using a softer tone while reaching out tentatively and petting her hair as though she were an unruly animal. "Take it easy. We'll have you something to eat right away." As he speaks Leatherface wanders out of the kitchen, but the Old Man angrily orders him back, presumably to finish readying the evening meal.

Leatherface still wears his shirt and tie, but he has now exchanged the yellow vinyl apron for a blue cloth one with white polka dots. His hair is also different, gray and tied up in the back. While the movement and lighting make it hard to notice, he is also wearing a different human-skin mask, one more feminine-appearing as though to indicate further he has switched from the masculine position of breadwinner to a more domestic, "motherly" role. Soon we will learn he has a third mask as well, signifying both a string of "personalities" for the character as well as a series of murders extending well before the ones occurring on this day.

While we wait with Sally, noises of moving furniture come from above. The Hitchhiker slides to the top of the stairs the chair on which sits the cadaverous, emaciated elderly man Sally saw before, the action dimly recalling the Hitchhiker's earlier digging up of corpses. "Hey, Leatherface!" he yells, the first of only a couple of instances of the name being uttered in the film. "Give me a hand with Grandpa!" Leatherface hustles up the stairs and the pair carefully carry the chair with the man sitting in it downstairs where they set it down next to Sally. "Look, Grandpa! Look! Look!" the Hitchhiker giggles. The Hitchhiker then frees one of Sally's arms and holds his knife up to her neck while Leatherface takes her hand and with a kitchen knife slices her finger, the ritual-like nature of their actions making it seem as though they have performed them many times. Leatherface directs Sally's bleeding finger into Grandpa's mouth and he begins to suck. As Grandpa does his body becomes weirdly animated, creating the impression that he is being invigorated somehow, his flailing limbs making him look like a baby receiving a mother's milk. The screenplay highlights that latter idea in the stage direction (typos all [*sic*]): "Once the finger is in his mouth the grandfather begins to suckle like and an infant his arms and legs suddenly have life and begin to squirm. He buts Sallys finger with his hands as if it were a reluctant breast."[312]

The day after his election win in 1968, Nixon visited Eisenhower, a.k.a. "America's grandfather," at Walter Reed Army Medical Center.

Sally watches, terrified and wide-eyed, her mouth still forced open as though locked in a permanent scream. Finally overcome she blacks out, and the scene ends.

When Sally earlier encountered Grandpa during her flight from Leatherface, it was not clear whether or not he might be dead like his female companion, although now we see he is alive. Neither the screenplay nor the film specifies the character's age, but most references indicate he is intended to be more than 100 years old. Most commonly he is referred to as aged 108, which would make the year of his birth exactly coincide with the end of the Civil War. (In the 1986 sequel where a matching opening crawl sets events 13 years later, Grandpa is said to be 137.) Interestingly, the actor John Dugan, brother-in-law to Kim Henkel, was the youngest cast member at the time of filming at age 20, and he was forced to endure many hours in the makeup chair for the arduous application of liquid latex and prosthetics to create Grandpa's corpse-like appearance.

Grandpa is a widower, it appears. The female figure sitting in the chair upstairs who reminds us of Mrs. Bates in *Psycho* is evidently his dead wife. The relationship of the entire family remains somewhat ambiguous, however, as it is unclear whether the Old Man is the father or older brother to Leatherface and the Hitchhiker. The character of Grandpa provides a parallel to Sally and Franklin's deceased grandfather who once owned the neighboring house. Franklin had mentioned how his grandfather used to sell cattle at the slaughterhouse they pass, while the Hitchhiker explained his grandfather (and brother, whom we know now is Leatherface) had been employed there.

While the other family members are all outrageous in different ways, Grandpa is perhaps the least believable character in the film, although his late entrance into the story does not seriously threaten *Chain Saw*'s sense of realism. Especially when considering the film's political satire, one consequence of Grandpa's strange status as a sort of living dead creature is that he seems the most obviously symbolic character, the literal embodiment of the Hitchhiker's earlier argument that the "old way" is preferable to the "new way." He represents a reactionary, older generation intolerant of change and ready to maintain its authority by all available means, including by weakening (or even eliminating) the younger generation that threatens them. Not only does Grandpa gather sustenance by his vampire-like sucking of Sally's blood, but his strengthening directly incapacitates her. He becomes more alive, and she faints dead away.

In the world of *The Texas Chain Saw Massacre*, power resides with a (wholly) patriarchal group who live in a white house and who firmly impose upon others a peculiar understanding of order informed not by moral or legal definitions but rather by the practical requirements of self-preservation. In this world, Grandpa is obviously a distinguished champion of the "old way." Like a decorated war veteran, he stars as the hero in the family's oft-repeated tales of his triumphs. He is the one who has taught all of the others and whose example they revere. An omitted detail from this scene that appears in the screenplay (discussed above)—"On the back of the grandfather's chair is painted the symbol the hitchiker [*sic*] scrawled on the van"[313]—would further indicate Grandpa's special status as a respected elder in this powerful secret society. In the context of American politics, he is akin to earlier leaders or administrations that provide a model for those who come after, existing as a justifying precedent or (depending on your point of view) a rationalization. Of course, he is also enfeebled and physically helpless, making his "power" now essentially figurative and only actual in a distant past, although that does not prevent the others from still believing in his literal strength.

Dwight D. Eisenhower, the two-term president under whom Nixon served as vice president, stood as the most recent, immediate Republican model for Nixon, although in truth once Nixon assumed the office himself he was more desirous to achieve Eisenhower's high level of popularity than to emulate his method of governing. While Nixon respected Eisenhower's military service as a five-star general and Supreme Commander of the Allied Forces in Europe during the Second World War, he was generally less enamored with his abilities as a politician, a realm in which Eisenhower was always an outsider. The pair were never close, either, enduring several famous clashes starting with their first campaign in 1952 and the "fund crisis" that nearly forced Nixon off the ticket. In *Six Crises*, Nixon tells how Eisenhower "tended to make a visitor feel like a junior officer coming in to see the Commanding General."[314] It is safe to say Nixon never quite rid himself of this same sense of inferiority with regard to Eisenhower, even if publicly he communicated only admiration and esteem. Even so, when later campaigning for president himself, Nixon promoted his association with well-liked Ike at every opportunity.

Joe McGinniss tells a story in *The Selling of the President 1968* that he elaborates upon in Emile de Antonio's 1971 documentary *Millhouse: A White Comedy* about the Nixon campaign's ultimately futile effort that year to recruit Eisenhower to make a short campaign ad for his former vice president. Just a few months from dying at age 78, a weakened Eisenhower lay bedridden in Walter Reed Army Medical Center in Washington, D.C. After suffering his first heart attack while president in 1955 and a variety of ailments thereafter, Eisenhower had been mostly out of the public eye for three years before enduring four heart attacks and multiple cardiac arrests during the spring and summer months of 1968, including his seventh heart attack in mid-August. As McGinniss explains in *Millhouse*, the election was drawing close when Nixon political strategist Murray Chotiner, a longtime cohort whose association with Nixon dated back to his first Congressional campaign, decided "some film of Eisenhower endorsing Nixon from his deathbed would be a very effective 60-second spot." Chotiner assembled a camera crew and traveled to Walter Reed. "They put a Lavalier microphone around Eisenhower's neck and they propped him up in the bed," says Mc-

Ginniss. "It was a terrible thing to see because he really looked skeletal and very, very sick. He was dying, and it was indecent to send cameras into that room." Chotiner nevertheless persisted, and ultimately collected about 20 minutes' worth of footage of Eisenhower, obtained with great difficulty since "he was losing his faculty for speech and found it impossible to utter more than two or three coherent sentences in a row and he kept garbling words." In his book McGinniss tells how Chotiner screened the material to campaign consultant Harry Treleaven who objected to the idea of showing the former president and war hero in such a state. "That's one thing I'm not going to do," Treleaven insisted to Chotiner. "I'm not going to make a commercial out of that."[315]

Nixon did not shy away from exploiting Eisenhower's infirmity, however, when opening his speech accepting his party's nomination for president at that year's Republican National Convention. "General Eisenhower, as you know, lies critically ill in the Walter Reed Hospital tonight," said Nixon. "I have talked, however, with Mrs. Eisenhower on the telephone. She tells me that his heart is with us. And she says that there is nothing that he lives more for and there is nothing that would lift him more than for us to win in November and I say let's win this one for Ike!"[316] In *Millhouse*, de Antonio delivers a withering blow by showing Nixon make this statement, then juxtaposing it with the "Win one for the Gipper" locker room speech from the 1940 film *Knute Rockne, All American* in which then-governor of California and future U.S. president Ronald Reagan portrays the dying George Gipp for whom Coach Rockne successfully rallies his men. In de Antonio's film the sequence forms part of a larger argument regarding Nixon's lack of scruples and indifference toward others, though it emphasizes as well how Nixon relied on his association with Eisenhower when presenting himself as a reliable patron of the "old way."

Nixon visited Eisenhower in the hospital the day after the election in November. When Eisenhower died in March 1969, the new president eulogized him as "an authentic hero" and "one of the giants of our time." Nixon also made a point to emphasize Eisenhower's toughness and vigor. "He had a side more evident to those of us who worked with him than to the rest of the world," said Nixon. "He was a strong man."[317]

Is Grandpa a shriveled up, decayed version of a former American president? He might be read that way. In any event, the fact that he physically resembles a grotesque version of Eisenhower who during his presidency and after was nicknamed "America's grandfather" is at least suggestive.

Leatherface and the Nixon Mask (1:13:04)

The full moon, positioned and framed almost exactly as the shot of the sun with which the film begins.

Sally's blackout crossfades to a shot of the outside of the house, a rapid zoom as though swiftly backing away from the finger-sucking scene in distaste. There is another crossfade to the night sky where a shot of the full moon gradually comes into focus while the generator can be heard continuing to chug along. The framing of the shot of the moon is nearly identical to the post-opening credits filtered shot of the sun, adding to the sense of claustrophobic circularity already present in the narrative. There is a cut to a battered and beaten Sally with her head leaned back and eyes closed. Her head tilts down as she slowly regains consciousness, a changing rack focus indicating how she successively looks at the items positioned down the center of a long dining table. Each of these items—a chicken head, an armadillo, and a cow skull—have been shown before and thus again signal a kind of return back through the story. Finally her dawning awareness reaches the end of the table and she sees the person sitting opposite her, Grandpa. He appears asleep, but Sally is now fully awake and loudly screams. The disappearance of her friends, the butchering of her brother, and her abduction are not part of some nightmare. It has all really happened, and it is still happening. (We recall her foreboding horoscope and its prediction for Sally and other Capricorns, "There are moments when we cannot believe that what is happening is really true. Pinch yourself and you may find out that it is.")

Thus begins the dinner scene, much celebrated in *Chain Saw* lore as having been produced under trying circumstances during an unfathomably arduous, marathon day of shooting.

Leatherface as "Pretty Woman," a.k.a. the "Clarabell Clown."

The Hitchhiker, Leatherface, and the Old Man all howl mockingly in response to Sally's screams until the Old Man undergoes another personality shift and yells at the others to shut up. In the background a human skeleton with a light inside of it hangs in the corner of the room, and a close-up reveals the shade for the light hanging overhead has been made from yet another skinned human face. The Hitchhiker objects to the Old Man's antagonism, saying they are merely having fun, but the Old Man is unyielding. "You think this is a *party*?" he cries, suggesting that despite appearances there is still work to do. Recognizing Grandpa as an authority sitting at the head of the table, Sally begs to him, "please, you can make them stop." But the Hitchhiker mocks her again, saying "no, he can't" and grinning madly. As she continues her futile appeal to zombie-like Grandpa, the Old Man chimes in that whatever her fate might be, "it can't be helped." At that Leatherface and the Hitchhiker both stand and from other side of the table approach their captive. They lean forward, moving uncomfortably close to the camera and to Sally.

"You *like* this face?" giggles the Hitchhiker from the left, and the camera pans over to Leatherface on the right. The screenplay clarifies the Hitchhiker is asking Leatherface if he likes Sally's face. "Leatherface seems to see Sally's face for the first time," says the stage direction. "He studies it briefly and then nods happily."[318] The camera adopts Sally's perspective, and the close-up helps us see Leatherface is wearing yet another mask, this one another woman's face with lipstick and makeup heavily applied in clownish fashion.

As earlier noted, Leatherface has not one mask, but several of them. Gunnar Hansen spells out in *Chain Saw Confidential* how each of the three different masks he wears in the film represents a distinct personality. "We called the first the 'Killing Mask,'" he explains, referring to the one he wears during each of the four murders. The second mask worn during the meal preparations Hansen calls the "Old Lady"

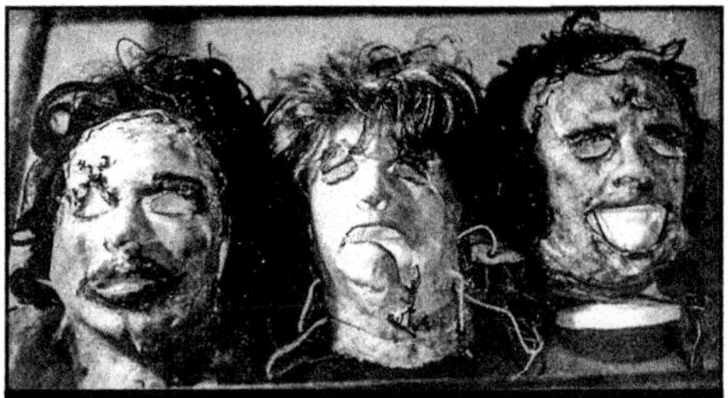

The three Leatherface masks.

thanks to the gray hair arranged in a bun, suitable for "making dinner and being 'mom' for a while." The third and last mask he says was referred to on set as the "Pretty Woman" which Hansen says Leatherface wears in order "to dress up for dinner."[319] The screenplay's description of the third mask is especially detailed: "He now wears a new mask. It is the face of a woman who might once have been beautiful. The process of tanning the flesh has shrunken the size of the features and given them a deep mahogany tint. The mask has been made up with white powder and has some of the starkness of stage make up. The lips are heavily ringed with a dark red lipstick, the eyebrows penciled in darkly with mascara, the lashes have been covered with false ones and around the eyes there is a greenish eye shadow."[320] Henkel called the third mask the "Clarabell Clown," a reference to Howdy Doody's sidekick, a male clown with a woman's name who like Leatherface did not speak.[321] There is also mention of the long dark hair attached to the mask, as well as the fact that Leatherface is wearing Pam's bracelet, both details that appear in the film. To complete the ensemble, he has donned a black dinner jacket.

Leatherface's accessorizing provides fruitful material for those wishing to explore the film's commentary on gender roles as articulated within the domestic sphere, its challenge to traditional assumptions of the significance of family, or to pursue psychoanalytic or feminist approaches to the character and story. However the masks in particular also carry an immediate and conspicuous political significance linking his character on a psychological level with Richard Nixon.

Hansen describes how "the masks are theatrical for Leatherface" insofar as each one enables him to engage in a kind of "performance" of various roles. That said, "Behind the mask he is, in essence, unknown and unknowable."[322] In terms of horror film history, Leatherface harkens back to old B-movie monsters deliberately kept hidden or only partially shown as a means to heighten suspense regarding them. Even in cases where elusiveness was merely a consequence of budgetary constraints, the withholding of detail about the monster's physical appearance often had the desired effect of increasing audience anxiety over the threatening figure. As Hooper explains of Leatherface, "when you can't see his face, your imagination goes wild. When you can't see, you fill in the blanks with something that's far more interesting than what can actually be shown."[323] Leatherface prefigures later mask-wearing slasher villains like Michael Myers in *Halloween*, Jason Voorhees in the *Friday the 13th* sequels, and countless other horror films with ambitions to present similarly frightening nihilistic killers. Of course Leatherface differs from many of these latter characters insofar as each of his masks supplies him a temporary identity corresponding to recognizable familial roles. Thus while Leatherface shares with the other killers a similar absence of "self," his identification with his mask is unique in its totality. Even the name used by family members to address him is not a name at all, but rather a label that describes his mask. "Everything was in the mask, and beneath it there really was nothing at all," says Hansen. "Eventually this extended to my thinking of Leatherface as having no face at all. Take off his mask and you find nothing—featureless skin or even nothingness itself."[324]

One of the most recognizable pop cultural artifacts from the time of Richard Nixon's presidency was the famous "Nixon mask." Like the masks worn by Leatherface, the Nixon mask often inspired similar interpretations of its symbolism, with some commentators finding it an apt metaphor for a president whose elusive identity and shifting policy positions often seemed wholly dictated by poll results and political expediency. The most frequently sported versions of the mask accentuated the same eminently spoofable Nixon facial features long exploited by political cartoonists, almost always lengthening the already large nose to Pinocchio-like proportions as an indication of Tricky Dick's aversion to speaking the unvarnished truth. In fact, the *idea* of the Nixon mask predated the actual item, gaining particular relevance during the 1968 campaign when hired ad execs crafted a "New Nixon" to help enable their candidate's improbably successful comeback. A political science undergraduate at Columbia University named Lenny Glynn, later a speechwriter for Michael Dukakis and Bill Clinton, made such a point in his review of the 1968 presidential campaign published on the eve of the election in the

Nixon masks first appeared worn by protestors at the 1969 Inauguration.

student newspaper, the *Columbia Daily Spectator*. In his feature, Glynn skeptically reports on an end-of-campaign rally held by the Nixon campaign in Madison Square Garden a few days before on October 31. Emphasizing the lack of substance in both the event's specious pomp and Nixon's stump speech, Glynn's description shows how the concept of Nixon concealing himself behind a figurative disguise was already well in play. "The night was Halloween, and with a Republican's respect for tradition, Tricky Dick obliged us by coming in costume," writes Glynn. "Here was the old Nixon wearing the New Nixon mask, the hawk in dove's feathers, the cold warrior in the negotiator's suit, the hanging judge dressed as a firm but gentle minister, the miser wearing the United Way button, and the groin kicking politician in statesman's robes."[325]

It was at Nixon's inauguration in January 1969 that the physical manifestation of the idea suggested by Glynn—that is, a *literal* Nixon mask—fully emerged onto the national consciousness. Starting over the weekend prior to the Monday swearing-in ceremony, anti-war protestors converged on Washington for a three-day gathering consisting of workshops, lectures, seminars, and a number of public performances dubbed a "counter-inauguration." A government-commissioned report on the protest activities and police response tells how on Saturday, "A guerilla theater group, wearing white face masks intended to resemble the President-elect, imitated pigs and the gestapo. A rubber doll was pulled apart and burned while demonstrators chanted 'Kill for Peace.'"[326] On Sunday came the protestors' marquee event, a processional parade of thousands marching west-to-east

Dr. John E. Fryer appears as "Dr. Henry Anonymous" in an altered Nixon mask at the annual meeting of the American Psychiatric Association in May 1972.

down Pennsylvania Avenue, the direction deliberately chosen as opposite of the one Nixon would take the following day from the Capitol to the White House. "One youth wearing a Nixon mask marched the entire 20-block distance in a mime of picking his nose," reports the *New York Times*.[327] The masks came out again during the actual inauguration, periodically dotting the crowd of spectators lining the streets. The masks were all white and without the added coloring and features that came with later iterations, inspiring writers of later accounts to focus on their sinister appearance with adjectives like "macabre," "ghost-like," and "haunting."[328] Contemporary reports also pointed out how the "chalky white" masks were meant "to emphasize the 'theme of death.'"[329] When introducing the scene for his 1970 book *Nixon Agonistes*, Garry Wills starts out fixating on the masks and likewise noting their sickly look: "At the 1969 inauguration, the streets were full of ashen Nixons."[330]

The masks continued to turn up with increasing frequency after Nixon took office. While spending his first Fourth of July as president in Key Biscayne, Florida attending an Independence Day parade, Nixon reportedly "shook with laughter when he saw a man wearing a Nixon mask atop a float."[331] During the first Moratorium to End the War in Vietnam demonstrations in October 1969, a student group in New York City acted out an anti-war skit at Columbus Circle One in which a student wore a Nixon mask and directed another to kill Vietnamese.[332] By February 1970 came more stories centering upon the masks, such as one out of New Jersey of a successful holdup and getaway at a bank in Hillsdale during which the robber hid his identity behind a Nixon mask.[333] The masks appeared again at the many protests that followed the National Guard killings at Kent State in May 1970. In one widely circulated UPI photo, a young man perched atop the Boy Scout Memorial in The Ellipse park in Washington, D.C. is shown holding his fist aloft while wearing a Nixon mask, the features of which had been darkened into a pronounced sneer. The masks became a regular detail in reports of most public demonstrations going forward, especially those opposing the war, although Nixons would also pop up in protests criticizing the United Nations' admission of the People's Republic of China, the treatment of Jews by the Soviets, and other causes.[334]

Following the Saturday Night Massacre, a protestor in a prison outfit invites passersby to "Honk for Impeachment."

An interesting and momentous use of the Nixon mask occurred in May 1972 at the annual meeting of the American Psychiatric Association in Dallas. Among that year's sessions was one titled "Psychiatry: Friend or Foe to the Homosexual? A Dialogue" where Dr. John E. Fryer was one of the participants. As both a psychiatrist and a homosexual, Fryer brought a unique perspective to the topic and spoke persuasively about the need for change, earning a standing ovation in response to his presentation. It proved a landmark moment both in psychiatric history and American culture, directly influencing the removal of homosexuality from the APA's *Diagnostic and Statistical Manual of Mental Disorders* the following year. Fryer's contribution earned the session even more notice than might have been the case otherwise, however, thanks to his decision to appear with his identity hidden in order not to risk his position on the medical faculty at Temple University. Calling himself "Dr. Henry Anonymous," Fryer spoke through a machine that distorted his voice while wearing a multi-colored and oversized tuxedo, a dark-haired fright wig, and a customized rubber Nixon mask. Fryer and a friend had modified the mask by removing the eyebrows, altering the openings, and introducing other surface irregularities.[335] Interestingly, the changes made to the Nixon mask made it resemble one of the skin-masks created for Leatherface

"Dirty Tricks or Treat," Halloween 1974.

a little over a year later.

Nixon masks became even more popular after the arrests at the Watergate, remaining so all of the way through to Nixon's resignation and afterwards. Delegates from New Jersey and West Virginia each wore Nixon masks on the floor of the Democratic National Convention in July 1972.[336] In October 1972, a group called W.A.R.N. (Women Against Richard Nixon) assembled in front of a Nixon campaign office on Madison Avenue in New York. Describing the demonstration as a "kiss-off," the fifty women wore shrouds, fake noses, and Nixon masks while carrying signs stating "Kiss Nixon and Kiss Day-Care Goodbye" and "Nixon Kisses Like Bela Lugosi."[337] The masks continued to appear at fundraisers, at various gatherings on and around election day, and once again at Nixon's second inauguration in January 1973. As that year progressed the mask was a frequently spotted item worn by protestors calling for Nixon's removal from office. In October 1973 picketers gathered outside the White House following the Saturday Night Massacre, and an AP photo of one wearing a Nixon mask, a prison outfit, and holding a sign reading "Honk for Impeachment" was reprinted in many of the nation's newspapers.[338] *Time* magazine reported that at a Halloween party in New York in 1973, a child wearing a Nixon mask won first prize for "most frightening costume."[339] In February 1974, an attorney in Portland who had also worn a Nixon mask to a party was arrested afterwards for violating a city ordinance prohibiting wearing a disguise in public.[340] There was another arrest of a Nixon mask wearer outside a D.C. courthouse in March 1974 where the president's aides were being arraigned on felony counts, not for wearing the mask but for dropping his pants.[341] There were also Nixon masks, and even a Henry Kissinger one, worn by those waiting outside the Supreme Court building in late July 1974 to hear the unanimous ruling against Nixon requiring him to hand over the subpoenaed tapes that ultimately would force him from office.[342]

Hunter S. Thompson swimming with a Nixon mask.

On the night of August 8, *Chicago Sun-Times* reporter Tom Fitzpatrick observed a crowd of 3,000-plus who had gathered outside of the White House while Nixon announced his resignation on television. As sirens blared over protestors singing "Jail to the king," Fitzpatrick noticed the curtains being pulled back from a second floor window. "The noise of the crowd rose to a fever pitch at the sight of the President's daughter," he writes. "Then the most bizarre thing happened," he continues before describing what sounds almost like a horror movie scene. A man was lifted onto others' shoulders up above the crowd. His dress was strangely formal as he wore a blue suit. He also was wearing a large rubber Nixon mask. "Tricia stood there, almost transfixed at the man," who upon realizing that she could see him began to shout obscenities while raising his middle finger. "Tricia's mouth opened in shock," writes Fitzpatrick. "Quickly, she drew the curtain shut. The crowd roared in triumph."[343]

Over subsequent weeks the mask became a top-selling item nationwide, sold in a variety of styles in vinyl, plastic, or rubber. From the time of Ford's pardon of Nixon in early September to the end of October, the famous Dave Miller Costume Shop in downtown Milwaukee sold thousands of Nixon masks before running out of stock, a phenomenon experienced by other retailers throughout the country. Some of the masks were purchased as collector's items, although many youngsters wore them that Halloween, a few of whom carried bags on which was written "Dirty Tricks or Treat."[344] In other words, at the very moment a horror film depicting a killer wearing a human face as a mask was starting to be shown in the nation's theaters, the most popular Halloween mask in the country was one portraying the villainous ex-president.

Continuing the theme, Bob Dylan famously wore a Nixon mask to open a Halloween concert in 1975, an occasion preserved at the

An early cinematic example of a robber wearing a Nixon mask in the 1974 film *Cockfighter*.

start of the film *Reynaldo and Clara*. Dylan wears it while singing "When I Paint My Masterpiece," a song that among other themes meditates upon unrealized plans, potentially apt when considered from the perspective of a president whose time in office was cut short. *Sports Illustrated* captured Kansas City Royals star George Brett before a game in 1976 donning a Nixon mask and holding a bat aloft while delivering the former president's "V" for victory salute, a seemingly random bit of horseplay. For a 1978 episode of the BBC's *Omnibus* featuring Hunter S. Thompson, the reporter wore a Nixon mask while swimming the length of a pool, an obviously sarcastic visual chosen to match Thompson's devastating criticisms of Nixon as representative of "everything that's wrong with America."[345] Meanwhile in *Airplane II: The Sequel* from 1982, when the lunar shuttle hits one-half the speed of light, passengers undergo a "temporary metabolic change" humorously represented by all of them suddenly wearing Nixon masks.

Over time the Nixon mask evolved into a pop culture cliché, providing a kind of shorthand for makers of various entertainment media to identify a character as villainous, to indicate the creators' sense of humor, or both. Art has imitated life with frequent examples of fictional robbers wearing Nixon masks. The earliest example came in the 1972 blaxploitation film *Cool Breeze* that premiered a few months before the Watergate break-in, a scene in which a group pull off a diamond heist with the ringleader wearing a Nixon mask while his accomplices are disguised as Spiro Agnew and George Wallace. (Incidentally, the thief given the Wallace mask to wear laughingly objects before putting it on, joking "man, I could get shot looking like this," and in fact his character does. Two months after the film premiered came the actual assassination attempt on Wallace that saw the Alabama governor survive being shot four times.) Another early instance came in the Roger Corman-produced *Cockfighter* released just before the resignation in 1974, a scene in which a group of gunmen wearing rubber masks hold up an underground cockfighting ring with a Richard Nixon prominent among them. The 1987 neo-noir *Best Seller* opens with a scene set in 1972 involving a group of Nixon mask-wearing robbers murdering several police while pilfering evidence from a precinct. Meanwhile the best-known example is probably the 1991 action film *Point Break* that features a group of mask-wearing bank robbers known as the "Ex-Presidents," with the one disguised as Nixon shouting from behind his mask "I am not a crook!" The idea was repeated as well in the 1986 comic book series *Batman: The Dark Knight Returns* when a whole gang of Nixons tries to rob a convenience store. There has also been at least one slasher, the no-budget *Horror House on Highway Five* from 1985, that chose to have its killer wear a Nixon mask, often bloodied.

These and other instances of the Nixon mask being worn after the resignation suggest a variety of significances that sometimes but not always evoke direct criticism of the fallen president. Often in these post-1974 examples an effect of the mask has been to make light of the nightmare of Watergate, transforming the frightening and dangerous Nixon into a primarily comic figure at which America can (finally) laugh. But the mask has always potentially meant something more, and particularly did so during the time Nixon was still in office. Returning to Garry Wills's discussion of the masks' debut at the 1969 inauguration, Wills provides an early, insightful attempt to explain their symbolic significance. "Kids in town to cause trouble wore crinkly white masks with that undeniable nose," he writes. "But Nixon's car sped past their jeering ranks, and, up on the reviewing stand, his face bunched in its instant toothed smile, so circumspect, so vulnerable. He had this in common with the kids: he wears a Nixon mask."[346] Wills judges Nixon as an entirely political creature, "the least 'authentic' man alive."[347] Such a conclusion necessarily helps make the Nixon mask signify something more than just a comic novelty, but a commentary on the absence of any substantive identity behind Nixon's actual face and appearance. For Wills, even Nixon's ever-present suit and tie connoted the president's lack of genuineness. "Nixon is the most doggedly dressed man imaginable," he says, always "creased and encased" no matter what the context. "Nixon does not exist outside his role, apart from politics: take his clothes off, he would be invisible."[348] As David Greenberg would later write in

Nixon's Shadow: The History of an Image, "the Nixon mask is powerful because it is redundant—the mask of a man who seemed to be wearing a mask already."[349]

Such an assessment uncannily resembles Hansen's understanding of Leatherface as having no identity beyond the mask itself. With Leatherface, his masks and their attendant identities have literally been "lifted" from other presumed victims, allowing him temporarily to inhabit the different roles they provide. (The Hitchhiker's question to Leatherface about whether he likes Sally's face has a particular significance—he is asking if Leatherface likes Sally's face to wear.) Such a practice can be read as a variation on the family's cannibalism, which appears primarily motivated by survival although also carries the symbolic significance of assimilation ("you are what you eat"). Murdering those who pass through their rural hellscape not only provides Leatherface and his family sustenance via the meat they sell to others and that they consume themselves, but the lives they are sacrificing also give meaning to their own. In this way, the family's outlook is an entirely pragmatic, unaffected by conventional morality or concern for the welfare of others whose existence entirely functions as a means for their own self-preservation.

It is a perspective that was shared by Richard Nixon the politician, who similarly wore a "mask" or image entirely composed of what others provided to him. "There is one Nixon only," explains Wills, "though there seem to be new ones all the time—he will try to be what people want." Adlai Stevenson once summed up such a view by declaring of Nixon, "This is a man of many masks. Who can say they have seen his real face?" Lacking his own philosophical core, Nixon consumed others' beliefs and values and made them his own, building an identity out of those whose support he needed to subsist. The result was a complex, self-contradictory creature perhaps best explained by John Ehrlichman when complaining in 1982 about how the public release of the secret White House tapes would undoubtedly produce misleading interpretations of the man he once described as a "great prism with a thousand facets."[350]

"The problem is that historians are going to grab an hour of tape when these tapes come out, and if you listen to a snippet of tape, you're going to form an impression of this man that's going to be wrong," said Ehrlichman. "So sometime, hopefully, there will be a historian or a committee of historians who will listen to all the tapes and go into all the archives and then come out and say Richard Nixon was the strangest collection, the strangest paradoxical combination of any man I ever heard of. And they'll be right."[351]

Nixon was multi-faceted. Leatherface is multi-faced. A human-face mask serves as a rich and suitable symbol for both.

No Sex (1:14:11)

Maureen Dean watches as her husband John testifies before the Senate Watergate Committee on June 25, 1972.

The dinner continues with the nature of the family's business receiving further clarification after another argument breaks out between the Hitchhiker and the Old Man.

Responding to Sally's pleas to the Old Man for help, the Hitchhiker points out to her that the Old Man is as powerless as Grandpa to provide her any assistance. "He's nothing, he's just the cook," says the Hitchhiker. "Shut up, you bitch hog," growls the Old Man, but the Hitchhiker refuses to back down. "Me and Leatherface do all the work, he don't like it," he tells her while turning to face the Old Man. "Ain't that right? You're just the cook!" he says defiantly, repeating how he and his brother "do all the work." The Old Man's response makes it sound as though he understands and on some level accepts what the Hitchhiker is saying, but he still feels the need to defend himself.

"I just can't take no pleasure in killing," says the Old Man, sounding a little deflated. He seems to imply that he is willing to contribute in other ways to the family's workload, but prefers leaving to others the distasteful if necessary task of killing. Again he oddly shifts gears to address Sally, appearing to chide her for raising objections to being made to uphold her responsibility (as the victim) in this morbid enterprise. "There's just some things you have to do," he says to Sally. "It don't mean you have to like it."

Sally tries again, this time with the Hitchhiker. (Indeed, Leatherface is the only family member she does not try to persuade.) "I'll do... I'll do anything you want," she says. Her implication is clear enough, but her offer yields no acknowledgement whatsoever from the Hitchhiker or anyone else. In fact, there is not even a reaction shot of the Hitchhiker, only a continued shot of Sally recognizing her words are being ignored as she dissolves into terror.

Like the family in *The Texas Chain Saw Massacre*, all of the primary co-conspirators in the Watergate break-ins and cover-up were men. A few women did appear among the scandal's supporting cast of characters, although for the most part they played subordinate roles. During the final days Pat, Julie, and Tricia Nixon might have urged the president not to resign, though aside from Julie's public defenses of her father the first family was largely on the periphery throughout. Nixon's longtime secretary Rose Mary Woods momentarily found the spotlight during controversy over the eighteen-and-a-half-minute gap, being made to reenact the infamous "Rose Mary stretch" at her desk to show unconvincingly how she might have accidentally erased part of the tape. John Mitchell's wife, Martha, became a media sensation thanks to her vibrant personality and habit of phoning reporters to talk openly about a variety of topics. After the resignation and her death from cancer in 1976, Nixon attempted to make Martha a kind of ultimate scapegoat for the scandal, blaming her as a distraction that led to her husband's failure to prevent Watergate. Even so, during the scandal she was generally considered an interested commentator and only of minor importance. E. Howard Hunt's wife, Dorothy, played a key role handling hush money payments to the seven arrested men before her tragic death in a plane crash in December 1972.

During John Dean's week-long appearance before the Senate Watergate Committee at the end of June 1973, his attractive, blond-haired wife Maureen became nationally known simply by sitting stoically behind him as he testified. There were other women who were important to the story, among them Judy Hoback, the bookkeeper for the Committee for the Re-Election of the President who provided key information to Bob Woodward and Carl Bernstein for their reporting on Watergate, and of course *Washington Post* publisher Katharine Graham whose paper ran the pair's stories. But from a public perspective, the Watergate story was a drama in which the players were almost always entirely men.

It was Maureen Dean who in her 1975 book *"Mo": A Woman's View of Watergate* argues how the subordinate status of the "Watergate wives" in the story was perhaps a contributing factor making it worse. "Had all the wives of the Watergate principals rebelled against being relegated to insignificant roles everywhere but within the home, their families, like ours, might have been spared the years of trauma, bitterness and lasting shame that none of us will ever shed," she writes. "The country, too, would have been infinitely better off."[352] Whether a female presence in the *Chain Saw* household might have similarly mitigated the horrors perpetrated there is a matter left to the viewer to contemplate.

There was one belated attempt to bring sex into the Watergate story via an outlandish theory first advanced by the authors of a 1991 book, *Silent Coup*, and later amplified by G. Gordon Liddy. The book tries to advance the fantastic argument that John Dean ordered the DNC break-in as a means to collect and hide evidence implicating (his then-girlfriend) Maureen's participation in a prostitution ring. The book earned notice thanks to its sensational thesis, but its claims have been roundly dismissed by serious historians as conspiratorial fantasy, ultimately resulting in defamation suits brought by Dean and a settlement.

In other words, during the time Watergate played out the scandal touched on practically every type of political intrigue imaginable *except* sexual intrigue. Comedian Mark Russell alludes to this omission on his 1973 LP *Mark Russell's Wild, Weird Wired World of Watergate* recorded live shortly after the Senate Watergate Hearings began. While attending one of the early days of testimony, Russell tells how he found himself sitting next to a reporter from the (London) *Times*. "Hey, what do you think of our little scandal here?" asked Russell. "Not much, really," said the reporter. "Oh, why not?" asked Russell.

"No sex, you see."

Eye Under a Microscope (1:14:47)

What follows is nearly a minute's worth of experimental cinema in the vein of Hooper's early short films, *Eggshells*, and the opening of

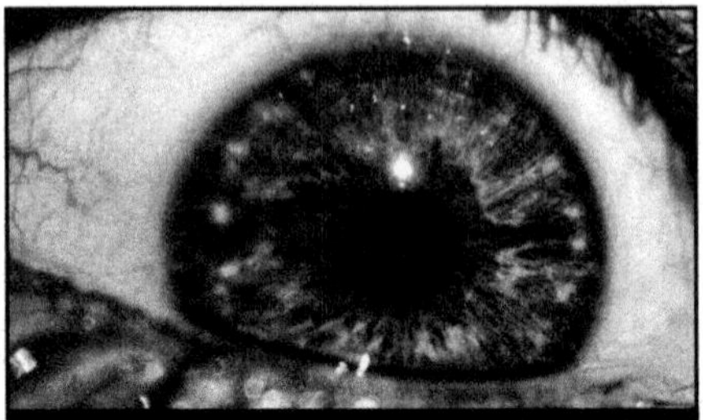
An extreme close-up of Sally's eye.

Chain Saw. As Sally continues to scream incessantly, a darkly ambient swirl of reverb and echo rises up on the soundtrack to challenge the noise she makes. Then comes a sequence of several extreme close-ups of Sally's open green eyes, wide with fright and moist with tears, cross-cut with shots of the Old Man giggling and the Hitchhiker mocking her cries. The shots of Sally's eyes begin with an alarmingly quick zoom producing the impression of the camera attacking her. After several shots of both bloodshot eyes, the attention shifts to just one of them with the edits successively bringing us close enough so the emerald globe, alternately viewed from the front and the side, nearly fills the screen.

Thematically the sequence parallels the rude handling of Sally by the Old Man and the uncomfortably close inspection of her by the Hitchhiker and Leatherface just before. It is as though the viewer, too, is invading her personal space. (Stories of rough treatment and injuries to the actress Marilyn Burns during the shooting of the dinner scene serve to further that impression.) Stylistically the sequence points directly back to the opening credits, with the slight tremors of the iris and pupil and the red veins popping in Sally's sclera recalling the almost abstract-seeming stock footage of solar flares. As with other self-referential moments in the film, the carefully constructed montage might serve to recall to us the film's artifice, *if* we were not so freaked out by it all. The fact is for most viewers the close-ups likely produce another specific effect, namely to eliminate whatever emotional distance they had managed to preserve up to this point, making it all but impossible to remain detached.

A couple of weeks before the dinner scene was filmed, Bob Haldeman began his testimony to the Senate Watergate Committee with an opening statement in which he defended the actions of the president, himself, and others during the cover-up. There Haldeman advanced a dubious thesis, suggesting that whatever peccadilloes he and others in the administration might have committed had been magnified unfairly by investigators, legislators, the media, and the American public. Such scrutiny, argued Haldeman, "spawned an unceasing barrage of charges and countercharges, allegations, innuendo, hearsay, rumor, speculation, [and] hypothesis" over the previous year that according to him caused the scandal to appear much greater and more significant than it actually was. "During this period with its intense concentration on every aspect of the Watergate and everything related to it, the sense of proportion regarding the time period under study becomes grossly distorted," he testified.

Haldeman then chose a curious analogy with which to further his point.

"In looking at the year 1972, it is important—especially now during these hearings—to try to keep a sense of perspective as to where things fit," he said. "The harmless eye of a fly viewed under a microscope can become a terrifying object in spite of its actual insignificance. Likewise, the Watergate viewed under the microscope of this hearing and the intensive coverage of all of its aspects can become a terrifying sight if one loses track of the perspective in which it should be viewed."[353]

It was a specious argument, one repeatedly forwarded by Nixon as well when complaining how investigations into Watergate unfairly invited extreme focus upon activities, conversations, and decisions that otherwise would have passed without notice. The problem, of course, was not the intensity of effort being exerted by investigators, but rather what those inquiries were uncovering. If the administration's actions had been as innocent they protested they had been, they would not have appeared so terrifying when viewed up close. Neither would the interstitial study of Sally's wild, staring eyes that interrupts the dinner scene be as potent if not for what it reveals, namely, Sally clearly "seeing" the utter hopelessness of her situation.

The Committee Meeting Will Come to Order (1:15:19)

Haldeman's analogy also implies a measure of self-pity with regard to his testifying before the Senate Watergate Committee insofar as he appears to be likening it to being placed under a microscope himself and mercilessly examined. That, too, resembles Sally's circumstance, as we are reminded of again when the montage of eye close-ups finally concludes and Leatherface once more approaches Sally, leaning over uncomfortably close to peer at her again while she screams.

The Hitchhiker continues his cheerful hooting. The Old Man likewise grins goofily as though taking a freakish delight in the proceedings before suddenly snapping out of his reverie and standing from the table. "No need to torture the poor girl," he declares, prompting the Hitchhiker once more to argue how the Old Man is "just the cook" and that he and Leatherface "will handle this," presumably in whatever fashion they choose. "Then get on with it," the Old Man mutters while turning away from the table. "I won't have this."

The dinner scene in *The Texas Chain Saw Massacre* seems much longer than it actually is. From the moment Sally regains consciousness at the table to her final escape, almost exactly seven minutes of screen time elapse. Yet Sally's suffering feels especially protracted, in part because with the other characters' murders there was a great deal less prologue, or none at all. In fact, when the Old Man turns from the table he mentions needing to "open up soon," an indication that several hours have passed since Sally was first brought into the house.

Another reason the scene feels drawn out is the fact that despite everyone sitting around a dinner table with food in front of them, there is very little eating happening. At the start of the scene the Hitchhiker nibbles a sausage and Leatherface briefly feeds something to Grandpa who chews silently at the far end of the table. But thereafter the food is entirely neglected, and while there is a plate with meat before Sally, she obviously is not meant to eat as her arms are tied to the chair. During the van ride the Hitchhiker had invited Sally and the others to dinner, and here he again recalls their excuse for not accepting the invitation when he tells her "We ain't in no hurry, because *you* ain't going no place!" However in actuality the "dinner" appears more like a strange bit of theater concocted for their amusement as though attempting to stage a domestic scene with female representation in a conventional family gathering. Sally is the guest of honor, in a way, although eventually it becomes clear the purpose of the meeting is to kill her and, ostensibly, carve her up and store her remains like the others in preparation for cooking and serving. In other words, she has not been invited to dine, but to be dined *upon*.

For Hooper at least, the dinner scene importantly provided a

The family gathers for dinner.

means to emphasize how the strange group of characters living in the white house were, in fact, a family, with their bickering at the table resembling what might be considered expected, normal behavior among a traditional "family unit." A dinner scene punctuates the 1986 sequel as well, and when asked in the DVD commentary about the significance of the scene's inclusion, Hooper there describes dinner as "central" to the "*Texas Chain Saw Massacre* family," adding in particular that in his experience dinner was where familial conflicts generally rose to the surface. "As I recall, as a young boy growing up in Texas, dinner time, especially if it's a large family occasion, was the place that you could get in more trouble with your family," explains Hooper. "I mean it's kind of where resentment and all kind of things spark up, out of dinner time. That is, in a world that I have observed."[354] It is certainly the case in *Chain Saw* that dining itself appears secondary to the airing of grievances during what might be understood as another episode in an ongoing negotiation of power between family members as they revisit and reconfirm their roles. Meanwhile in this case, perhaps adding an extra layer of tension between the family members, there is particular business to be settled upon and carried out concerning their guest. In that respect, the dinner is more like a meeting than a meal.

If the dinner scene seems long, the Senate Watergate Committee hearings genuinely were. As noted the committee was first formed in early February 1973. After three months' worth of negotiations and planning, the televised hearings finally began in May. Most days lasted five or six hours with some of the key witnesses testifying for multiple days. John Dean's appearance for a full week in late June was the longest, lasting nearly 30 hours total. Six months after the hearings began the last witness testified, and it would take another seven months before the committee submitted its final report in late

Senators Howard Baker (left) and Sam Ervin (right) consulting with one another during the Senate Watergate Committee hearings.

June 1974. Especially during the hearings' first phase from May to September when the committee trained its focus upon the break-ins at the Watergate and subsequent cover-up, television audiences were captivated. In a pre-cable world, the hearings helped create an impressive and at the time novel news "cycle" that utterly dominated the national political conversation just before, during, and after *Chain Saw* was filmed. Bombshells dropped frequently, and when Senator Howard Baker dramatically asked John Dean "What did the President know and when did he know it?"[355] there was a genuine sense that if and when an answer to the question came, the consequences would be historic.

The suspense increased with each passing day, and while millions watched from the edge of their seats, the ultimate purpose of the hearings was not immediately obvious. As legislators, the committee members were empowered to alter laws or write new ones, but could not make legally binding judgments or deliver punishments. As Baker noted on the hearings' first day and he and others would reiterate many times over the coming months, the committee's purpose was "not... to pass judgment on the guilt or innocence of anyone," but rather "to achieve a full discovery of all the facts that bear on the subject of this inquiry,"[356] namely, to investigate "illegal, improper, or unethical activities" during the 1972 presidential campaign. Witnesses might have sworn oaths to be truthful, but the hearing room was not a courtroom, and in fact a constant concern from many quarters was whether or not witnesses' testimony would interfere with their ability to receive fair trials. The report the committee eventually sent to the full senate would recommend legislative action designed to ensure future campaigns would be free of the illegalities and irregularities the hearings helped to expose. Meanwhile the delivering of indictments, the conducting of trials, the imposing of penalties and sentences, and the eventual launching of impeachment proceedings in the House were all for others to pursue. In retrospect it is clear the hearings were especially meaningful, directly influencing the investigations and ultimately helping to ensure Nixon's downfall. While they were playing out, however, their significance was not always so obvious.

For six months, the Senate Watergate Committee grilled witness after witness.

Senator Sam Ervin chaired the committee, and nearly every session began with him announcing through a thick Southern accent "the committee meeting will come to order." Ervin was a Democrat from North Carolina in his mid-seventies and nearing the end of a lengthy career in public service that included two decades in the senate. A grandfatherly figure with a penchant for referencing the Bible, Shakespeare, history, or folksy anecdotes in order to interject relevant maxims, Ervin often described himself self-deprecatingly as "just a country lawyer" although most understood it was unwise to underestimate either his intellectual prowess or his unshakable authority. His entertaining asides and colorful personality made him a national celebrity as the summer progressed, even inspiring a Sam Ervin Fan Club for admirers of "Uncle Sam." At times Ervin's management of the proceedings evoked a family gathering at which he functioned as a kind of respected patriarch. Even if significant strategic maneuvering was being separately pursued by the two political parties behind the scenes, during the hearings themselves partisanship largely appeared set aside. Ranking member Baker, a Republican from Tennessee, often expressed admiration for Ervin's wit and wisdom, with their collegiality occasionally calling to mind a curious sort of Southern hospitality being maintained in the midst of the surrounding D.C. maelstrom. A consistent level of professional etiquette was maintained with witnesses, too, even those such as Mitchell, Ehrlichman, and Haldeman who could be occasionally recalcitrant with their answers (or non-answers).

Was it all political theater? *Variety* described the hearings that summer as "the hottest daytime soap opera."[357] Indeed while much of the "show" was spontaneously generated, most of the participants often followed a kind of prearranged scenario that indicated just what would be discussed and revealed. As later recounted by Mark Lackritz, assistant chief counsel on the Senate Watergate Committee staff, constant negotiations with lawyers representing all interested parties as well as pre-testimony interviews of witnesses significantly shaped how their appearances would go. "There was an enormous gap between what the public saw and what was going on behind the scenes," explains Lackritz. "We were like the script writers of a soap opera."[358] The many cliffhangers and surprise revelations throughout the hearings well supported such a comparison. Then again, to pundits describing what was happening as an ongoing nightmare, the hearings were more horror show than melodrama.

Meanwhile, there was a lot of levity on display, too, with practically every day of testimony producing several humorous exchanges interspersed among the increasingly grave revelations. Sometimes, such as during Tony Ulasewicz's streetwise quips or when other low-ranking staffers earned chuckles from their forthright accounts of having misplaced their trust in their superiors, the mood was light-hearted. Occasionally the gallery's laughter seemed a reflexive response to something shocking, such as when John Mitchell joked about silencing Watergate conspirators by shooting them on the White House lawn. Often it was the absurdity of either the actions undertaken or the positions being maintained by administration officials that caused the greatest mirth among observers and sometimes even among the participants themselves. As the chairman, Ervin often had to bang his gavel in order to settle the audience down, and on multiple occasions he had to admonish the audience to restrain themselves during the proceedings. Once when Bob Haldeman's lawyer complained about audience laughter, Ervin acknowledged the problem yet could not resist sharing a lengthy aside that "the only thing that distinguishes humanity from a lofty attitude of disdain called a brute creation is the fact that man laughs and brute creation does not."[359] Unsurprisingly, that observation earned still *more* laughter. On another occasion a comment by Ervin about the secret tapes and the White House's resistance to sharing them similarly produced merriment among those in attendance. "The President says he has heard the tapes or some of them, and they sustain his position," said

Ervin. "But he says he's not going to let anybody else hear them for fear they might draw a different conclusion."[360] Again the audience roared, although all fell quiet when Ervin continued with an oration regarding the separation of powers and a thorough condemnation of Nixon's efforts to impede the investigation of criminal activities. If it were indeed theater, the Watergate hearings represented a curious hybrid, constantly alternating between uproarious comedy and somber tragedy.

The Senate Watergate Hearings were also like one long dinner scene, by turns breathtakingly sensational and tortuously repetitive as committee members and their counsel grilled one witness after another, feasting on their guests while going through each day's menu.

Viewers ate it up.

Killing With Honor (1:16:47)

"Why, old Grandpa's the best killer there ever was."

Ervin usually had to pound his gavel multiple times in order for the committee's work to continue. Still, that was much more efficient than Grandpa's handling of the sledge, despite the latter's vaunted reputation.

During Nixon's first term and the start of his second, his oft-repeated "peace with honor" justification for prolonging the war in Vietnam angered many who opposed America's continued engagement in Southeast Asia. Critics viewed the phrase as not just misleading but cynical, a rhetorical ploy to obscure the lethal and devastating reality of war. As Watergate unfolded, some revised Nixon's mantra to satirize the president's plight, creating a new slogan that appeared on bumper stickers, picket signs, and lapel pins: "Impeachment with Honor." As it turned out, the joking phrase prophetically described Nixon's ultimate fate, in a way, when he avoided the direct rebuke of impeachment by resigning instead ("I have impeached myself," Nixon would later say[361]). In his resignation speech Nixon characterized himself as having chosen to "put the interest of America first," coloring the act as selfless.[362] His "honor" was then further preserved, in a way, when his successor Gerald Ford granted him a "full, free, and absolute pardon" for all offenses committed while president, either known or to be discovered.[363]

After being told to "get on with it," the Hitchhiker has an idea. "I've been thinking about letting Grandpa have some fun," he says to the Old Man. "You always say he's the best." The Old Man confirms the assessment. "He's the best, all right," he says, and the Hitchhiker responds excitedly. "Hey Grandpa!" he yells. "We gonna let you have this one!"

The Hitchhiker enters the kitchen then returns carrying the same wide metal bucket earlier positioned beneath Pam when hanging on the meat hook, placed so as to catch the blood. He sets the bucket next to Grandpa's chair, then unties Sally and with difficulty forces her to the other end of the table where he pushes her to knees and holds her head over the bucket. Meanwhile the Old Man delivers a brief monologue commemorating Grandpa's legendary skills as demonstrated at the slaughterhouse years ago. "Now you... you just hush," he says to Sally. "It won't hurt none. Why, old Grandpa's the best killer there ever was. Why, it never took more than one lick, they say. Why, he did 60 in five minutes once. They say he could've done more if the hook and pull gang coulda gotten the beeves [the cows] out of the way faster. Now, now don't you cry none. Old Grandpa's the best. It won't hurt a bit."

Affecting a Southern oratory style not unlike the one employed by Ervin in the hearings, the Old Man interestingly uses "why" as an interjection to begin three straight sentences, the only instances of anyone doing so in the entire film. The testimonial calls to mind the Hitchhiker's earlier, less garrulous espousal of "the old way," in this case presenting "Old Grandpa" as the foremost exemplar of slaughterhouse efficiency. The review of Grandpa's résumé is weirdly intended to persuade Sally to accept her fate, as though dying at the hands of "the best killer there ever was" confers a kind of honor upon her. The speech also promises her death will be swift and painless, a patently obvious lie as big as those told about Vietnam or Watergate.

The subsequent action is shown via rapid cutting, including an overhead shot that contains the Hitchhiker holding Sally on the right and Leatherface standing behind Grandpa's chair on the left. Leatherface repeatedly places the sledgehammer in Grandpa's hand in order for him to strike Sally with it, though he lacks the strength even to hold it. He drops it eight times, sometimes in his lap, sometimes on the floor, and sometimes in the bucket. At least once Leatherface guides the hammer well enough for it to connect with Sally's head as it falls, and blood is shown at the base of her skull. But it is obvious that despite encouragement from the Hitchhiker ("Hit that bitch!") and the Old Man ("Get her, get her Grandpa!") that their revered slaughterhouse warrior cannot execute the task. It is a chaotic, farcical scene, topping even the Hitchhiker's van ride with its dizzying mixture of horror and (extremely dark) comedy.

The Hitchhiker finally grows impatient and for a moment loosens his hold on Sally in order to grab the hammer himself—a crucial mistake, and as it will turn out for the Hitchhiker, a fatal one. Still screaming and waving her arms wildly, Sally seizes the opportunity to break away and races out of the dining room toward the front of the house. Without hesitation she crashes through the front window in much the same way she did earlier when escaping Leatherface.

The repetition again calls to mind the story's claustrophobic circularity. It also inspires doubt that Sally has really and truly escaped.

You Have to Laugh (1:21:33)

Surviving the nightmare, though much worse for wear.

The final minutes of *The Texas Chain Saw Massacre* are bonkers, one of the most inspired and genuinely chest-tightening action sequences in horror film history.

After breaking through the window, Sally lands on all fours on the ground outside, shattered glass surrounding her. It is light outside, a disorienting though welcome change after the oppressively dark dinner scene. The camera pans around in front of Sally to reveal her bloodied face and terrified look. Like us, she also seems momentarily confused by the daylight. There is a cut to a wide angle, a nearly extreme long shot that shows the contrast between her small form and the large, imposing white house behind her as she struggles to stand and begins to limp away. The generator can be heard faintly in the distance, but its noise is abruptly drowned out by the much louder sound of the chainsaw starting. The Hitchhiker emerges from the house to chase Sally, and a long, moving shot shows him quickly close the gap as they both run down the driveway. Leatherface follows him out of the house, running while holding the whirring chainsaw before him with both hands. The Hitchhiker has his knife out again and as he reaches Sally he starts swiping with it wildly. Her torn shirt exposes her back, and the pattern of her screams indicates he is connecting.

As they reach the road the Hitchhiker appears to have grabbed Sally's shirt while he continues his fitful stabbing. A red eighteen-wheeler suddenly bears down upon on them, the same color as the one from the start of the film that caused Franklin to spill down the hill. While the earlier truck looked to be carrying gravel, this one is clearly designed to transport cattle (a seemingly deliberate irony). The truck horn blares, causing the Hitchhiker to look up and allowing Sally to break free, and in a flash the front of truck smacks the Hitchhiker down onto the asphalt. His body is violently crushed beneath the vehicle's multiple sets of wheels, killing him instantly.

Sally, her face now blood-soaked, screams again. The driver emerges, an overweight African American man with a beard and dirty yellow t-shirt. The first non-white character in the film, his appearance suggests Sally has at last found a path leading her outside of the family's insular (and inbred?) world. Soon, however, Leatherface swings out from the truck's rear and both the driver and Sally scramble back into the cab, closing the door just before Leatherface lunges at it with his saw. He marks up the door with his chainsaw in a strangely deliberate fashion that recalls the Hitchhiker's smearing of blood on the side the van as well as his own destruction of the front door during the earlier chase of Sally. Meanwhile Sally and the driver exit through the passenger's side, the driver grabbing a monkey wrench from the floorboard as he does. Leatherface races around the front of the truck and down the other side after them. A few seconds later the driver spins around and from a short distance throws the wrench at Leatherface, hitting him squarely on the forehead. Leatherface falls and drops the running chainsaw onto his leg, and we see it start to cut through his pants and into his leg before he cries out and pulls it away.

As Sally and the driver continue to run away from the eighteen-wheeler and Leatherface, a light blue Chevrolet pickup truck appears coming from the other direction. Sally stumbles out into the middle of the road and waves her arms for it to stop, forcing the driver to swerve to miss her. Once beyond her, he slams the brakes, then quickly spins the truck around to face the opposite direction toward Sally and Leatherface before the engine stalls. The driver of the eighteen-wheeler continues to run up the highway, but Sally makes a beeline toward the pickup. With a now somewhat hobbled Leatherface nearing once again and the pickup truck driver struggling to restart the engine, shots rapidly alternate between long, medium, and close as Sally tries and fails twice to pull herself up and into the back of the truck. Finally on the third attempt she succeeds, throwing herself over the side just as Leatherface arrives to miss hitting her with the chainsaw. Leatherface gives chase for a short distance until they pull away, still swinging the chainsaw back and forth while Sally screams "Go!" and the driver floors it, on a couple of occasions turning back over his right shoulder to look through the back window himself.

We stay with Sally in the back of the truck for a few seconds as she continues to look back at Leatherface, her frantic screams unmistakably changing into uncontrollable, harrowing laughter. A final shot shows Leatherface crazily whipping the chainsaw around and up over his head in the foreground as the sun with which the story began appears over the horizon behind him. The screen goes black.

Uncertainty over Sally's fate and the final answer to the question "Who will survive and what will be left of them?" considerably ramps up the tension during the final sequence. So does uncertainty over what the filmmakers might be capable of, with any confidence in their self-restraint having been lost well before, most likely the moment Pam is dropped on the meat hook. As director John Landis once observed while contrasting the films of Alfred Hitchcock with ones like *Chain Saw*, when experiencing suspense in a Hitchcock film, the knowledge of being "in the hands of a master" creates what he calls a "comfortable scary feeling" that generally prevents the viewer from feeling *too* vulnerable or uneasy. Meanwhile when watching *Chain Saw*, the viewer does not have such confidence, and instead suspects "the people making the movie are untrustworthy.... You're *not* the hands of a master. You're in the hands of a *maniac*!"[364]

Having no assurance about how things might end adds to the

scene's realism as well, even though the remarkable variety of angles and shot types, rapid cuts, and expertly timed edits again demonstrate how cleverly information being conveyed onscreen has been manipulated by the filmmakers. (Speaking of Hitchcock, with 75 separate shots in a little over three minutes, the final sequence's meticulous construction rivals that of the *Psycho* shower scene.) So, too, do the several callbacks—a return to the highway (and to roadkill, in way), another red eighteen-wheeler, another idiosyncratic marking of a vehicle, the sun's reprise—provide a final reminder of the film's artistry while also reaffirming the "nightmare syntax" of its circular narrative. Even Leatherface's dance resembles the film's similarly lit opening shot of the corpses posed in the cemetery, bookending *Chain Saw* with another image both aesthetically alluring and menacingly macabre.

Following Nixon's resignation in August and his pardon in September, *The Texas Chain Saw Massacre*'s October 1974 premiere was timed in such a way that when viewed as political satire, the parting message delivered by its audacious finale was uncannily apt. Like Sally, America had been thoroughly traumatized, having survived its "long national nightmare" though only barely and much worse for wear. She looks back bloodied and bruised, watching Leatherface pirouetting in the middle of the highway, seemingly unconcerned about his dead brother and swinging his chainsaw as though it were a dancing partner. When America looked back on what it had endured, it saw something similarly disturbing.

"The monster goes unpunished," explains Gunnar Hansen, pinpointing the last bit of dread *Chain Saw* leaves us to contemplate. "He is still there capable of returning. The normality, the predictability of the world is gone. There is no punishment. There is no relief of suffering. There is no justice. There is no order. Without justice and order, how can we have meaning? It is all nothing. This is the real horror."[365] Hansen is referring to the character he portrayed in *Chain Saw*. But he also describes the disquieting uncertainty a departing Nixon left in his wake.

A myth of Watergate, articulated immediately afterwards and often still perpetuated, is that Nixon being forced to leave office proved the American government's system of checks and balances had functioned as intended. As such, Watergate's abrupt conclusion was championed by some as a first step toward a return to those ideals Hansen lists and that a well-run democracy typically promises its citizens—normality, predictability, justice, order, meaning. "Our Constitution works," declared Gerald Ford in his first remarks upon assuming the presidency. "Our great republic is a government of laws and not men. Here the people rule."[366] Narrowly speaking and in a technical sense, Ford was right. Nixon's downfall was directly facilitated by the considerable efforts of the legislative and judicial branches whose work was importantly assisted by a free press. But if it were not for the leakers, the flippers, and especially the multiple acts of self-sabotage committed by Nixon and his men, the most significant being the introduction of a secret taping system that ultimately supplied objective evidence of their corrupt and criminal words and deeds, it is unlikely the Watergate scandal would have ended as it did.

In the film, Sally's escape and survival depends upon her tormentors' shortcomings. If not for the Old Man's impotency, Grandpa's infirmity, the Hitchhiker's impatience, and Leatherface's inelegance, as well as the family's general dysfunction as collaborators (or co-conspirators), she would not have survived. America likewise needed Nixon and his men to slip up, else there would have been no check, really, on Watergate or on other White House horrors.

Then came the pardon, and the soundness of the system was thrown into question once more. Following Ford's decision, many agreed with the *New York Times* that the act dealt "a body blow" both to Nixon's credibility and to "the public's reviving confidence in the integrity of its Government."[367] The House responded by passing multiple resolutions requiring the White House to provide information regarding how the decision to pardon was made. In fact before Congress would allow Ford's nomination of his own vice president, Nelson Rockefeller, to go forward, Ford himself had to appear before a House subcommittee to answer questions about the "very dark suspicions that have been created in the public's mind" (as one representative put it) and deny any pre-resignation deal had been made.[368] The Senate also passed a resolution declaring its opposition to any further Watergate-related pardons until after defendants were tried and found guilty (and had run through all appeals). The American Bar Association issued a declaration calling the pardon unwarranted. Even Ford's own Press Secretary Jerry terHorst resigned in protest after just one month on the job. Over the decades that followed opinions would evolve regarding the pardon, with Ford's subsequent loss in the 1976 presidential election making the decision appear to some selfless in retrospect, a courageous placing of national interests ahead of personal political ambitions. (Ford would even later receive the John F. Kennedy Profile in Courage award for the pardon.) At the time, however, many viewed Ford's action in precisely the opposite manner, with the ultimate failure of Congress to investigate satisfactorily how the pardon came about casting serious doubt on both Ford and the legitimacy of the American government. "Gerald Ford, by putting self-interest and political loyalty to a benefactor above his duty, did not give the American legal system a chance to work," judged reporter and historian Seymour Hersh. "The transfer of power in August of 1974 was not a triumph of democracy."[369]

It *was* unsettling. The monster went unpunished.

On the surface, Sally's laughter matches our own sense of relief. Like her, we have survived *The Texas Chain Saw Massacre*. It appears to escape from her involuntarily, as though to signal a loss of control or perhaps even sanity. It also parallels Leatherface's odd and exuberant ballet, an act that hardly connotes defeat but rather a strange kind of rejoicing.

In a deeper sense, her laughter reflects the film's satirical purpose to respond to a national crisis with dark humor delivered via a scary movie. Arthur Dudden, quoted earlier characterizing Watergate satire as commonly "violent and destructive" in its withering ridicule of Nixon, speculates further why America so often responded to the scandal and crisis with humor. As he explains, such a response can be understood as a way of coping, a kind of survival strategy. Humor helps to minimize and/or to avoid dealing directly with a highly unpleasant, overwhelmingly stressful, even despairing reality. Indeed sometimes in the face of unrelenting trauma, there seems to be no other available response. As Dudden says, "The people's laughter expressed their defense against the national shame."[370] When facing a situation as grim and absurd as the one created by Watergate, sometimes you have to laugh.

Completed before Nixon stepped down and first shown to audiences shortly afterwards, *The Texas Chain Saw Massacre*'s lack of resolution directly reflected the ongoing nightmarish open-endedness of

Watergate. The film is not an allegory of Watergate, but its many cues and suggestions unmistakably invite comparisons between the outrageous story that plays out on the screen to the outrageous one that played out in the White House and the country during the time the film was conceived, written, shot, produced, and distributed to its first audiences.

Several of these cues encourage the identification of Watergate's central villain, Richard Nixon, with *Chain Saw*'s most destructive and arguably most enigmatic character whose name supplied the film's working title, Leatherface. Hooper and Henkel created their mask-wearing killer first and foremost to frighten, but also as a means to criticize by way of exaggeration the damage being inflicted upon the country by a corrupt president. Just as more obvious parodies and caricatures of Nixon from comedians and satirists presented outlandish versions of the president in order to communicate disapproval of him, so, too, was Leatherface and the story in which he appears a means to register the same sort of discontent. In such cases the invented "Nixon" character might nominally have represented its real-life counterpart, but also existed as a kind of fictional combatant designed to fight the real Nixon. In the same way, those who wore Nixon masks were not supporting or endeavoring to emulate the president. They were attacking him.

So was Leatherface, right through to that last upward swipe of his chainsaw just before the screen turns dark.

★ ★ ★ ★ ★

The monster goes unpunished.

Notes

Epigraphs

1 Dryden, iii.
2 Hooper *et al.*, Audio Commentary, *The Texas Chain Saw Massacre.*

Introduction

3 Ford, "Remarks on Taking the Oath of Office."
4 Ford, *A Time to Heal*, 25.
5 United States Senate, Select Committee on Presidential Campaign Activities of 1972, vol. 1, bk. 3, 1309. Dean memo (Exhibit No. 34–45) dated 12 Apr. 1973.
6 Nixon, *RN*, 633.
7 *Ibid.*, 949.
8 *Ibid.*, 1088.
9 Halberstam, 809.
10 Nixon, *RN,* 783.
11 Kristol, 20.
12 Riesel, "Political Alliance," 4; Thompson, Hunter S., "Fear and Loathing in the White House," 262; White, William S., 4.
13 *Masters of Horror*, Bloom, Zwilling.
14 Jaworzyn, 28, 30.
15 Macor, 20.
16 West, 9.
17 Bloom.
18 *Masters of Horror.*
19 Hansen, 100.
20 Baumgarten.
21 Zinoman, 134.
22 *Ibid.*
23 Rev. of *Night of the Living Dead*, *Variety*, 6.
24 Canby, 59.
25 Ebert, "Just Another Horror Movie," C1.
26 Gross, 98.
27 Pym, 258.
28 Koch, 108, 110.
29 Ebert, Rev. of *The Texas Chain Saw Massacre.*
30 Hoberman and Rosenbaum, 112.
31 Berrigan, 159.
32 Malcolm, 10.
33 Reed, 23.
34 Andrews, 3; Walker qtd. in Phelps, 84.
35 Wood, Robin, 211.
36 Wood, Robin, 210–213.
37 Wood, Robin, 211.
38 Phipps.
39 Hooper *et al.*, Audio Commentary, *The Texas Chain Saw Massacre.*
40 Farley and Knoedelseder Jr., "Real," Calendar 3.
41 Phelps, 84.
42 *The American Nightmare.*
43 *Texas Chain Saw Massacre: The Shocking Truth.*
44 Jaworzyn, 39.
45 *Ibid.*, 38.
46 Hansen, 224.
47 Wood, Robin, 214.
48 *Ibid.*
49 *Ibid.*
50 Lanza, 121–43.
51 "The de Antonio Legacy (Part

2)."
52 *Hail*, "History."
53 Dudden, 65.
54 Buchwald, "What to Say," 155–7.
55 "Watergate Brings Novelty Items."
56 Nevin, George, 23.
57 Wax, 24–25.
58 The "Secret Empire" story arc by Steve Englehart and Mike Friedrich (writers) and Sal Buscema (artist) appeared in *Captain America*, issues #169–#175 (Jan.–Jul. 1974).
59 "Show Business: Watergate Wit."
60 Sobel, 1; "Billboard's Top Single Picks: Chartalk," 61.
61 Inside Track," 66; Ritter, 12.
62 Dryden, lii.
63 Addison.
64 Klosterman.
65 *The American Nightmare*.
66 Ford, "Remarks on Signing a Proclamation."

Caught in the Vortex (0:00)

67 Farley and Knoedelseder Jr., "Real," Calendar 4.
68 *Ibid.*
69 Bloom.
70 Farley and Knoedelseder Jr., "Real," Calendar 4.
71 Jaworzyn, 45, 74; Martin, 39.
72 Farley and Knoedelseder Jr., "Real," Calendar 2.
73 *Ibid.*
74 Bloom.
75 Hansen, 185–86.
76 Farley and Knoedelseder Jr., "Real," Calendar 6.
77 *Texas Chain Saw Massacre: The Shocking Truth*.
78 Farley and Knoedelseder Jr., "Tangled," Calendar 3.
79 "Two Big Names," 14.
80 Abramson, 1. "Former Chairman," 10.
81 Riesel, "Dead man's tales," 4.
82 Bernstein and Woodward, *All the President's Men,* 73–74.

Writing Partners (0:00)

83 Jaworzyn, 27.
84 Hooper *et al.*, Audio Commentary, *The Texas Chain Saw Massacre*; Jaworzyn, 31.
85 Macor, 20.
86 Bernstein and Woodward, *All the President's Men*, 19.
87 Szulc, 24.
88 Nixon, "The President's News Conference," 22 Jun. 1972.
89 Bernstein and Woodward, "GOP Security Aide," 1.
90 Semple Jr., "Mitchell Quits Post," 1.
91 Bernstein and Woodward, "Bug Suspect," 1.
92 Evans and Novak, 4.
93 Nixon, "The President's News Conference," 5 Oct. 1972.
94 Crouse, 299.
95 Gallup, Inc., "Presidential Approval Ratings."
96 "Still No Real Answers," 213.
97 "Remarks by Principals," 12.
98 Bernstein and Woodward, *All the President's Men*, 22.
99 Hooper *et al.*, Audio Commentary, *The Texas Chain Saw Massacre.*

"What Happened Is True." That Was a Lie (0:14)

100 Hooper *et al.*, Audio Commentary, *The Texas Chain Saw Massacre*.
101 Jaworzyn, 91.
102 Hansen, 209–13.

103 Bowen, 16.

One of the Most Bizarre Crimes in the Annals of American History (0:48)

104 Nixon, Conversation No. 739–4.
105 *Ibid.*, "The President's News Conference," 29 Aug. 1972.
106 *Ibid.*, "Remarks Announcing Procedures," 17 Apr. 1973.
107 Ziegler qtd. in Apple Jr., 1; Gray qtd. in United States Senate, Select Committee on Presidential Campaign Activities of 1972, vol. 1, bk. 9, 3488. Gray testimony 6 Aug. 1973
108 Nixon, "Address," 30 Apr. 1973.
109 Ripley, 1, 20.
110 Nixon, "Address," 15 Aug. 1973.
111 *Ibid.*, "Address," 29 Apr. 1974.
112 *Ibid.*, Conversation No. 741–2.
113 *Ibid.*, *RN*, 629.
114 Ambrose, "Why Didn't Nixon Burn the Tapes," 1776.

Another Saturday Night Massacre (1:03)

115 Hansen, 33.
116 Jaworzyn, 52.
117 *The Texas Chain Saw Massacre: A Family Portrait*.
118 Bloom.
119 Macor, 33–34.
120 Jaworzyn, 91.
121 Macor, 33–34.
122 Hansen, 175–76.
123 Macor, 33.
124 Henkel and Hooper, 26.
125 Safire, 643–44.
126 Broder, qtd. in Wang.
127 Wang.
128 Worland, 211.
129 Hooper and Black, Audio Commentary, *Eggshells*.
130 Zwilling.
131 Nevin, David, 24–31.
132 Jaworzyn, 92.
133 Macor, 34.

Flash Photography in the Dark (1:26)

134 Baumgarten.
135 Hansen, 170, Pereira.
136 Pereira.
137 Hooper *et al.*, Audio Commentary, *The Texas Chain Saw Massacre*.
138 United States Senate, Select Committee on Presidential Campaign Activities of 1972, vol. 1, bk. 1, 106. Leeper testimony 17 May 1973.
139 Liddy, 320–21.
140 *Ibid.*, 331.

One of a Series of Indictments (2:16)

141 *The World This Week*.
142 Weaver Jr., 1, 13.

A Sinister Force (4:01)

143 Baumgarten.
144 Knipp et al.
145 "Immense Solar Flares."
146 Jaworzyn, 76, 256.
147 Bernstein and Woodward, *The Final Days*, 94–95.
148 The National Archives and Records Administration, 9.
149 Haig.
150 Bernstein and Woodward, *The*

Final Days, 96.

No Explanation for the Attack (4:47)

151 Wood, Jennifer M.

How to Read Roadkill (4:51)

152 *Texas Chain Saw Massacre: The Shocking Truth*.
153 Hooper *et al.*, Audio Commentary, *The Texas Chain Saw Massacre*.
154 For instance, see Tongeren.
155 Zitz, D2.
156 Franks, 34.

It's All Downhill From Here (6:16)

157 Wood, Robin, 210.
158 Thompson, Hunter S., "Fear and Loathing in the Bunker," 19.

Saturn in Retrograde (6:43)

159 Jaworzyn. 34.
160 Smallwood, 20–24.
161 Anderson and Blumenthal, 12.
162 Tyler, 7.
163 *Ibid.*
164 Nixon, Conversation No. 490–17.
165 Nixon, Conversation No. 783–25.
166 Nixon, Conversation No. 784–7.
167 Naftali, 59–61.

Expletive Deleted (7:28)

168 Russo, 252.
169 "Sen. Scott Shocked," 1.
170 Aikman, 217.
171 "Dean Reportedly Finds Deletions in Transcripts," 29.
172 *The White House Transcripts*, 155; Nixon, Conversation No. 886–8; Transcript of a Recording of a Meeting, 59.
173 Ambrose, *Nixon: Volume Three*, 328–29.
174 *The White House Transcripts*, 145; Nixon, Conversation No. 886–8; Transcript of a Recording of a Meeting, 30.
175 Ambrose, *Nixon: Volume Three*, 329.

Please Change the Subject (9:57)

176 "Per Capita Consumption of Poultry and Livestock, 1960 to Forecast 2020, in Pounds."
177 "U.S. Cattle Inventory Per Year."
178 Nixon, "Radio Address: 'A Salute to Agriculture.'"
179 Lappé, *Diet for a Small Planet*, 42.
180 *Ibid.*, *Diet for a Small Planet: Twentieth Anniversary Edition*, 13.
181 Nixon, "Remarks of Vice President Nixon."
182 Haller and Aronson, 84–85.
183 *Ibid.*, 130–31.

The CREEPs (10:27)

184 West, 9.
185 United States Senate, Select Committee on Presidential Campaign Activities of 1972, vol. 1, bk. 6, 2263. Ulasweicz testimony 18 Jul. 1973.

186 United States Senate, Select Committee on Presidential Campaign Activities of 1972, vol. 1, bk. 6, 2237. Ulasweicz testimony 18 Jul. 1973.
187 *Ibid.*, vol. 1, bk. 3, 915.

The Southern Strategy (10:52)

188 *Texas Chain Saw Massacre: The Shocking Truth.*
189 *Ibid.*
190 *Ibid.*
191 Dent, 212.

The Old Way and the New Way (11:37)

192 U.S. Bureau of Labor Statistics, Labor Force Statistics.
193 U.S. Bureau of Labor Statistics, United States Inflation Rate by Year.
194 Urquhart and Hewson, 4.
195 Schlosser, 41.
196 United States Senate, Hearing Before the Committee on Foreign Relations, 79.
197 Gallup, Inc., "Election Polls."
198 Thompson, Bob, W16.
199 "She Has Nightmares."
200 Schlesinger, 128–30, 237–40, 250–52.

Law and Order (17:42)

201 Nixon, "Remarks." Most transcripts (including one prepared by Nixon's staff) erroneously give the line as "you won't have Nixon to kick around anymore" even though he actually said "don't."
202 White, *Theodore S.*, 47.
203 CBS News.
204 Witcover, 165.
205 Cronkite, *CBS Evening News.*
206 *Ibid., A Reporter's Life*, 278.
207 White, 48.
208 McGinniss, 181–83.
209 *Ibid.*, 247.
210 *Ibid.*, 16–17.
211 Jamieson, 245–47.
212 Nixon, "The President's News Conference," 15 Mar. 1973.
213 Semple Jr., "Nixon Meets Heads," 1.
214 Naughton, *Theodore S.*, 12.
215 Nixon, "Question-and-Answer Session," 17 Nov. 1973.
216 Kilpatrick, A1.

The Events of the World Are Not Doing Much, Either, to Cheer One Up (18:09)

217 Oakley, A6; Bacon, A4; Lerner, 4.
218 Front page headlines from *The New York Times*, 18 Aug. 1973.

American Astrology (18:18)

219 Hendler, 317.
220 Campion, 75–76.
221 "The Exorcist Letter."

The Old Man (19:19)

222 Hansen, 42.
223 Nixon, "Remarks on Departure."
224 Buchanan, 314.

No Gas (19:39)

225 Jacobs.
226 Bird, 77.

YOU THINK YOU COULD DO THAT TO YOURSELF? (22:05)

227 Nixon, Interview with Frank Gannon, 8 Apr. 1983.
228 "Origin and Distribution," 1.
229 *The Nixon Interviews with David Frost*, "War at Home and Abroad."
230 Bernstein and Woodward, *All the President's Men*, 356–57.
231 Rosenbaum, "Hunt Says," 28.
232 United States Senate, Select Committee on Presidential Campaign Activities of 1972, vol. 1, bk. 4, 1689. Dean memo (Exhibit No. 48) dated 16 Aug. 1971.
233 House of Representatives, Hearings Before the Committee on the Judiciary House of Representatives, bk. 3, 453. Colson testimony 16 Jul. 1974.
234 United States Senate, Select Committee on Presidential Campaign Activities of 1972, vol. 1, bk. 3, 915. Dean testimony 25 Jun. 1973.
235 United States Senate, Select Committee on Presidential Campaign Activities of 1972, vol. 1, bk. 4, 1610. Mitchell testimony 10 Jul. 1973.
236 United States Senate, Select Committee on Presidential Campaign Activities of 1972, vol. 1, bk. 5, 1837. Mitchell testimony 11 Jul. 1973.
237 United States Senate, Select Committee on Presidential Campaign Activities of 1972, vol. 1, bk. 3, 933. Dean testimony 25 Jun. 1973.
238 United States Senate, Select Committee on Presidential Campaign Activities of 1972, vol. 1, bk. 2, 791–92. Magruder testimony 14 Jun. 1973.
239 Liddy, 405.
240 Dean, *Blind Ambition*, 71–72.
241 Kristol, 20.

LOOKS LIKE HE WAS TRYING TO WRITE SOMETHING (23:40)

242 Henkel and Hooper, 56.
243 Qtd. in "The Nation: Pentagram Papers," 18.
244 Henkel and Hooper, 89.

MESSING AROUND AN OLD HOUSE (26:03)

245 Henkel and Hooper, 43.

UNCOVERING A PATTERN (32:19)

246 Henkel and Hooper, 46.
247 *Ibid.*, 50; Hooper *et al.*, Audio Commentary, *The Texas Chain Saw Massacre*.
248 Baumgarten; Zinoman, 134.
249 Ambrose, *Nixon: Volume Three*, 138.

KILLER IN A TIE (35:24)

250 Rinzler, 69.
251 "To Save the Presidency," 260.
252 Dean, *Blind Ambition*, 281.
253 Feeney, 14, 347.
254 Silverstein, 105, 116–17.
255 Crist, 71.
256 Buchwald, "Watergate," 5.
257 Cook, 116–17.
258 Kermode.
259 Hansen, 53.
260 Greene, 29.

THE WHITE HOUSE HORRORS (35:51)

261 Henkel and Hooper, 46.
262 'White House Horrors,' 34.
263 United States Senate, Select Committee on Presidential Campaign Activities of 1972, vol. 1, bk. 4, 1653. Mitchell testimony 10 Jul. 1973.

THE MADMAN THEORY (37:43)

264 Bernstein and Woodward, *The Final Days*, 395.
265 Gwertzman, 1.
266 Bernstein and Woodward, *The Final Days*, 403.
267 Morgan, 13.
268 Haldeman and DiMona, 83.
269 United States Senate, Select Committee on Presidential Campaign Activities of 1972, vol. 1, bk. 6, 2599–2600. Ehrlichman testimony 25 Jul. 1973.
270 Roth, 185–86.
271 Whitfield, 122.
272 Thompson, Hunter S., "He Was a Crook," 42.

THE HOOK (39:30)

273 Jaworzyn, 73.
274 Hansen, 75.
275 Peary, 347.
276 Lanza, 209.
277 Hansen, 177.
278 Bloom.

HEARING IS BELIEVING (39:39)

279 Willis, 393.
280 Nixon, Conversations No. 741–2, 779–2, and No. 886–8.
281 Rosenthal, "The chief electronic witness," 5.

EVERYTHING MEANS SOMETHING, I GUESS (42:45)

282 Henkel and Hooper, 56.

A THEORY OF CONTAINMENT (46:46)

283 Nixon, Conversation No. 886–8.
284 Armstrong, SR3.
285 Nixon, Conversation No. 886–8. Dean outlines the extent to which Nixon feigned ignorance and surprise during this conversation in *The Nixon Defense*, 308–36.
286 Hansen, 56.

THE NIXON SHOCK (52:11)

287 Ambrose, *Nixon: The Education of a Politician*, 68.
288 Nixon, Interview with Frank Gannon, 9 Feb. 1983.
289 Bullock, 330.
290 *Ibid.*, 337.
291 Nixon, *In the Arena*, 254.
292 Ronan, 29.
293 Morgan, 153–54.

WHO WILL SURVIVE AND WHAT WILL BE LEFT OF THEM? (58:35)

294 *First Line Report*.
295 Clover, 35–36.

A LARGE AND WELL-ORGANIZED

West Coast Jewel Theft Ring (1:00:06)

296 Davie, 25.
297 Bernstein and Woodward, *All the President's Men*, 131.
298 Liddy, 271–76.

The Instinct to Cover Up (1:02:07)

299 Lanza, 122–23.
300 United States Senate, Select Committee on Presidential Campaign Activities of 1972, vol. 1, bk. 3, 1091. Dean testimony 26 Jun. 1973.

This Little Moment About Capitalism (1:03:03)

301 Hooper *et al.*, Audio Commentary, *The Texas Chain Saw Massacre*.
302 U.S. Bureau of Labor Statistics, Price Inflation for Electricity Since 1913.
303 Smith, 55.

You Damn Fool, You Almost Got Caught (1:05:04)

304 Hooper *et al.*, Audio Commentary, *The Texas Chain Saw Massacre*.
305 Nixon, Conversation No. 741–2.
306 *Ibid.*
307 Haldeman, 474–75.
308 Nixon, Conversation No. 741–10.
309 *Ibid.*, Conversation No. 741–2.

Look What Your Brother Did to the Door! (1:06:22)

310 Emery, 67–70.

Conspiracy (1:06:59)

311 Henkel and Hooper, 86–87.

Grandpa (1:10:51)

312 Henkel and Hooper, 90.
313 Henkel and Hooper, 89.
314 Nixon, *Six Crises*, 76.
315 McGinniss, 132.
316 Nixon, "Address Accepting the Presidential Nomination."
317 *Ibid.*, "Eulogy."

Leatherface and the Nixon Mask (1:13:04)

318 Henkel and Hooper, 92.
319 Hansen, 53–54.
320 Henkel and Hooper, 90.
321 Hansen, 54.
322 *Ibid.*
323 Mulleavy, 138.
324 Hansen, 54–55.
325 Glynn, C7.
326 National Commission, 94.
327 Franklin, 21.
328 Gibbs and Duffy, 173 ("macabre"); Light, 1 ("ghost-like," "haunting").
329 "Protestors Say," 3.
330 Wills, 403.
331 "President Sees Parade," A6.
332 "NYC Observes Moratorium," 2.
333 "Bandit Wears Nixon Mask," 2.
334 "Thant, Red Chinese," C8; "Demonstrate for Soviet

Jewry," 6.
335 Glass.
336 "Nixon Nods," 3; "Never Dull Moment," 2.
337 Johnston, 31.
338 "White House Picketed," A6.
339 Whitfield, 129.
340 "Nixon Mask," 19.
341 Rosenthal, "Indicted Nixon aides," A4.
342 Nelson, 1.
343 Fitzpatrick, 16.
344 Apostola, 1.
345 "Fear and Loathing in Gonzovision."
346 Wills, 403.
347 Wills, 406.
348 Wills, 407.
349 Greenberg, xvi.
350 Stevenson qtd. in Nixon, RN, 178; Ehrlichman qtd. in Rowland, 1
351 *Nixon by Nixon*.

No Sex (1:14:11)

352 Dean and Gorey, 206.

Eye Under a Microscope (1:14:47)

353 United States Senate, Select Committee on Presidential Campaign Activities of 1972, vol. 1, bk. 7, 2868. Haldeman testimony 30 Jul. 1973.

The Committee Meeting Will Come to Order (1:15:19)

354 Hooper and Gregory, Audio Commentary, *The Texas Chainsaw Massacre 2*.
355 United States Senate, Select Committee on Presidential Campaign Activities of 1972, vol. 1, bk. 4, 1466. Dean testimony 28 Jun. 1973.
356 United States Senate, Select Committee on Presidential Campaign Activities of 1972, vol. 1, bk. 1, 5. Baker opening statement 17 May 1973.
357 Johnson.
358 Neyfakh.
359 United States Senate, Select Committee on Presidential Campaign Activities of 1972, vol. 1, bk. 8, 3151. Haldeman testimony 1 Aug. 1973.
360 United States Senate, Select Committee on Presidential Campaign Activities of 1972, vol. 1, bk. 6, 2479. Strachan testimony 23 Jul. 1973.

Killing With Honor (1:16:47)

361 *The Nixon Interviews with David Frost*, "Watergate."
362 Nixon, "Address," 8 Aug. 1974.
363 Ford, "Remarks on Signing a Proclamation."

You Have to Laugh (1:21:33)

364 *The American Nightmare*.
365 Hansen, 229.
366 Ford, "Remarks on Taking the Oath of Office."
367 "The Failure of Mr. Ford."
368 Rosenbaum, "Ford Defends," 85.
369 Hersh, 78.
370 Dudden, 65.

★ ★ ★ ★ ★

CHRONOLOGY OF EVENTS RELATED TO WATERGATE AND ★ THE TEXAS CHAIN SAW MASSACRE ★

5 Nov. 1946 Political newcomer Richard Nixon wins election to the U.S. House of Representatives, representing California's 12th district. Two years later he is re-elected to a second term.

* *

26 Sep. 1950 During the 1950 U.S. Senate race, the campaign of Nixon's opponent Helen Gahagan Douglas sends a press release to a Democratic-leaning publication in Los Angeles that describes Nixon as "this tricky young man." Three days later the paper runs an editorial criticizing "Tricky Dick Nixon," and the nickname sticks.

* *

7 Nov. 1950 Nixon wins election to the U.S. Senate, representing California.

* *

23 Sep. 1952 As a candidate for Vice President, Nixon delivers his famous "Checkers" speech on television to defend himself against accusations of inappropriately using a secret campaign fund for personal reasons.

* *

4 Nov. 1952 Dwight D. Eisenhower wins election to become President, with Nixon his Vice President. Four years later they are re-elected and together serve a second term.

* *

24 Jul. 1959 During a diplomatic visit to Russia, Vice President Nixon engages in an unplanned debate with Soviet First Secretary Nikita Khrushchev. Subsequently televised in both countries, the debate takes place in the kitchen of a model American home (part of a larger exhibit meant to foster cultural exchange), causing the interaction later to be called the "kitchen debate."

* *

8 Nov. 1960 Nixon loses the presidential election to John F. Kennedy in a close race. Kennedy receives 49.72 percent of the popular vote, while Nixon earns 49.55 percent. Kennedy wins the Electoral College 303-219.

* *

6 Nov. 1962 Nixon loses the California gubernatorial election to Pat Brown. Brown earns nearly 52 percent of the vote, Nixon just under 47 percent. Nixon punctuates his concession speech by announcing his retirement from politics, telling reporters "You don't have Nixon to kick around any more, because, gentlemen, this is my last press conference."

* *

11 Nov. 1962 ABC airs a half-hour news special titled "The Political Obituary of Richard Nixon."

* *

22 Nov. 1963 President John F. Kennedy is assasinated. Lyndon B. Johnson becomes President.

* *

3 Nov. 1964 Johnson wins the presidential election by a wide margin over his opponent, Barry Goldwater. Nixon remains largely behind the scenes during the campaign, the only presidential race between 1948 and 1976 in which he did not appear on the Republican ticket as a nominee for either President or Vice President.

8 Nov. 1966 With Nixon actively campaigning for Republican candidates though not running himself, Republicans gain 47 seats in the U.S. House and three U.S. Senate seats. Nixon earns signficant credit in the G.O.P. for his contributions, and emerges from the elections positioned to retake his role as party leader.

5 Nov. 1968 Nixon wins the presidential election in a close race against Democratic opponent Hubert Humphrey and third-party candidate George Wallace. Nixon receives 301 electoral votes and 43.4 percent of the popular vote, Humphrey 191 electoral votes and 42.7 percent, and Wallace 46 electoral votes and 13.5 percent.

4 May 1970 During a peace rally protesting the Vietnam War on the campus of Kent State University, Ohio National Guard soldiers open fire, killing four students and wounding nine more. Ten days later at a similar protest at Jackson State University in Mississippi, two students are shot and killed by police and 12 others are injured.

8 May 1970 Anti-war protestors gathered in lower Manhattan are met by approximately 200 construction workers supportive of Nixon and the war effort, resulting in the "Hard Hat Riot" that caused dozens of injuries and property damage. Later in the month, a group of 22 labor union leaders meet with Nixon at the White House, presenting him with a hard hat.

27 Jul. 1970 Acknowledging objections raised by FBI Director J. Edgar Hoover, Nixon formally withdraws approval of the so-called "Huston Plan" that among other measures would allow wiretapping, mail intercepts, break-ins and burglaries when surveilling protestors. Elements of the plan would resurface, however, in the later work of the White House's Special Investigations Unit.

13 Jun. 1971 The *New York Times* begins publishing excerpts from the leaked Pentagon Papers, prompting a legal battle with the White House over their publication.

24 Jun. 1971 A new Special Investigations Unit (a.k.a. the "White House Plumbers") is established by the White House in order to discover and stop leaks of classified information. Egil "Bud" Krogh and David Young are the nominal heads, although former FBI agent G. Gordon Liddy and former CIA agent E. Howard Hunt are the lead operatives. Under Liddy and Hunt's influence, the group's activities swiftly expand to include other clandestine and in some cases criminal operations.

* *

30 Jun. 1971 The U.S. Supreme Court rules against the government in *New York Times Co. v. United States*, requiring the White House to remove its injunction forcing *NYT* to cease its publication of the *Pentagon Papers*.

* *

3 Sep. 1971 Members of the White House's new Special Investigations Unit break into the Los Angeles office of Pentagon Papers leaker Daniel Ellsberg's psychiatrist, Lewis Fielding, in an attempt to discover files on Ellsberg to be used to discredit him. The operation is a failure, producing no useful information. The event becomes a crucial part of the Watergate backstory, as part of the motivation to hide the White House's connection to the DNC break-in also involved keeping the Fielding break-in from becoming public.

* *

27 Jan. 1972 Working for the Committee for the Re-Election of the President as its finance counsel, although more particularly charged with gathering "political intelligence" on opponents, G. Gordon Liddy first presents his "Operation Gemstone" plan to then-Attorney General John Mitchell in the AG's office. (Mitchell subsequently would step down in March to chair the re-election committee.) An elaborate plan with a $1 million budget, Liddy's outlandish scheme includes buggings, break-ins, kidnappings, and the use of prostitutes, and is rejected by Mitchell.

* *

28 Jan. 1972 At a White House performance by the Ray Conniff Singers, one of the performers, Carole Feraci, delivers a speech protesting the Vietnam War and criticizing Nixon prior to the first song.

* *

4 Feb. 1972 Liddy returns to Mitchell's office to present a scaled-down, smaller-budgeted version of "Operation Gemstone." The plan is again rejected, with the meeting cut short by White House Counsel John Dean who declares discussion of such criminal activities should not be taking place in the Attorney General's office.

* *

30 Mar. 1972 A meeting in Miami between Mitchell and two deputy directors of the re-election committee, Jeb Magruder and Fred LaRue, results in Liddy's operation being approved with a budget of $250,000, although accounts by those involved regarding what exactly was being approved differ.

* *

28 May 1972 The first break-in (undiscovered) at the Democratic National Committee Headquarters at the Watergate Hotel and Office Building in Washington, D.C. by individuals working for the Committee to Re-Elect the President.

* *

12 Jun. 1972 *Deep Throat* premieres, financed by the Peraino crime family whose Bryanston Distributing Company will later distribute *The Texas Chain Saw Massacre*.

* *

17 Jun. 1972 The second break-in at the DNC, this time followed by arrests. Seven men are arrested, five burglars and two conspirators.

19 Jun. 1972 White House Press Secretary Ron Ziegler refuses to answer a question about the DNC break-in, stating "I'm not going to comment from the White House about a third-rate burglary attempt."

20 Jun. 1972 Nixon and Haldeman have their first recorded conversation following the Watergate arrests. The tape of the conversation is later discovered to contain an eighteen-and-a-half-minute gap omitting part of their discussion about Watergate.

22 Jun. 1972 "The White House has had no involvement whatever in this incident," says Nixon when asked at a press conference about the Watergate break-in.

23 Jun. 1972 Nixon and Haldeman meet again to discuss the Watergate break-in. They explicitly outline a plan to cover up the White House's connection to the crime by having the CIA convince the FBI to stop its investigation. In early August 1974, the public release of the transcript of a recording of this conversation earns it the nickname the "smoking gun" thanks to the fact that it definitively confirms Nixon's early involvement in the cover-up.

15 Sep. 1972 The seven men arrested for the break-in at the DNC are all indicted: G. Gordon Liddy, E. Howard Hunt, James McCord, Bernard Barker, Virgilio Gonzalez, Eugenio Martinez, and Frank Sturgis. That afternoon, John Dean meets with Nixon and Haldeman in the Oval Office where they have a conversation in which the president compliments Dean for his management of the cover-up to that point.

7 Nov. 1972 Nixon re-elected as President by a wide margin over his Democratic opponent George McGovern, earning 60.7 percent of the popular vote and 520 of 538 electoral votes.

Nov. 1972 Loudon Wainwright III releases the novelty folk single "Dead Skunk," a song popularly misinterpreted as satirizing Nixon and Watergate. Hooper later mentions both the song and Watergate as primary influences upon *Chain Saw*.

Dec. 1972 While Christmas shopping, film director Tobe Hooper visits the hardware section at a crowded Montgomery Ward department store in Austin, Texas. Standing before a display of chainsaws, the director has an idea.

Jan.-Feb. 1973 Tobe Hooper and Kim Henkel write first draft of *Leatherface*.

8 Jan. 1973 Trial of the seven Watergate defendants begins with U.S. District Court Judge John Sirica officiating. One pleads guilty three days later, and four others do the same the following week. By the end of the month the other two defendants are found guilty as well.

27 Jan. 1973 The U.S., North and South Vietnam sign the Paris Peace Accords, signaling the end of U.S. engagement in Vietnam. The last U.S. combat troops leave South Vietnam on 30 Apr. 1973. Two years later (to the day), South Vietnamese capital Saigon falls to the North Vietnamese and Viet Cong.

29 Jan. 1973 A Gallup poll reports Nixon's job approval rating at 67 percent, equaling the highest of his entire presidency.

7 Feb. 1973 The U.S. Senate votes 77-0 to establish the Select Committee on Presidential Activities, a.k.a. the Senate Watergate Committee.

21 Mar. 1973 Dean explains to Nixon how the cover-up likely will not be able to be contained, comparing the situation to a "cancer—within—close to the presidency." Among the items discussed in this meeting are the continuing of hush money payments to the Watergate burglars. Dean suggests as much as $1 million will be needed over the next couple of years, and Nixon responds by saying he knows a way to secure the money (in cash).

23 Mar. 1973 A letter becomes public that James W. McCord Jr. (one of the seven Watergate defendents) has written to Judge John Sirica informing him that perjury has been committed in the trial as a result of pressure from the White House.

18 Apr. 1973 Nixon delivers a speech to Congress announcing the implementation of several strategies designed to increase domestic production of energy sources and reduce reliance on foreign imports. One of those measures, however, was to end the Mandatory Oil Import Program that placed limits on the amount of oil the nation's companies could import, which helped in the short term but would serve to increase America's vulnerability later when facing an oil embargo imposed by the Organization of Arab Petroleum Exporting Countries.

30 Apr. 1973 Nixon delivers his first "Watergate speech" in which he announces the resignations of White House Chief of Staff H.R. "Bob" Haldeman, Domestic Affairs Advisor John Ehrlichman, Attorney General Richard Kleindienst, and the firing of White House Counsel John Dean.

May 1973 (approx.) Hooper and Henkel meet with Bill Parsley, Vice President for Public Affairs at Texas Tech University, who delivers an initial investment in the film. Hooper and Henkel form a production company, Vortex, Inc. Others will invest as well, with the final budget often estimated between $125,000 and $155,000.

17 May 1973 Public, televised hearings of the Senate Watergate Committee begin.

25 May 1973 Elliot Richardson is sworn in as the new Attorney General. He chooses Archibald Cox to serve as the Justice Department's special prosecutor for Watergate.

* *

25-29 Jun. 1973 John Dean testifies for an entire week before the Senate Watergate Committee.

* *

10 Jul. 1973 During testimony before the Senate Watergate Committee, former Attorney General and director of the Committee for the Re-Election of the President John Mitchell and others repeatedly characterize White House-sponsored crimes and corrupt activities that took place prior to the break-ins at the Watergate as "the White House horrors."

* *

15 Jul. 1973 *The Texas Chain Saw Massacre* begins filming at Quick Hill Road in Round Rock just outside of Austin, Texas with shots of the large white house.

* *

16 Jul. 1973 During public testimony before the Senate Watergate Committee, former Deputy Assistant Alexander Butterfield reveals the existence of a secret White House taping system. After having been installed in early 1971, the system is shut off two days later.

* *

15 Aug. 1973 Nixon delivers his second Watergate speech in which he argues against allowing recordings of conversations involving himself and other White House officials to be made public.

* *

18 Aug. 1973 The date on which *The Texas Chain Saw Massacre* is set. Also the last day of filming, according to some accounts. (Others suggest filming did not conclude until later in August or September.)

* *

Oct. 1973 Post-production on *The Texas Chain Saw Massacre* begins.

* *

10 Oct. 1973 Facing investigations for bribery, criminal conspiracy, extortion, and tax fraud (none related to Watergate), Vice President Spiro Agnew resigns.

* *

12 Oct. 1973 Nixon nominates Gerald Ford as his new Vice President. He will be confirmed in early December.

* *

19 Oct. 1973 In response to the U.S. providing aid to Israel during the Yom Kippur War, the Organization of Arab Petroleum Exporting Countries imposes an embargo on oil exports to the U.S. and other countries, thus precipitating an oil crisis. The embargo is not lifted until March 1974.

* *

20 Oct. 1973 In an afternoon speech, Watergate Special Prosecutor Archibald Cox makes clear he believes a compromise suggested by the White House to avoid handing over subpoenaed tapes is unacceptable. In response,

Nixon orders his Attorney General Elliot Richardson to fire Cox, but Richardson refuses and instead resigns. Deputy Attorney General William Ruckelshaus also refuses to carry out the order and resigns. Next in line of succession, Solicitor General Robert Bork does fire Cox. The episode comes to be known as the "Saturday Night Massacre" and dramatically brings to the fore allegations of Nixon's abuse of power.

30 Oct. 1973 Following a week's worth of resolutions brought by multiple lawmakers, the House Judiciary Committee votes to begin an impeachment inquiry. The 21–17 vote is strictly along party lines, with all Democrats on the committee voting in favor and all Republicans voting against.

1 Nov. 1973 Nixon appoints Leon Jaworski as the new Watergate Special Prosecutor.

17 Nov. 1973 Nixon holds a televised press conference with the nation's newspapers editors during which he infamously defends himself by saying, "I am not a crook."

21 Nov. 1973 Nixon's lawyer discloses to Judge Sirica that the subpoenaed 20 Jun. 1972 recording of a conversation between Nixon and Haldeman contains an unexplained eighteen-and-a-half-minute gap. Sirica immediately makes the news public in a hearing that afternoon and launches an investigation.

Dec. 1973-Jan. 1974 Likely when the title *The Texas Chain Saw Massacre* was first proposed, apparently by someone in production manager Ron Bozman's poker game. Most accounts credit Warren Skaaren as having suggested the title.

1 Mar. 1974 The other "Watergate Seven" comprised of White House staff and aides are indicted: John Mitchell, Bob Haldeman, John Ehrlichman, Charles Colson, Gordon Strachan, Robert Mardian, and Kenneth Parkinson.

Mar.-Apr. 1974 Approximately when post-production on *The Texas Chain Saw Massacre* is completed. The final items created for the film include the opening crawl with John Larroquette's narration, the opening shot of the exhumed corpses in the Newt graveyard, and the opening credit sequence backed by stock footage of solar flares purchased from NASA in Houston.

29 Apr. 1974 Nixon delivers his third and final Watergate speech, this time announcing the White House's intention to publish edited transcripts of subpoenaed tapes in lieu of handing over the actual tapes.

30 Apr. 1974 *The White House Transcripts* are published, a carefully curated and edited selection of transcripts of the White House tapes. Over fifty newspapers reprint them in full, and three million copies are sold within one week. Omissions and edits are highly criticized, and after the White House is ordered once again to supply the actual subpoenaed tapes, the issue moves to the Supreme Court to decide.

9 May 1974 The U.S. House Judiciary Committee opens formal impeachment proceedings.

15 Jun. 1974 *All the President's Men* by Bob Woodward and Carl Bernstein is published.

27 Jun. 1974 The Senate Watergate Committee issues its "Report on Presidential Campaign Activities."

24 Jul. 1974 U.S. Supreme Court unanimously rules against Nixon's claim of executive privilege in United States v. Richard Milhous Nixon, compelling Nixon to surrender subpoenaed tape recordings and other materials.

27-30 Jul. 1974 The House Judiciary Committee votes to adopt three articles of impeachment against President Richard Nixon: obstruction of justice (27 to 11 in favor), abuse of power (28 to 10), and contempt of Congress (21 to 17). The votes mean all three articles are sent to the full House to be voted upon, and if at least one of the articles is adopted by the full House that will trigger an impeachment trial in the Senate.

5 Aug. 1974 A transcript is made public of the "smoking gun" recording of Nixon and Haldeman of 23 Jun. 1972 discussing the plan to instruct the CIA to block the FBI's investigation of the Watergate break-in.

8 Aug. 1974 In a prime time television address, Richard Nixon announces his intention to resign the office of President of the United States the following day.

9 Aug. 1974 After bidding goodbye to his staff in an emotional farewell, Nixon resigns. Gerald R. Ford is sworn in as President of the United States.

28 Aug. 1974 Distribution rights to *The Texas Chain Saw Massacre* are sold to Bryanston Distributors, a movie company created with profits from the 1972 film *Deep Throat*. A week later Bryanston runs a full-page ad in *Variety* announcing the film's October release.

8 Sep. 1974 President Ford grants Nixon a "full, free, and absolute pardon" of all offenses committed by him while in office (known or yet to be discovered).

1 Oct. 1974 *The Texas Chain Saw Massacre* premieres in Dallas, Texas.

Works Cited

Abramson, Rudy. "Troubleshooter Buzhardt May Be in Trouble." *The Los Angeles Times*, 2 Dec. 1973, 1.

Addison, Joseph. *The Spectator*, 512, 17 Oct. 1712.

Aikman, David. *Billy Graham: His Life and Influence*. Nashville: Thomas Nelson, Inc., 2007.

Ambrose, Stephen E. *Nixon: The Education of a Politician 1913–1962*. New York: Simon & Schuster, 1987.

——. *Nixon: Volume Three, Ruin and Recovery 1973–1990*. New York: Simon & Schuster, 1991.

——. "Why Didn't Nixon Burn the Tapes and Other Questions About Watergate." *Nova Law Review* 18.3 (1994): 1775–86.

The American Nightmare. Dir. Adam Simon. The Independent Film Channel, 2000.

Anderson, Jack and Fred Blumenthal. "Washington's Incredible crystal-gazer." *Parade*, 13 May 1956, 11–12.

Andrews, Nigel. "Brunnhilde Is Alive and Well." *Financial Times*, 19 Nov. 1976, 3.

Apostola, Elaine. "Pardon Me, 'er Trick or Treat." *Oshkosh Advance-Titan*, 31 Oct. 1974, 1.

Apple Jr., R.W. "Dean Is Rebuked." *The New York Times*, 20 Apr. 1973, 1, 11.

Armstrong, Scott. "What to Remember About Watergate." *The New York Times*, 21 May 2017, SR3.

Bacon, Don. "Nixon Strikes Low Chord." *Charleston Daily Mail*, 18 Aug. 1973, A4.

"Bandit Wears Nixon Mask." *Ames Daily Tribune*, 6 Feb. 1970, 2.

Baumgarten, Marjorie. "Tobe Hooper Remembers 'The Texas Chainsaw Massacre." *The Austin Chronicle*, 20.9, 27 Oct. 2000, <austinchronicle.com/screens/2000-10-27/79177/>.

Bernstein, Carl and Bob Woodward. *All the President's Men*. New York: Warner Books, 1974.

——. Bug Suspect Got Campaign Funds." *The Washington Post*, 1 Aug. 1972, 1.

——. "GOP Security Aide Among Five Arrested in Bugging Affair." *The Washington Post*, 19 Jun. 1972, 1.

——. *The Final Days*. New York: Simon & Schuster, 1976.

Berrigan, Donald R. Rev. of *The Texas Chain Saw Massacre*. *The Cincinnati Inquirer*, 17 Nov. 1974, 159.

"Billboard's Top Single Picks: Chartalk." *Billboard*, 85.28, 14 Jul. 1973, 61.

Bird, David. "'Gas' Shortage Traces Erratic Pattern." *The New York Times*, 20 May 1973, 77, 92.

Bloom, John. "They Came, They Sawed." *Texas Monthly*, Nov. 2004, <texasmonthly.com/articles/they-came-they-sawed/>.

Bowen, John W. "Return of the Power Tool Killer." *Rue Morgue*, 42, Nov.–Dec. 2004, 16–18.

Buchanan, Patrick J. *Nixon's White House Wars: The Battles That Made and Broke a President and Divided America Forever*. New York: Crown Forum, 2017.

Buchwald, Art. "Watergate Is Like 'Godfather.'" *The Oil City Derrick*, 5 Dec. 1974, 5.

——. "What to Say About Watergate." 12 Jul. 1973. Rpt. in *I Am Not a Crook*, New York: G.P. Putnam's Sons, 1974. 155–57.

Bullock, Paul. "'Rabbits and Radicals': Richard Nixon's 1946 Campaign Against Jerry Voorhis." *Southern California Quarterly*, 55.3, Fall 1973, 319–59.

Campion, Nicholas. *Astrology and Popular Religion in the Modern West*. New York: Routledge, 2012.

Canby, Vincent. Rev. of *Night of the Living Dead. The New York Times*, 5 Dec. 1968, 59.

CBS News. Special coverage of the assassination of John F. Kennedy, 23 Nov. 1968.

Cook, David. "1974: Movies and Political Trauma." *American Cinema of the 1970s*. Ed. Lester Friedman. New Brunswick, NJ: Rutgers UP, 2007. 116–34.

Crist, Judith. "All in the Family." Rev. of *The Godfather Part II*. *New York Magazine*, 23 Dec. 1974, 70–71.

Cronkite, Walter. *CBS Evening News*. 27 Feb. 1968.

——. *A Reporter's Life*. New York: Random House, 1996.

Crouse, Timothy. *The Boys on the Bus*. New York: Random House, 1973.

Davie, Michael. "The Riddle of the White House." *The Observer*, 22, Apr. 1973, 25.

"The de Antonio Legacy (Part 2)." *Alternative Views*, Alternative Information Network, April 1993.

Dean, John W. *Blind Ambition*. New York: Pocket Books, 1976.

——. *The Nixon Defense: What He Knew and When He Knew It*. New York: Viking Penguin, 2014.

Dean, Maureen and Hays Gorey. *"Mo": A Woman's View of Watergate*. New York: Simon & Schuster, 1975.

"Dean Reportedly Finds Deletions in Transcripts." *The New York Times*, 3 May 1974, 29.

"Demonstrate for Soviet Jewry." *The Williamsport Sunday Grit*, 19 Mar. 1972, 6.

Dent, Harry S. *The Prodigal South Returns to Power*. New York: John Wiley & Sons, 1978.

Dryden, John. "A Discourse Concerning the Original and Progress of Satire," from *The Satires of Decimus Junius Juvenalis: Translated into English Verse by Mr. Dryden and Several Other Eminent Hands*. London, 1693.

Dudden, Arthur. "The Record of Political Humor." *American Quarterly* 37.1 (Spring 1985): 50–70.

Ebert, Roger. "Just Another Horror Movie—Or Is It?" Rev. of *Night of the Living Dead. The Chicago Sun-Times,* 5 Jan. 1969, C1.

——. Rev. of *The Texas Chain Saw Massacre*. *The Chicago Sun-Times*, 1 Jan. 1974 [*sic*], <rogerebert.com/reviews/the-texas-chain-saw-

massacre-1974>.
Emery, Fred. *Watergate: The Corruption of American Politics and the Fall of Richard Nixon.* New York: Simon & Schuster, 1994.
Evans, Rowland and Robert Novak. "The Watergate Specter." *The Syracuse Post-Standard*, 22 Aug. 1972, 4.
"The Exorcist Letter." *Zodiac Letters and Ciphers*, 29 Jan. 1974, <zodiackiller.com/ExorcistLetter.html>.
"The Failure of Mr. Ford." *The New York Times*, 9 Sep. 1974, 34.
Farley, Ellen and William K. Knoedelseder Jr. "The Real Texas Chainsaw Massacre." *The Los Angeles Times*, 5 Sep. 1982, Calendar 2–7.
—. "A Tangled Web Clogs 'Chainsaw.'" *The Los Angeles Times*, 12 Sep. 1982, Calendar 3–5.
"Fear and Loathing in Gonzovision." *Omnibus*, season 12, episode 8, BBC 1, 2 Nov. 1978.
Feeney, Mark. *Nixon at the Movies: A Book About Belief*. Chicago: U of Chicago P, 2004.
First Line Report. CBS radio network, 6 Aug. 1974.
Fitzpatrick, Tom. "Cruel crowd sheds no tears." *Columbia Missourian*, 10 Aug. 1974, 1, 16.
Ford, Gerald R. "Remarks on Signing a Proclamation Granting Pardon to Richard Nixon." The East Room of the White House, Washington, DC, 8 Sep. 1974.
——. "Remarks on Taking the Oath of Office." The East Room of the White House, Washington, DC, 9 Aug. 1974.
——. *A Time to Heal: The Autobiography of Gerald R. Ford*. New York: Berkley Books, 1979.
"Former Chairman of SEC faces trial for perjury." *The Pittsburgh Press*, 6 Jun. 1974, 10.
Franklin, Ben A. "Thousands of War Foes Stage Counter-Inaugural March Down Pennsylvania Ave." *The New York Times*, 20 Jan. 1969, 21.
Franks, Alan. "It's a Family Affair." *The London Times*, 26 Jul. 2008, 34.
Gallup, Inc. "Election Polls—Vote by Groups, 1968–1972." Washington, DC: Gallup Organization.
——. "Presidential Approval Ratings—Gallup Historical Statistics and Trends." Washington, DC: Gallup Organization.
Gibbs, Nancy and Michael Duffy. *The Preacher and the Presidents: Billy Graham in the White House*. New York: Center Street, 2007.
Glass, Ira. "204: 81 Words." *This American Life*, Chicago Public Media, 18 Jan. 2002.
Glynn, Lenny. "Four nights in the garden of delight." *Columbia Daily Spectator*, 108.31, 4 Nov. 1968, C1–C2, C7.
Greenberg, David. *Nixon's Shadow: The History of an Image*. New York: W.W. Norton & Company, 2003.
Greene, Bob. *Fraternity: A Journey in Search of Five Presidents*. New York: Crown Publishers, 2004.
Gross, Linda. "'Texas Massacre' Grovels in Gore." *The Los Angeles Times*, 30 Oct. 1974, 98.
Gwertzman, Bernard. "Pentagon Kept Tight Rein in Last Days of Nixon Rule." *The New York*

Times, 25 Aug. 1974, 1.

Haig, Alexander. Interview by Timothy Naftali, Douglas Brinkley and John Powers, 30 Nov. 2007, Yorba Linda, CA, Richard Nixon Oral History Project of the Richard Nixon Presidential Library and Museum.

Hail. "History." American Film Institute, AFI Catalogue of Feature Films: The First 100 Years, 1893–1993. <catalog.afi.com/Catalog/MovieDetails/54580>.

Halberstam, David. *The Best and the Brightest*. Greenwich, CT: Fawcett Publications Inc., 1972.

Haldeman, H.R. *The Haldeman Diaries: Inside the Nixon White House*. New York: G.P. Putman's Sons, 1994.

Haldeman, H.R. and Joseph DiMona. *The Ends of Power*. New York: Times Books, 1978.

Haller, Henry and Virginia Aronson. *The White House Family Cookbook*. New York: Random House, 1987.

Hansen, Gunnar. *Chain Saw Confidential: How We Made the World's Most Notorious Horror Movie*. San Francisco: Chronicle Books, 2013.

Henkel, Kim and Tobe Hooper. *Leatherface*. Unpublished film script. 1973.

Hendler, Herb. *Year by Year in the Rock Era*. New York: Prager, 1983.

Hersh, Seymour M. "The Pardon: Nixon, Ford, Haig and the Transfer of Power." *The Atlantic Monthly*, 252.2, Aug. 1983, 55–78.

Hoberman, J. and Jonathan Rosenbaum. *Midnight Movies*. New York: Harper & Row, 1983.

Hooper, Tobe and David Gregory. Audio Commentary. *The Texas Chainsaw Massacre 2: Gruesome Edition*, Twentieth Century Fox Entertainment, 2006.

Hooper, Tobe and Louis Black. Audio Commentary. *Eggshells (Tobe Hooper's Early Works)*, Arrow Video, 2013.

Hooper, Tobe, Gunnar Hansen, Daniel Pearl. Audio Commentary. *The Texas Chain Saw Massacre*, Elite Entertainment DVD, 1996.

"Immense Solar Flares in '72 Had Wide Impact on Earth." *The New York Times*, 8 May 1973, 10.

"Inside Track," *Billboard*, 85.33, 18 Aug. 1973, 66.

Jacobs, Meg. "America's Never-Ending Oil Consumption." *The Atlantic*, 15 May 2016, <theatlantic.com/politics/archive/2016/05/american-oil-consumption/482532/>.

Jamieson, Kathleen. *Packaging the Presidency: A History and Criticism of Presidential Campaign Advertising*. New York: Oxford UP, 1984.

Jaworzyn, Stefan. *The Texas Chain Saw Massacre Companion*. London: Titan Books, 2003.

Johnson, Ted. "When Congressional Hearings Become 'The Hottest Daytime Soap Opera.'" *Variety*, 7 Jun. 2017, <variety.com/2017/biz/news/john-dean-watergate-hearings-tv-moments-1202456418/>.

Johnston, Laurie. "Anti-Nixon Rally Ends in Arrests." *The New York Times*, 24 Oct. 1972, 31.

Lanza, Joseph. *The Texas Chain Saw Massacre: The Film That*

Terrified a Rattled Nation. New York: Skyhorse Publishing, 2019.

Lappé, Frances Moore. *Diet for a Small Planet*. New York: Ballantine Books, 1971.

——. *Diet for a Small Planet: Twentieth Anniversary Edition*. New York: Ballantine Books, 1991.

Lerner, Max. "Decline of Authority." *Oil City Derrick*, 18 Aug. 1973, 4.

Light, Ken. Foreword. *Black and White: 1968–1974* by Howard Epstein. Berkeley, CA: Inworks Press, 2017.

Liddy, G. Gordon. *Will: The Autobiography of G. Gordon Liddy*. New York: St. Martin's Press, 1980.

Kermode, Mark. "Jaws, 40 years on: 'One of the truly great and lasting classics of American cinema.'" *The Guardian*, 31 May 2015, <theguardian.com/film/2015/may/31/jaws-40-years-on-truly-great-lasting-classics-of-america-cinema>.

Kilpatrick, Carrol. "Nixon Tells Editors, 'I'm Not a Crook.'" *The Washington Post*, 18 Nov. 1973, A1.

Klosterman, Chuck. "*The Shining*, Immersion Criticism, and what might be the documentary of the year." *Grantland*, 29 Mar. 2013, <grantland.com/features/documentary-year/>.

Knipp, Delores J. et al. "On the Little-Known Consequences of the 4 August 1972 Ultra-Fast Coronal Mass Ejecta: Facts, Commentary, and Call to Action." *Space Weather*, 16, 1635–1643.

Koch, Stephen. "Fashions in Pornography." *Harper's Magazine*, 253, 1 Nov. 1976, 108–112.

Kristol, Irving. "The Nightmare of Watergate." *The Wall Street Journal*, 17 May 1973, 20.

Martin, Bob. "The Real Tobe Hooper." *Fangoria*, Apr. 1981: 38–40.

Masters of Horror. Directed by Mike Mendez, Dave Parker. Flixmix, The Sci-Fi Channel, 2002.

Macor, Alison. *Chainsaws, Slackers, and Spy Kids: Thirty Years of Filmmaking in Austin Texas*. Austin: U. of Texas Press, 2010.

Malcolm, Derek. Rev. of *The Texas Chain Saw Massacre*. *The Guardian*, 18 Nov. 1976, 10.

Morgan, Iwan W. "Nixon Biographies." In *A Companion to Richard M. Nixon*. Ed. Melvin Small. Malden, MA: Wiley-Blackwell, 2011. 7–26.

Mulleavy, Kate and Laura. "Tobe Hooper." *Interview*, 44.5, Jun.-Jul. 2014, 24–25, 138–39.

Naftali, Timothy. *Blind Spot: The Secret History of American Counterterrorism*. New York: Basic Books, 2005.

"The Nation: Pentagram Papers." *Time*, 99.24, 12 Jun. 1972, 18.

The National Archives and Records Administration. Nixon Grand Jury Records, Folder 9/25, Exhibits 2 of 3, Part 2, "Tape Hearings Before Sirica," 6 Dec. 1973.

National Commission on the Causes and Prevention of Violence. *Rights in Concord: The Response to the Counter-Inaugural Protest Activities in Washington, D.C., Jan. 18–20, 1969*. Washington, D.C.: U.S. Government Printing Office, 1969.

Naughton, James N. "Agnew Assails

Protestors as 'Misfits' and 'Garbage.'" *The New York Times*, 30 Oct. 1970, 12.

Nelson, W. Dale. "Supreme Court Decides President Must Surrender Tapes and Papers." *The Hagerstown Daily Mail*, 24 Jul. 1974, 1.

"Never Dull Moment for Demos." *Columbia Missourian*, 13 Jul. 1972, 2.

Nevin, David. "Texas Sniper's Murder Rampage." *Life*, 12 Aug. 1966: 24–31.

Nevin, George. "The Watergate Game Is Here." *San Rafael Daily Independent Journal*, 24 May 1973, 23.

Neyfakh, Leon, narrator. "Lie Detectors." *Slow Burn*, season 1, episode 4, Slate Group, 19 Dec. 2017.

Nixon, Richard. "Address Accepting the Presidential Nomination at the Republican National Convention in Miami Beach, Florida." Miami Beach Convention Center, Miami, FL, 8 Aug. 1968.

———. "Address to the Nation About the Watergate Investigations." The Oval Office at the White House, The United States Government, Washington, DC, 30 Apr. 1973.

———. "Address to the Nation About the Watergate Investigations." The Oval Office at the White House, Washington, DC, 15 Aug. 1973.

———. "Address to the Nation Announcing Answer to the House Judiciary Committee Subpoena for Additional Presidential Tape Recordings." The White House, Washington, DC, 29 Apr. 1974.

———. "Address to the Nation Announcing the Decision to Resign the Office of President of the United States." The White House, Washington, DC, 8 Aug. 1974.

———. Conversation No. 490–17. Oval Office, 4 May 1971, White House Tapes, Richard Nixon Presidential Library and Museum, Yorba Linda, CA.

———. Conversation No. 739–4. Oval Office, 21 Jun. 1972, White House Tapes, Richard Nixon Presidential Library and Museum, Yorba Linda, CA.

———. Conversation No. 741–2. Oval Office, 23 Jun. 1972, White House Tapes, Richard Nixon Presidential Library and Museum, Yorba Linda, CA.

———. Conversation No. 741–10. Oval Office, 23 Jun. 1972, White House Tapes, Richard Nixon Presidential Library and Museum, Yorba Linda, CA.

———. Conversation No. 779–2. Oval Office, 15 Sep. 1972, White House Tapes, Richard Nixon Presidential Library and Museum, Yorba Linda, CA.

———. Conversation No. 783–25. Oval Office, 19 Sep. 1972, White House Tapes, Richard Nixon Presidential Library and Museum, Yorba Linda, CA.

———. Conversation No. 784–7. Oval Office, 21 Sep. 1972, White House Tapes, Richard Nixon Presidential Library and Museum, Yorba Linda, CA.

———. Conversation No. 886–8. Oval Office, 21 Mar. 1973, White House Tapes, Richard Nixon Presidential Library and Museum, Yorba Linda, CA.

———. "Eulogy Delivered at the Capitol During the

State Funeral of General Eisenhower." The Rotunda of the Capitol, Washington, DC, 30 Mar. 1969.

——. *In the Arena*. New York: Simon & Schuster, 1990.

——. Interview with Frank Gannon. 9 Feb. 1983. The Nixon-Gannon Interviews. Walter J. Brown Media Archives & Peabody Awards Collection, U of Georgia Libraries, Athens, GA.

——. Interview with Frank Gannon. 8 Apr. 1983. The Nixon-Gannon Interviews. Walter J. Brown Media Archives & Peabody Awards Collection, U of Georgia Libraries, Athens, GA.

——. "The President's News Conference." The Oval Office at the White House, Washington, DC, 22 Jun. 1972.

——. "The President's News Conference." The Briefing Room at the White House, Washington, DC, 15 Mar. 1973.

——. "The President's News Conference." San Clemente, CA, 29 Aug. 1972.

——. "The President's News Conference." The Oval Office at the White House, Washington, DC, 5 Oct. 1972.

——. "Question-and-Answer Session at the Annual Convention of the Associated Press Managing Editors Association, Orlando, Florida." Contemporary Hotel at Walt Disney World, Orlando, FL, 17 Nov. 1973.

——. "Radio Address: 'A Salute to Agriculture.'" Palm Springs, CA, 2 May 1971.

——. "Remarks." Beverly Hilton Hotel, Beverly Hills, CA, 7 Nov. 1962.

——. "Remarks Announcing Procedures and Developments in Connection With the Watergate Investigations." The Briefing Room at the White House, Washington, DC, 17 Apr. 1973.

——. "Remarks of Vice President Nixon, Kamehameha Shopping Center." Honolulu, HI, 3 Aug. 1960.

——. "Remarks on Departure from the White House." The East Room at the White House, Washington, DC, 9 Aug. 1974.

——. *RN: The Memoirs of Richard Nixon*. New York: Simon & Schuster, 1978.

——. *Six Crises*. Garden City, NY: Doubleday & Company, Inc., 1962.

Nixon by Nixon: In His Own Words. Directed by Peter W. Kunhardt. HBO Documentary Films, Home Box Office, 2014.

"Nixon Family Sees Parade; President Visits Bahamas." *The Albuquerque Journal*, 5 Jul. 1969, A6.

The Nixon Interviews with David Frost. "War at Home and Abroad." Syndicast, 19 May 1977.

——. "Watergate." Syndicast, 4 May 1977.

"Nixon Mask Gets Lawyer Arrested." *Cedar Rapids Gazette*, 5 Feb. 1974, 19.

"Nixon Nods as McGovern Clinches It." *The Doylestown Daily Intelligencier*, 12 Jul. 1972, 3.

"NYC Observes Moratorium." *Middletown Times Herald Record*, 16 Oct. 1969, 2.

Oakley, Don. "Questions Unanswered." *Iowa City Press*

Citizen, 18 Aug. 1973, A6.
"Origin and Distribution of the Huston Plan." Central Intelligence Agency, General CIA Records Collection, 19 Feb. 2003, <cia.gov/library/readingroom/docs/CIA-RDP87B01034R000700230008-6.pdf>.
"Per Capita Consumption of Poultry and Livestock, 1960 to Forecast 2020, in Pounds." United States Department of Agriculture and National Agricultural Statistics Service, <nationalchickencouncil.org/about-the-industry/statistics/per-capita-consumption-of-poultry-and-livestock-1965-to-estimated-2012-in-pounds/>.
Pereira, Korey. "Wayne Bell: The man behind the sounds of The Texas Chainsaw Massacre." *Designing Sound*, 25 Oct. 2018, <designingsound.org/2018/10/25/wayne-bell-the-man-behind-the-sounds-of-the-texas-chain-saw-massacre/>.
Phelps, Guy. "Family Life." *Sight & Sound*, 45.2, 84–85.
Phipps, Keith. "Tobe Hooper." *AV Club*, 11 Oct. 2000, <avclub.com/article/tobe-hooper-13680>.
"Protestors Say They're Peaceful." *The San Antonio Express and News*, 19 Jan. 1969, 3.
Pym, John. Rev. of *The Texas Chain Saw Massacre*. *Monthly Film Bulletin*, 143.515, Dec. 1975, 258.
Reed, Rex. "Being Bored in Cannes." *Manchester Journal Inquirer*, 24 May 1975, 23–24.
"Remarks by Principals in Watergate Sentencings." *The New York Times*, 24 Mar. 1973, 12.
Rev. of *Night of the Living Dead*. *Variety*, 16 Oct. 1968, 6.
Riesel, Victor. "Dead man's tales: White House ready to woo big labor again." *Austin Daily Herald*, 14 Jun. 1974, 4.
——. "Political Alliance of Inouye Jack Hall Scrutinized." *Manitowoc Herald-Times Reporter*, 7 Aug. 1973, 4.
Rinzler, J.W. *The Making of Star Wars Return of the Jedi: The Definitive Story*. New York: Del Ray, 2013.
Ripley, Anthony. "Guideline Issued for Prosecutor." *The New York Times*, 18 May 1973, 1, 20.
Ritter, Bill. Rev. of *Richard Nixon: A Fantasy* by David Frye. *Door*, 5.5, 13–27 Sep. 1973, 12.
Ronan, Thomas P. "Lindsay Says Nixon Follows 'Doctrine of Unpredictability.'" *The New York Times*, 2 Oct. 1971, 29.
Rosenbaum, David E. "Ford Defends Pardon Before Panel in House and Denies Any 'Deal' With Nixon." *The New York Times*, 18 Oct. 1974, 85.
——. "Hunt Says He Fabricated Cables on Diem to Link Kennedy to Killing of Catholic." *The New York Times*, 25 Sep. 1973, 28.
Rosenthal, Harry F. "Indicted Nixon aides could get long jail sentences if found guilty." *The Lowell Sunday Sun*, 10 Mar. 1974, A1, A4.
——. "The chief electronic witness: Hearing is believing." *The Tampa Bay Times*, 18 Oct. 1974, 5.
Rowland, Barbara. "Former Nixon advisor describes colleagues, boss and Watergate." *The University of Delaware Review*,

105.40, 6 Mar. 1981, 1, 6.

Russo, John. *Making Movies: The Inside Guide to Independent Movie Production*. New York: Dell, 1989.

Safire, William. *Safire's Political Dictionary: Revised Edition*. Oxford: Oxford UP, 2008.

Schlesinger Jr., Arthur M. *The Imperial Presidency*. Boston: Houghton Mifflin Company, 1973.

Schlosser, Eric. "The Chain Never Stops." *Mother Jones*, Jul.–Aug. 2001, 26.4, 38–47, 86–87.

Semple Jr., Robert B. "Mitchell Quits Post, Putting Family First." *The New York Times*, 2 Jul. 1972, 1, 20.

——. "Nixon Meets Heads of 2 City Unions, Hails Support." *The New York Times*, 27 May 1970, 1.

"Sen. Scott Shocked." *The Philadelphia Inquirer*, 8 May 1974, 1.

"She Has Nightmares." *The Austin American*, 6 Apr. 1972, 38.

"Show Business: Watergate Wit." *Time*, 101.26, 25 Jun. 1973, 94.

Silverstein, Norman. "*The Godfather* a Year Later—An Examination of the Movie's Internal Structure." *Italian Americana*, 1.1, Autumn 1974, 104–17.

Smallwood, Christine. "Astrology in the Age of Uncertainty." *The New Yorker*, 28 Oct. 2019, 95.44, pp. 20–24.

Smith, Gene. "Electricity Rates Jumped 55.4% in 1974 Half." *The New York Times*, 15 Oct. 1974, 55, 57.

Sobel, Robert. "Watergates Flood Market." *Billboard*, 85.22, 2 Jun. 1973, 1, 76.

"Still No Real Answers." *The New York Times*, 4 Feb. 1973, 213.

Szulc, Tad. "Ex-G.O.P. Aide Linked to Political Raid." *The New York Times*, 20 Jun. 1972, 1, 24.

The Texas Chain Saw Massacre: A Family Portrait. Dir. Brad Shellady. MTI Home Video, 1988.

Texas Chain Saw Massacre: The Shocking Truth. Dir. David Gregory. Blue Underground, 2000.

"Thant, Red Chinese Held First Meetings." *The Findlay Republican-Courier*, 15 Nov. 1971, C8.

Thompson, Bob. "Richard Nixon and the Oobie-Doobie Girl." *The Washington Post Magazine*, 27 Jul. 1997, W16.

Thompson, Hunter S. "Fear and Loathing at the Watergate: Mr. Nixon Has Cashed His Check." *Rolling Stone*, 144, 27 Sep. 1973. Rpt. in *The Great Shark Hunt: Strange Tales from a Strange Time*. New York: Simon & Schuster, 1979. 248–82.

——. "Fear and Loathing in the Bunker." *The New York Times*, 1 Jan. 1974, 19.

——. "He Was a Crook." *Rolling Stone*, 684, 16 Jun. 1994, 42–44.

"To Save the Presidency." *The New York Times*, 5 May 1974, 260.

Tongeren, Phil van. "De vloek van een meesterwerk." *Schokkend Nieuws*, 8 Aug. 2017, <schokkendnieuws.nl/interviews/4850-de-vloek-van-een-meesterwerk>.

Transcript of a Recording of a Meeting Among the President, John Dean, and H.R. Haldeman in the Oval Office, on March 21, 1973, from 10:12 to 11:55 a.m. Prepared by the Impeachment

Inquiry Staff of the House Judiciary Committee, 8 Jul. 1974. <nixonlibrary.gov/sites/default/files/forresearchers/find/tapes/watergate/trial/exhibit_12.pdf>.

"Two Big Names Caught in the Hottening Watergate Vortex." *The Indiana Evening Gazette*, 9 Apr. 1973, 14.

Tyler, H. "The Unsinkable Jeane Dixon." *The Humanist*, 37.3, May 1978, 6–9.

United States House of Representatives. Hearings Before the Committee on the Judiciary House of Representatives. House Resolution 803, Washington: U.S. Govt. Print. Off., 1974.

United States Senate. Hearing Before the Committee on Foreign Relations. Senate Resolutions 2640 and 3429, House Resolution 15628, Washington: U.S. Govt. Print. Off., 1970.

United States Senate. Select Committee on Presidential Campaign Activities of 1972. Senate Resolution 60: Watergate and Related Activities, 3 vols., Washington: U.S. Govt. Print. Off., 1973–74.

Urquhart, Michael A. and Marillyn A. Hewson. "Unemployment continued to rise in 1982 as recession deepened." *Monthly Labor Review*, Feb. 1983, 3–12.

"U.S. Cattle Inventory Per Year." Department of Agriculture and National Agricultural Statistics Service. <beef2live.com/story-united-states-cattle-inventory-1867-2014-90-108169>.

U.S. Bureau of Labor Statistics. Labor Force Statistics from the Current Population Survey. <data.bls.gov>.

——. Price Inflation for Electricity Since 1913, Consumer Price Index. <data.bls.gov>.

——. United States Inflation Rate by Year. <data.bls.gov>.

Wang, Amy B. "Who coined 'Saturday Night Massacre'? A birthday party at a YMCA may hold the key." *The Washington Post*, 12 May 2017, <washingtonpost.com/news/retropolis/wp/2017/05/12/how-a-washington-post-humorist-became-connected-to-the-saturday-night-massacre/>.

"Watergate Brings Novelty Items." *The New York Times*, 29 May 1973, 18.

Wax, Judith. "The Waterbury Tales." *The New Republic*, 169.10, 15 Sep. 1973, 24–25.

Weaver Jr., Warren. "Nixon's Lawyers Insist He Can End a Criminal Case." *The New York Times*, 18 Aug. 1973, 1, 13.

West, Richard. "Texas Monthly Reporter: Scariest Movie Ever?" *Texas Monthly*, 2.3, Mar. 1974, 9.

White, Theodore, H. *The Making of the President 1968*. New York: Harper Perennial Political Classics, 1969.

White, William S. "Nixon may rise again." *The Newport Daily News*, 8 Jan. 1974, 4.

"White House Horrors." *The New York Times*, 13 Jul. 1973, 34.

"White House Picketed." *Eau Claire Leader-Telegram*, 23 Oct. 1973, A6.

The White House Transcripts. New York: The Viking Press, 1974.

Whitfield, Stephen J. "Richard Nixon as a Comic Figure."

American Quarterly, 37.1, Spring 1985, 114–32.

Willis, Donald C. *Horror and Science Fiction Films II*. Metuchen, NJ: Scarecrow Press, 1982.

Wills, Garry. *Nixon Agonistes: The Crisis of the Self-Made Man*. Boston: Houghton Mifflin Company, 1970.

Witcover, Jules. *The Resurrection of Richard Nixon*. New York: G.P. Putnam's Sons, 1970.

Wood, Jennifer M. "11 Things You Didn't Know about *The Texas Chainsaw Massacre*." *Esquire*, 21 Oct. 2014, <esquire.com/entertainment/movies/a23810/texas-chainsaw-things-you-didnt-know/>.

Wood, Robin. "An Introduction to the American Horror Film." 1979. Rpt. in *Movies and Methods: Volume II*, ed. Bill Nichols. Berkley: University of California Press, 1985. 195–220.

Worland, Rick. *The Horror Film: An Introduction*. Oxford: Blackwell Publishing, 2007.

The World This Week. CBS radio network, 18 Aug. 1973.

Zinoman, Jason. *Shock Value: How a Few Eccentric Outsiders Gave Us Nightmares, Conquered Hollywood, and Invented Modern Horror*. New York: Penguin Press, 2011.

Zitz, Michael. "Folk star plays at Birchmere." *The Free Lance-Star*, 12 Sep. 2003, D1–D2.

Zwilling, Marcia. "Commentary: Tobe Hooper's Austin youth shaped 'Texas Chain Saw Massacre.'" *Statesman*, 29 Aug. 2017, <statesman.com/news/opinion/commentary-tobe-hooper-shocked-america-austin-shaped-his-film-genius/gmOgMCOFLukLwM4kmJQtTK/>.

★ ★ ★ ★ ★

Index

★ ★ ★ ★ ★

★ About the Author ★

MARTIN HARRIS is an author and teacher who writes about horror film, literature, and popular culture. An English Ph.D., he teaches American Studies at UNC Charlotte where his courses include "Tricky Dick: Richard Nixon, Poker & Politics."

★ ★ ★ ★ ★